Praise for Taking A Shot and Richard O'Connor

Rich O'Connor could have been king of the court, but he had more than hoop dreams on his mind. In "Taking a Shot," he delivers a fast-break look at his journey from basketball wiz to celebrated writer. At times exuberantly funny and at other times poignantly reflective, O'Connor's story scores on multiple levels, from unveiling the stakes at play with collegiate sports to the joy that comes with nailing the perfect paragraph. You'll laugh plenty riding shotgun as O'Connor retraces his life's unpredictable travel route — and be reminded that the unscripted life often produces the best memories.

Charles Butler, Co-Author of The Long Run: A New York City Firefighter's Triumphant Comeback from Crash Victim to Elite Athlete

~

Richard O'Connor's beautifully written book is about paths taken and not taken. Rubbing shoulders with the giants of the game, basketball takes O'Connor from the playgrounds of Union City, New Jersey to Cameron Indoor Stadium to all of Europe, on a journey of curiosity and self-discovery. From dreaming of being on the cover of *Sports Illustrated* to seeing his byline in that same publication, O'Connor shares life-lessons in perfect prose.

Ben Guest, author of Zen and the Art of Coaching Basketball

~

A young man abruptly gives up a chance at stardom in the game he seemed born to play. Surely, such an impetuous decision might haunt the rest of one's life. But instead of "what-if?" Rich O'Connor asks, "what's next?" Again and again, in a life that takes him from elite-level basketball, to writing, journalism, publishing, business, fatherhood. In Taking A Shot, we meet a man who has embraced the next and the new at every step—and provides, in addition to a darn good yarn, a template for many who might be stuck at similar crossroads; fearful of making course-changing decisions in their own lives. As we learn in this masterfully-written memoir, Rich O'Connor took a shot. Will you?

John Hanc, author of The Coolest Race on Earth: Mud, Madmen, Glaciers and Grannies at the Antarctica Marathon, He also co wrote the multi-award-winning memoirs, Not Dead Yet: My Race Against Disease: From Diagnosis to Dominance, by Type 1 diabetic bike racer Phil Southerland; and Your Heart, My Hands by cardiac surgeon Arun Singh, MD.

The beauty of "Taking a Shot" lies between who O'Connor was and who he became. Thanks to his many mentors—a gangster and a rabbi, celebrities and athletes—he learned to win in the game of life. In many ways, this book is a basketball version of "The Tender Bar."

Andrea Witzig, Senior Editor, ABB Zurich

~

Popular sports stories often adhere to one of two opposing narratives: stories of champions (if they "defied all odds" even better), and stories of "busts." These are the men and women with amazing talent and potential but who — usually due to hubris or injuries — never make it. Richard O'Connor's sports story is different, one I've never seen (and I'm a former sports scribe): An elite, successful athlete takes a hard look at his sport and all it entails--and walks away. "Willingly," he writes. "Without remorse. Without shame." In abandoning the basketball life he'd known--the one he'd dreamed of and worked obsessively toward-- O'Connor had no preparation, no design, no example to follow. It took courage and creativity, qualities vital to his next, truer vocation, that of writer.

He didn't renounce the game completely, working as an NBA scout; instead he engaged with it on his own terms. As he describes in vivid detail and engaging prose, through renouncing one self and reincarnating as another, he gained an education--and a richer, fuller life. Both sports fans and general memoir readers will be captivated by this original untold story.

John Capouya, Author of Florida Soul and Gorgeous George: The Outrageous Bad-Boy Wrestler Who Created American Pop Culture

~

I'm not a student of college or NBA basketball. Hardly a fan. But I know the names Grant Hill, Christian Laettner, Bobby Hurley, JJ Redick. All legendary Duke basketball players who moved on to great NBA careers.

Richard O'Connor was also a heralded player. But you probably don't know his name. That's because for some god forsaken reason he quit playing his junior year. No one in their right mind does that. Give up an almost certain NBA career.

O'Connor did because he wanted and needed more. He chose, very painfully, to take a shot at a life he had no freaking idea where it would take him. But it turned out his journey proved stimulating and fascinating.

Bradley Siegel, Former President TNT, TBS, TCM
and Cartoon Network / Current CEO Brand New World Studios

~

Taking A Shot

Quitting Duke Basketball, Starting a Life

Richard O'Connor

Print ISBN: 979-8-9874760-3-1
Library of Congress Reg #1-12442886531

ENHANCED COMMUNICATIONS, LLC
John Hanc, Writer/Educator/Journalist/Publishing Consultant

Tender Fire Books

www.TenderFireBooks.com

For my father, Big Tom, and my mother, Geri, and my grandfather John Barrett. They all gave me more love and support than I could ever thank them for. I miss them dearly.

For Peg, who was always there.

For Tracey, who is always there.

And, of course, for my son, Tim. The Tim Man. Who has made my life bigger, better and brighter. He makes every day Father's Day.

How lucky am I.

Foreword

In the 1940s and 50s, many parents preached to their children one of two aphorisms as the keys to success, or failure, in their lives.

"Jack of all trades, master of none."
William Shakespeare, 1600s.

"Don't put all your eggs in one basket."
Miguel de Cervantes, 1600s

By the time Richard O'Connor was five years old in Union City, New Jersey, he had "put all his eggs in one basket." He describes himself in his just published memoir, "Taking a Shot" (Enhanced Communications) already being "addicted" to "the narcotic" of basketball at that age. His only goal in life from then on was to be an All-American college player drafted into the NBA where he'd have a Hall of Fame career.

By the age of eight, O'Connor was already calling attention to his "ruthless" game, according to his grammar school coach. He played a "blue collar" style which he emulated after his "blue collar" father's work ethic. Tom O'Connor was a big, amiable man, who worked all his adult life as a milk man, beginning at 3 a.m. and returning home at 4 p.m., six and seven days a week.

"He never missed a day of work," writes O'Connor, "Nor was he ever fired." Often, "Big Tom," brought his young son to work with him in the early morning darkness. One such morning "Big Tom," was robbed by thugs with knives while he was unloading his truck. He quickly surrendered to the thugs the only thing he had of value, a few cases of orange juice, while concealing his young son behind him. After the thieves left, "Big Tom" told his shaking son, "There's a lot of bad people in this world. You can't escape them. But you never provoke them." Then he went back to work for the rest of the day.

In O'Connor's amiable memoir, without the anger that so many memoirs are consumed by these days, he describes his parent's long love affair. His mother, Geri, was a tall, beautiful, blue-eyed, Norwegian blonde, a gregarious woman who always spoke her mind. She was her high school Prom Queen when she met her husband at a town dance. She was 17, he was 25, and instantly smitten. "My God!," he said, "You're the prettiest Irish girl I've ever seen."

"I'm not Irish." She looked him over. "I like a fella who's tall and funny."

"Well, Miss Norway you got the right fella."

O'Connor remembers their home being filled with laughter and music because, his mother said, "A life without music is a long walk in the dark."

Big Tom and Geri realized that at a young age, their son, Richie, was a basketball protégé. They encouraged his obsession despite their precarious finances. They always made sure he had the best sneakers and was well-fed. By his late teens, O'Connor was 6'4 and weighed 190 pounds.

As a young basketball player, O'Connor was determined not just to "play" the game, but rather "choreograph it." By the time he was ready for high school, O'Connor's game had attracted the attention of coaches of the best high school basketball teams in the Massachusetts and New York City area. One of those coaches who recruited him, said, "because you see patterns where others see chaos."

From his freshman year at St. Michael's High School in Union City, O'Connor was the star of the team for his next four years. With his stardom, he learned, came certain perks. As a freshman, he and a teammate stole some candy from a delicatessen. When they were found out they were summoned to the principal's office. His teammate was suspended from school, while O'Connor was "given a warning." When his friend learned of their disparate punishments, he said, that's "the upside of being you."

O'Connor was already becoming aware as a freshman that his basketball talents warranted him special treatment. Flattery from adults he barely knew, flirtations from pretty girls, and a blind eye from teachers that he never cracked open a book. At the end of his freshman year, it was announced that St. Michael's would be closing because of "financial mismanagement." The school's director, Father Matthew Martin, called a meeting of parents and alumni in an attempt to keep the school open. His major argument for not closing the school was, "How can we close the school when we have a player like Richie O who has done so much for the school?" A famous school alumnus, Tommy Heinsohn, then a star with the Boston Celtics, told the director, "It would be a shame not to let O'Connor finish his career here."

O'Connor did finish his career at St. Michaels and became one of the mostly highly recruited players in the country by over fifty of the best college basketball schools. His writing about those recruiting experiences is some of his best in his memoir and the most perceptive.

One famous college coach and ex-NBA star had a stretch limousine deliver O'Connor to an expensive restaurant where he dined with an alumnus. The alumnus told O'Connor the coach was "a tower of integrity." Then the alumnus handed the 18-year-old a folded envelope with a stack of twenty-dollar bills in it. "It's yours. Every month," the alumnus said, "If you choose our school."

When O'Connor visited an Ivy League college in the East, he arrived in the midst of an anti-Vietnam War riot. He couldn't leave that campus fast enough. When he visited a Florida college, he was given a tour of the campus by "a buxom blonde cheerleader," who suggested "we make sexual music together." When the embarrassed O'Connor said he had a girlfriend, the blonde gave him a fake pout and said, "Does that mean you won't be coming to the U?"

By far, the sweetest, most humble college coach who recruited O'Connor was an NBA Hall of Famer, whose team had won numerous NBA championships. When O'Connor answered the house phone he refused to believe the coach on the other end was really who he claimed to be. In a Tweety Bird voice, the coach said, "I weally am (who he claimed to be)." O'Connor said, "Really?" The coach said, "Weally." Although that coach was the most famous of all those who recruited O'Connor, he was the only one who never talked about his own playing career. He also never praised O'Connor's talents obsequiously, despite the fact that both the coach and O'Connor had a lot in common. They both were acknowledged as playing a selfless game on the court that depended on crisp, blind passes to teammates rather than their own 30 foot jump shots. O'Connor also appreciated that the famous coach never gave him "grandiose promises....just pure straight talk."

Eventually, O'Connor accepted a scholarship from Duke University, one of the most powerful basketball colleges in the country. He chose Duke because he respected the team's assistant coach, who recruited him, and with whom he had already formed a relationship. O'Connor writes, "His pitch was always upbeat and positive. Truthful and knowledgeable... He was a player whisperer."

At Duke, O'Connor learned as a freshman that the perks of being a basketball player at Duke were more carnal than at St. Michael's High School. One of his older teammates told the freshman, "Getting laid (as a basketball star at Duke) is easier than getting grits."

One can only imagine the Northeasterner O'Connor replying, "Really? What are grits?"

O'Connor became a star of a Duke freshman team that went undefeated—the only undefeated freshmen team in Atlantic Coast Conference history. O'Connor spent his first three years at Duke as one of its best players but also "the dumbest kid" in school who rarely went to class. When a professor asked him a question about Karl Marx, O'Connor thought Marx was one of the Marx Brothers. The professor warned him that he might be "cheered" on the basketball court, "jeered" off it if he didn't apply himself more.

By his junior year O'Connor was the varsity's leading scorer on an underachieving team. Despite his success, he was disillusioned about his basketball career because the game wasn't fun anymore as it had been at St. Michaels. O'Connor, as the ultimate team player, had discovered that his teammates were not a close-knit family, as they had been in high school. They were fierce rivals in practice in order to get playing time in games.

O'Connor decided he wanted to be more than "just a basketball player." He began to notice interesting students around campus who had nothing to do with basketball. He tried to cultivate them as friends. When he attempted to strike up a conversation in the library with a beautiful co-ed, she asked him why should she want to talk to him, because he was "a dumb jock." He told her he was tired of being a dumb jock and wanted to be "more than I am."

The co-ed relented and gave O'Connor books by authors such as Sartre, Camus, Emerson, Thoreau, and Kierkegaard. He read them. And their words and thoughts inspired him to believe that he could become knowledgeable about things other than basketball.

His next attempt at connecting with a counter-basketball-culture student was rebuffed, too. O'Connor noticed a student named John, who was ostracized in the cafeteria by some athletes because he was gay. So Richie decided to give John a blessing — the basketball star who would befriend him. Essentially John told the clueless jock to fuck off, he didn't need O'Connor's condescension. O'Connor was stunned by John's reaction, but when he thought about it he realized that John was right. But O'Connor didn't give up and eventually he and John became friends. John told him about the cosmopolitan rewards of New York City, other than watching Knicks' basketball games, such as going to plays, concerts, movies and museums.

O'Connor eventually quit the basketball team and withdrew from Duke before he graduated. He transferred to Fairfield University, where he spent his time commuting from Connecticut to Manhattan. He sought out poets and novelists and the best magazine writers. He went to jazz clubs, book readings, art exhibitions and Broadway plays. Then basketball again intervened in his life. A pro basketball team in Spain offered him a contract to play for a year at a beautiful seaside resort town. O'Connor rarely got off the bench, but he used his free time to travel across Europe.

He learned about food and wine from a Swiss chef, bought books from Shakespeare & Co in Paris, and philosophized with a rabbi over coffee in Tel Aviv. O'Connor told the rabbi he was sick of basketball. He wanted to be an artist, maybe a writer, but he feared he had no talent. The rabbi told him, "You're only confined by the walls you build around yourself."

When O'Connor returned to the states in 1975, he was determined to become a writer. He pursued his new career with the same, all his eggs in one basket intensity, as he had pursued basketball. He read all the quality magazines with stories in them by his favorite writers, John McPhee and Gay Talese. He interviewed as many writers as he could about the nuts and bolts craft of becoming a free-lance magazine writer, mainly of profiles. When they told him it would take discipline and perseverance, he knew he possessed those virtues in spades. They told him don't expect to make big money as a freelancer, but if you're lucky you could make enough to support a family.

He wasn't discouraged. In 1977 he sold his first story to Sport magazine, and then others to Sports Illustrated, GQ, People, and The New York Times. He sold over 50 stories, mostly about sports, between 1977 and the early 80s. He won awards for his stories such as being included in The Sporting News Best Sports Stories Anthology. Sports Illustrated talked to him about a staff position as a basketball reporter. O'Connor turned it down because he wanted to write more complex personality profiles, not game stories. Besides, he wanted to remain a freelancer in control of his own destiny.

By the mid-80s, O'Connor had a nice writing career which afforded him enough money to support himself and his young wife, Peg, and their son, Tim, born in 1986.

By 1989, O'Connor had essentially stopped writing for a living. He published only a few magazine stories from 1989 to the present, along with two mystery novels, "Gaelic Force" in 1997 and "Foul Shot" in 1999. Both were well-received, garnering decent reviews, but no big money. Then, O'Connor published nothing until 2023, with the publication of his memoir, "Taking a Shot."

Beginning in the late 80s until "Taking a Shot," O'Connor had abandoned his "all his eggs in one basket" philosophy, and became instead a "Jack of All Trades, Master of None," businessman. Over the next 30 years, he worked at a number of different jobs. Sometimes three at a time. He was the editor of SportsWise Magazine New York, then the editor of SportsTravel Magazine. He published stories by his favorite writers, but few of his own. When he totally moved over to the business side of magazines he became a division president at Nielsen Business Media, in charge of 18 magazines, 12 trade shows, generating $70 million in revenue. As a sideline, he scouted players for the NBA's Dallas Mavericks and Detroit Pistons for 17 years. He also ran a successful real estate business restoring homes. He even managed to fulfill every Irish American's dream of returning back to the glories of the Old Sod. He got a gig as Chairman of the Shamrock Games, an Olympic-style sporting event. There he discovered his roots. And had more than a few pints of Guinness.

O'Connor says that during this period in his life he wanted as many experiences and jobs as he could attain, in as many different fields as possible, to prove himself. Because all his jobs were high paying, he was able to retire at age 55, he writes, so he could devote his life to his son Tim, who today, at age 37, is a big man, 6-4, 230 pounds—the same size as his father and grandfather.

Timothy O'Connor was diagnosed with extreme autism in 1990. The diagnosis meant that Tim might need institutionalized care for his entire life, or at the very least close parental supervision along with help from a host of special teachers, doctors, and autism psychologists. In either case, Tim's care would be very, very expensive.

Besides Tim's expenses, O'Connor had another price to pay. As a highly successful businessman, he found himself away from home for long stretches of time—traveling the world to see clients, having expensive late-night dinners. Peg stayed home with Tim, "doing the heavy lifting," O'Connor writes.

By the age of ten, Tim had become violent. During his autistic rages, he threw things, punched holes in walls, and one day he physically attacked his 5'4" mother who was forced to call the police. The police subdued Tim and brought him to Morristown Hospital, where he was sedated and released a few days later.

The O'Connor's were now left with two choices. Either put Tim in a home that specialized in dealing with extreme autistic cases or Richie could quit his business jobs and become a stay-at-home father. He could return to his free-lance writing knowing that his writing wouldn't support his son's extensive treatments, at home or in a facility.

It was an agonizing decision to make. Whichever choice they made would have a profound affect on all their lives.

In "Taking a Shot," O'Connor confronts their final decision, the most momentous in their lives, which makes his memoir such a heart rending and poignant read. The fact that he decided to write this memoir as he approached 70, after 35 years removed from his freelance days, was a risk he had to take. The result is a wonderful book which has inspired him to return full time to his writing career of years ago. This book should gain O'Connor a legion of new readers, who have never known him as the award-winning sportswriter, Richie O'Connor, of years ago. He might even recapture his older fans from the seventies and eighties, who had lost track of him over the years. Now, with his new memoir, "Taking a Shot," they will have their answer to a question that has befuddled them for years.

"Yo! Richie! Where'd you go, man?"

-Pat Jordan

Jordan's memoir, A False Spring, was named by Sports Illustrated as one of the 100 best sports books of all time. His articles have been anthologized in Best American Sports Writing, Best American Mystery Stories, Best American Essays and The Norton Anthology of World Literature. Additionally, Allan Barra in an article for The Wall Street Journal wrote, "Who is the best sportswriter ever? The names that are mentioned most often are W. C. Heinz and Pat Jordan. I concur, but I'll take Jordan in a split-decision."

He is the author of twelve books, both non-fiction and fiction, including Tom Seaver and Me and My Father's Con.

Chapter One

February 1986. I'm sitting in a cab on my way to Madison Square Garden, looking out the window at a skinny young kid dressed in black jeans and an orange-and-blue New York Knicks sweatshirt. He's dribbling a ball around his back and through his legs, zig-zagging around the many pedestrians that block his way like unsuspecting defenders.

The kid reminds me of that boy who used to be me, the way I dribbled late at night through the streets of Union City, New Jersey. The noise—thump, thump, thump—drove our neighbors crazy. Some complained to my parents. Others glared at me, shook their heads and circled an index finger round and round their ear.

Back then my love for basketball was an obsession so consuming it verged on the pathological. My basketball coach at the time called me a "ruthless competitor."

I was all of eight years old.

Sharing the cab with me is Ryan Clark, a neighbor who I've only known for a few weeks. Tall, thin and twentyish, he's a basketball fanatic.

We watch as the kid performs a lightning-quick cross-over

dribble.

"Boy's got some moves," Ryan says.

"Sure does," I say as the kid makes a reverse dribble that almost knocks over an old lady pushing a laundry cart.

I immediately recall, with remarkable clarity, a time in Union City when I myself, while dribbling, knocked over an old lady carrying a big bag of groceries. The bag flew open. Apples rolled. A milk container leaked. As I bent down to retrieve the fallen goods, the old lady hit me over the head with her purse while at the same time screaming vulgarities loud enough to be heard by every butcher, baker and candlestick maker in town.

The cab lurches forward. Traffic is bumper to bumper, horns honking.

"Should be a good game tonight," Ryan says.

"Should be," I say. It's St. John's versus Syracuse. A big rivalry. A sellout.

"Must be a thrill for a kid to play in the Garden, huh?" Ryan says.

"Yeah, it's a great place to play," I say, feeling a gut-level recollection.

Ryan's eyebrows and voice rise simultaneously. "You've played there?"

"I have."

"Who'd you play for?

"Duke."

"Duke! Holy shit! That's fuckin' amazing. Did you play for Coach K?"

"No. I was before him."

"Who was your coach?"

"Bucky Waters was the head coach and Hubie Brown was the assistant."

"You mean to tell me you played for Hubie Fucking Brown, the Knicks coach?"

"I did."

"He's the best."

"Agreed."

"You ever play pro ball?"

I don't answer.

The cab has barely moved. It stops now for an interminable red light. We idle at a sizzling stretch of 7th Avenue: corner delis, dry cleaners, clothing boutiques, leather outlets, hair salons, banks and bars.

"Did you?" Ryan asks again.

"Did I what?" I say as the kid detonates a merengue-like spin around a cop. The cop grins. The kid disappears into the crowd.

"Play pro ball," he says.

I look out the window and watch steam clouds swirl skyward out from a manhole cover.

After a few seconds, I turn, stare at Ryan and say, "I quit the team mid-way my junior year."

"Why? Weren't you getting any playing time?"

"No, I was the team's leading scorer and cover boy on the 1971-72 media guide."

"So why'd you quit?"

I ignore his question. I think instead of a framed picture sitting on my desk at home. The picture was taken in Cameron Indoor Stadium my sophomore year, just a few minutes after I had gone one-on-one with Los Angeles Laker superstar Jerry West. My idol. He kicked my ass.

In the cover picture, I am wearing a T-shirt stenciled with the words "Union City Dept of Parks and Recreation." My shirt is gray and drenched with sweat. West's shirt is white and unblemished. The photographer told us to smile. We did. After the picture was taken, West shook my hand and said, "You got game."

Mind. Blown. It was as if I was being knighted by a king.

Ryan is staring at me with disbelief. He liberates a squashed pack of Marlboros, taps the bottom and offers me a smoke. I shake my head. I'm deep in thought, my mind extracting, like a chain of magicians handkerchiefs, past games. In particular, I'm remembering the night in the Garden when I scored thirty points against St. Bonaventure. It was 1972, my sophomore year. I was unstoppable, hop-scotching around the court, leading fast-breaks, swishing jumpers, hitting free throws, dishing assists and grabbing rebounds.

In the locker room after the game, Cas Rakowski, a sports reporter for The Jersey Journal, interviewed me and said, "You keep playing like you did tonight and there's no question you're destined for a great NBA career."

We approach the Garden. It's bedlam. Fans are pouring into the arena. Shouts, screams, songs, chants. Some kids blow whistles. Others blow horns. There are fathers with sons. Mothers with daughters. Boyfriends with girlfriends. College kids wearing the orange-and-black colors of Syracuse and the red-and-white of St. John's. It hits me that there's no greater sports atmosphere than a college basketball game in the World's Greatest Arena, Madison Square Garden.

The cab pulls to the curb. We get out. I pay the cabbie. Ryan grips my bicep.

"At least tell me this," Ryan says. "What happened after you left Duke?"

"Can't."

"Why?"

"Too long a story."

"Shorten it."

I think for a moment of all my worldly travels, bizarre experiences and unusual jobs I've had after leaving Duke. Even more, I open my mind's safety deposit box and withdraw from it a treasure trove of transformative people, including a Gangster and a Rabbi, who made every meeting, every conversation educational.

I learned from them—sometimes happily, sometimes painfully—about the need to live boldly and bravely, to take risks, to seize opportunities and accept that at any moment a treachery of fate can ambush you. Yet it's not the ambush that impacts you. It is, rather, how you deal with it.

Mentors like the Gangster and the Rabbi convinced me that anything was possible. Achievable. But only if you had moxie. Guts. And a fierce determination to succeed.

Walking toward the Garden now, Ryan says, "C'mon, man. Tell me something."

I grin. "Let's just say…I took a shot."

Ryan palms the sides of his head. "A shot!" he says. "A shot at what?"

Without a moment's hesitation, I answer: "Life." Even though at the time I quit I had no idea of the kind of life I wanted to live and the kind of man—the kind of person—I wanted to be.

We enter the Garden and walk into the arena.

It's almost game time. I find my seat, lean back and look at the court. I see the players shooting and the cheerleaders tumbling. I hear the bands rocking and the fans chanting.

I can't help but smile and think: sometimes walking away is the first step in finding yourself.

Chapter Two

My father was a milkman. He became one because his Irish immigrant parents with four sons barely had enough money to pay the rent. Typical of Irish families at the time, they sent their oldest son, James, to college. To help the family pay bills, my father, nineteen and the second oldest, was forced to follow his father, a milkman, into the milk business.

He never complained. He accepted his role. He grew to enjoy the job. He didn't care about making big money, buying fancy clothes or expensive cars. Didn't care about living in a large house or a fancy suburb. He was happy living in our four-story walkup, a railroad apartment with a small kitchen, two bedrooms, little heat, no shower and occasional mice and roaches.

For fifty years my father worked for a number of milk companies, including Farmland Dairies. He woke up at three a.m. and returned home at four p.m., delivering milk only to supermarkets and grocery stores. He worked six, often seven, days a week. He never missed a day of work. Nor was he ever fired.

One afternoon when I was seven, I came home and found him face down on the kitchen table, a cup of cold coffee and a half-eaten grilled cheese sandwich near his left ear. He was snoring loudly. I shook him awake. A big man—six-four, two-forty with arthritic knees—he ascended as slowly as a rusty car jack. "What? What?" he said, rubbing his eyes with his knuckles, his fingernails embedded with dirt.

"You okay?" I said.

"I'm fine."

He grabbed the coffee cup and drained it. His gray uniform was smudged with sweat and oil.

"Why do you work so hard, Daddy?" I said.

He scratched his stubbed jaw with a fingernail, making a rasping sound. "A man puts in a good day's work for a good day's pay." A pause. A grin. "It's simply a matter of taking care of business."

One night—I was nine and it was August—my father asked me if I wanted to work with him. I beamed and sang "Hi, ho, hi, ho, it's off to work we go." I figured I'd have more fun than a day at the beach.

The following morning we got up long before sunrise. My father made peanut butter and jelly sandwiches and put them in his dented metal lunch box. He made coffee and poured it into a cracked thermos. He gave me a Royal Crown Cola.

It was dark when we left our apartment. The streets were deserted. No people walking, no cars passing, no lights in the windows of the factory building across the street or the gas station on the corner.

My father, as always, wore his drab, gray uniform. I sported white gym shorts and a green and white Boston Celtics jersey.

We got into our car—an old, dented boxy blue and white two-door Ford Mercury sedan. Inside, the upholstery was worn, and a long strip of black electrical tape covered a rip on the passenger seat. The interior smelled like baking soda.

It took a while for the car to start; probably needed an oil change. It coughed and sputtered before rattling into life and moving forward as slowly as a rusted tank.

We drove to the Dairy. Traffic was light. The trip took less than an hour, most of it on Route 4—a highway littered with cheap motels, old diners, car dealerships, gas stations and hamburger joints.

Though very early, the car had no air-conditioning and it was already hot. We opened every window. It didn't help. The Mercury felt like one big, congested lung.

When we got to the warehouse, my father parked the car and got his truck, a big white one that had huge front windows and a sliding back door. He pulled the truck into a loading dock and lifted the door. It shuddered on its hinges.

"I'll load the truck," he said. "You can help later."

I watched as he lugged crate after crate of milk, orange juice and whipped cream, occasionally stopping, grimacing and massaging his lower back with both hands.

When the truck was packed, we hopped inside. The interior reeked of sour milk. The seats sagged like the jowls of a bulldog. My father cranked the ignition and gave the accelerator pedal little jabs with his right foot, making the engine cough and fart. He put the truck in gear and off we went, my father crouched over the steering wheel, his nose almost touching the windshield.

The Coasters hit "Charlie Brown" came on the radio. My

father loved that song. He tapped the rhythm of the tune with his fingertips on the steering wheel, deepening his voice as he sang along to Bobby Nunn's plaintive cry, "Why's everybody always picking on me?"

We began harmonizing. My father glanced over and pointed at me. I pointed at him. Simultaneously, we bellowed: "Who me— yeah you!" We laughed and slapped hands.

It took us less than an hour on the New Jersey Turnpike to get to the George Washington Bridge. The air seemed to get hotter with every mile. A blistering wind came through the opened windows, blowing our hair and stinging our eyes.

We crossed the bridge into Manhattan, and a few miles later entered the Bronx.

Compared to Union City, the Bronx was like another planet. There were crumbling buildings and faded billboards. A mattress laid in the street, soaking in a pool of water. A car outside a kid's playground was torched. Even the air seemed incendiary.

Yet, even in the midst of such poverty, people still rose in the morning, poured cream in their coffee, milk in their cereal and went off to work.

We got to a supermarket and pulled into a side loading dock. The dock smelled of excrement and vomit. A rat slithered behind a dumpster.

We exited the truck and the steamy morning air hit us like a blast from a furnace door. Instant sweat.

My father rubbed his hands together.

"Ready to work?" he said, grinning.

I nodded, jumping around as if on an invisible pogo stick.

My father slid open the back of the truck and we began

unloading crates. The crates were heavy. I could barely lift them. Sweat clung to my neck like a wet scarf.

After carrying a few loads I let drop a few words of complaint.

"This is hard work," I said, wiping perspiration from my forehead.

My father listened, but I saw no sympathy in his eyes, no voicing a "Yeah, it's tough, isn't it?"

Four young, shirtless men suddenly appeared out of the shadows. Their faces were clenched fists. They all wore sunglasses, gray sweatpants and white tank tops. They all had bowling balls for shoulders and grapefruits for biceps. One guy had a thick white scar along his jawline. Another tap tapped a switchblade in his palm.

I was scared shitless—not only because the men were so menacing looking but because I knew my father had already been assaulted twice while working. Once he was hit over the head with a broomstick; the cut required six stitches. The other time he was sucker punched and came home with a bruised cheek.

The men sauntered toward us, their massive shoulders swaying. I tugged convulsively on my shorts. Sensing my fear, my father took my arm and gently maneuvered me behind his back.

"Look fellas," my father said, holding his hands up, palms out. "I carry no cash. But if you want to take something, be my guest."

They all stared at him for a long moment like blind men trying to catch a ray of light.

The scarred one took a drag of his cigarette with a hissing intake of breath. He puffed out a big cloud of bluish smoke.

"That's what we intends to do," he said, his voice the soft purr of a loud diesel engine.

My father and I moved aside. My heart beat in slow, liquid thumps. The guys quickly grabbed a few cases of orange juice.

The scarred one looked at my father. He had the runny eyes of a recently opened oyster. He made a gun gesture, slowly lowering his thumb. He nodded. My father nodded back. The men disappeared like boats into a fog.

My father took me from behind his back. He squatted before me like a baseball catcher. Holding my forearms, he said, "You okay?" Shivering, I nodded yes.

"There's a lot of bad people in the world," he said. "You can't escape 'em. But you never provoke 'em."

Then, without another word, my father stood and went back to work. Within a half hour, his uniform was covered with sweat.

By day's end, my calves throbbed and my ribs ached. I had two cuts on my right hand. When we got home I was so tired I went right to bed.

I didn't work with my father the following day. But when he got home he asked me if I wanted to work with him again.

"I…a…I…"

My father made scooping gestures with his hands, as if trying to draw the words out of me.

"I…I don't know," I said

"Good," he said, smiling. "I'll wake you tomorrow morning at four."

I worked with my father the next day and the next and the next. I never once said another word about how tired or achy I was. I just tried to do my job. No complaining.

At the end of the week, my father took me to a corner candy store located around the block from our apartment: Jack's. We ordered ice cream cones: chocolate for me, vanilla for him. Both were topped with rainbow sprinkles.

We sat on a bench outside the store and for a while didn't exchange a word. My father's uniform was filthy. My Boston Celtics jersey was ripped.

We watched as cars passed—a Ford Thunderbird, a Buick Riviera, a Dodge Charger. Even a snazzy looking motorcycle.

"That's a Royal Enfield Continental GT," my father said, pointing.

I stopped licking my ice cream. "How you know that?"

My father winked. "I know things."

I smiled and resumed wolfing down my ice cream.

"Thing is, Rich…" my father said. He paused, dabbed the corners of his mouth with a napkin, then turned and stared at me for perhaps thirty seconds. "…you live to learn and learn to live."

Hardly a day goes by now that I don't remember him telling me this. Yet at the time his words floated away above my head, like a kite going skyward. It would be a long time before I would reel them in. Indeed, had I known then what I know now, I might never have put all my energies into dribbling a basketball under the bright lights in Madison Square Garden.

After we finished eating our ice cream we walked back to our apartment. It was dark. The streetlights glowed. My father, as always at the end of the workday, limped.

When we got to the front steps, my father stopped and extended his hand. I shook it. His hand was callused, rougher than sandpaper.

"You did good," he said. That was the full extent of our conversation.

I skipped up the steps behind him—no longer feeling tired.

For as long as I can remember, I always called my father "Big Tom." Never Dad.

He loved being called Big Tom. It made us pals, buddies. At his core, my father was a nice man, a charmer who worked hard at niceness. Part of his achievement as a human being was to make people feel as if they were special. I often told friends that the only thing bigger than his bicep was his heart.

Like my father, my mother, Geri, grew up in Union City. Her parents were Norwegians. Her mother was a housewife and her father worked on the docks as a steamfitter in nearby Hoboken. Or at least, that's what everyone thought, including my mother. But the truth was, in his younger days in New York City, my grandfather was a gangster and a cohort of mobsters Bugsy Siegal and Meyer Lansky. After he got married and moved to New Jersey he started a family and became a bookie.

My mother, by all accounts, was a beautiful child. She grew up tall and slender, blonde and blue eyed.

In high school, she was a prom queen. After graduating, she worked in New York, first as a receptionist and later for Beldoch Popper, a women's clothing manufacturer. It was there she began her career, modeling for prospective buyers.

How my ambitious, gorgeous model mother got together with my easy-going, muscular, milkman father was, as a kid, a mystery to me. I mean, how could two people who had such different looks, different styles and different ambitions become a couple and stay married for almost sixty years?

My father's younger brother, Pat, first introduced them at a town dance. Pat knew my mother from hanging around the neighborhood. She was seventeen, my father was eight years older.

He had just returned from being a sergeant in World War II, where he spent the majority of his time in Italy and France. There he saw friends riddled with bullets. Robbed of arms and legs. Of life.

The first words my father, wearing a wrinkled suit and army boots, said to my mother was, "My God! You're the prettiest Irish girl I've ever seen."

My mother, resplendent in a floral dress and slingback heels, said, "I'm not Irish."

"What are you?"

"Norwegian."

"I like Norwegians."

My mother squinted. "Why?"

"They're nice."

"Not all."

"Well, you're nice."

My mother tilted her head.

"How can you tell?"

My father rubbed a finger back and forth under his nose.

"You haven't told me to take a hike."

My mother laughed.

"You're funny," she said.

"Everybody says that."

"And you're tall."

"Everybody says that, too."

My mother smiled. Her blue eyes sparkled.

"I like a fella who's tall and funny."

My father clasped his hands and rubbed them over each other.

"Well, Miss Norway," he said, excitedly, "you've got the right fella."

They stared at one another for a long moment. The air between them seemed to crackle, as if a strong current of electricity had swept through it.

"Your brother says you're a good dancer," my mother said.

"Few in town better."

"Few?"

"Actually nobody," my father said. "I was just trying to be modest."

"And failing miserably."

The two broke out laughing.

A scratchy version of "You'll Never Know" by Dick Haymes came from a loudspeaker.

My father extended his hand. "Care to dance?"

Taking his hand, my mother said, "I'd love to."

The two danced the night away. Soon they began dating. And on June 3, 1946, thinking it would be a romantic thing to do, they eloped to Baltimore, Maryland and were pronounced man and wife by clergyman John J. Duncan.

To the day he died, my father always said that by marrying my mother he "won the human lottery" adding, "Think about it. How the hell did a guy like me get a gal like her? Miracles do happen."

Looking back, I guess it's true what they say about opposites attracting—though my parents did have one thing in common, aside from being a comedy team. Neither was very athletic, except on the dance floor. Put them on a basketball court or a tennis court and they'd have stumbled around worse than Inspector Clouseau.

Union City was populated with working-class people who lived in small homes or brick apartment buildings. The men were mostly blue-collar guys—truckers, plumbers, cops and firemen. Their spouses were mostly housewives and waitresses. Almost everyone in town was Irish, Italian, or Polish. There were few Blacks. Cubans and Puerto Ricans came later because housing was cheap and work in the many factories plentiful.

Our apartment was at 1619 Palisade Avenue. Picture Ralph Kramden's crib in The Honeymooners. I shared an itsy-bitsy bedroom with my brother, Tom, who was five years older. We slept in bunk beds.

On cold winter days when heat was scarce, we warmed ourselves by opening the oven and rubbing our hands together. At night, we buried ourselves in blankets. Sometimes getting out of bed in the morning was like stepping into a meat locker.

In the summer, we opened every window and tried cooling ourselves with small electric fans. Come August, I often slept with an ice bag on my neck.

The apartment was only a short walk from Bergenline Avenue, a suffocating street jammed with banks, delis, diners, dry cleaners and newspaper stands…David Burr's Men's Store…Davis' Toy Store. People ate out at one of three places: The Hearth, The Four-Star Diner or The New Moon, a Chinese restaurant where the food was cheap and barely edible, the sweet very sour and the sour very sweet.

My parents were sweet, too. And a hoot. A fun couple. They were like Lucy and Desi, June and Ward, Rob and Laura Petrie, Darrin and Samantha Stephens, though my mother was more bewitching than Samantha. When she smiled, it was as if she had swallowed the sun.

Most nights, after dinner—usually Swanson's TV dinners

or Mrs. Paul's Fish Cakes—my mother, father and brother Tom would gather in the living room and watch Gunsmoke, Bonanza, Paladin, Leave it to Beaver, I love Lucy or Father Know Best. (I especially loved it on days when we watched Dick Clark's American Bandstand or The Mickey Mouse Club. The only Mouseketeer I really cared about was Annette Funicello. Even at age eight, I could tell she was a hottie.)

So much of our life back then was stillness, tranquil. We were never rushing to get places, never dashing off on vacations, never running to restaurants, never hurrying to see the latest movie, never hastening to buy a new refrigerator or a new radio. We were content with what we had and didn't long for what we didn't. Or at least, that's how I remember it.

One thing we all shared was a love of music. It played constantly in our apartment, as if we had musical wallpaper. We listened to Frank Sinatra, Tony Bennett, Bing Crosby, Peggy Lee and Rosemary Clooney. My mother sang along. She had a good voice. Music made her happy. As it did my father—especially when he came home after "having a few."

I remember one time he bounced in the door, semi shit-faced, elated over getting a raise. He put one of his favorite LP's on the turntable: Anita O'Day singing Cole Porter. He placed the needle on the record, grabbed my mother by the hand, then twirled her around and the two of them started dancing the jitterbug.

My father didn't just cut a rug, he shredded it. When the song ended, he bent my mother backward tango-style, looked down at her and sang, "It's delightful, it's delicious, it's de-lovely." My mother's smile rose like bubbles in a champagne glass.

"A life without music," she often said, "is a long walk in the dark."

To this day, I am still serenaded by the music I grew up with: Elvis Presley singing "Hound Dog," Bobby Darin singing "Mack the Knife," Bill Haley & His Comets singing "Rock Around the Clock." Those songs activate the dopamine network in my brain. I seek them out whenever I think of the silly things my parents did.

I remember a day when they took me to Belmar at the Jersey Shore. I was nine. The beach was crowded. Lots of surfers and swimmers, kids and parents. A few bikinied girls held foil reflectors with two hands, their oily faces ablaze with summer light.

My mother was lying on a towel, sunning herself. My father suddenly picked her up like a groom carrying his bride across the threshold, raced down to the ocean and tossed her in. She emerged shaking water from her hair, then started splashing my father. He splashed her back. Shouts, squeals. The water fight lasted ten minutes. Even the young kids watching found them hilarious.

A few hours later, we left and stopped at Belmar Playland. Pinball machines. Dings and dongs. Cow bells. My father challenged my mother to Skee-Ball, a game played by rolling a ball up an inclined hill and over a hump that jumps the ball into bullseye rings. The idea is to collect as many points as possible by getting the ball into holes that have progressively higher values: 10-20-30-40-50.

Still wearing bathing suits—my father in tight plaid Jantzen shorts, my mother in a white Cole of California Lastex one-piece—they started playing. My mother quickly began racking up points. My father, impressed, started a routine. He blew out his right cheek like Popeye and said, "Well, well, shiver me timbers."

My mother stuck out her tongue. She quickly added more

points.

My father, joking, stomped his foot. "That's all I can stands, and I can't stands no more."

My mother put a finger to her lips and joined in. "Oh, dear," she said, imitating Olive Oyl.

Suddenly, as if injected with spinach, my father started hitting only the 40 and 50-point holes. He won easily.

My mother gave him a Bronx cheer.

"What can I tell ya," my father declared, "I yam what I yam!"

As we left the arcade, my father broke into a Charlie Chaplain walk, feet splayed, arms rocking, body tilting side to side. My mother held his hand. We ducked inside D'Jais Bar and Grill. My mother ordered a Pink Squirrel: vanilla ice cream, clear Crème de Cacao and Crème de Noyaux. My father ordered a Schlitz. I sat on a bar stool spinning round and round, sipping a Pepsi, chewing maraschino cherries and listening to them laugh and tell stories about their courtship.

The story I liked most happened a few nights after my father proposed to my mother.

They were sitting in an Italian restaurant in Union City. The restaurant was dimly lit and the tables were covered in red-and-white checkered oil cloths. Candles in jelly jars sat between tall wooden salt and pepper shakers. From a jukebox Louis Prima sang "Buona Sera."

My father wore a blue work shirt and black jeans. My mother sported a satiny silver dress, suede high heels and fish-net stockings. Pinned to her right shoulder was a white corsage.

My father twirled some spaghetti around his fork. Just as he was about to put it in his mouth, he dropped the fork and rubbed his chin as if acknowledging that he needed a shave. "Imagine this, Geri," he said, raising his index finger. "Imagine if we have a son and he gets your looks and my body."

My mother pondered this a moment, then said, "But what happens if he gets my body and your looks."

My father scrunched his face. "The kid's fucked." For the record, I got both Big Tom's looks and body.

My parents overfed my brother and me with attention and affection. They made sure we had the best of everything—even when money was scarce, which was often. They brought us the best basketballs, the best baseball gloves, the best sneakers.

My brother, Tom, wasn't as nuts about sports as I was; he wasn't as insistent about getting the best equipment. He approached sports more from an analytical perspective, which is why he became a basketball coach at Dartmouth and later the athletic director at George Mason University. In 2007, he was named the Chairman of the NCAA Selection Committee.

Unlike Tom, I pushed my father to get me the hottest equipment as soon as it hit the market.

I was ten years old when my father got me my first pair of Adidas. At the time, Adidas sneakers were the newest and hottest thing on the market—more popular than even Converse All Stars. Sporting goods stores simply could not get enough of them; they sold out instantly. But thanks to a friend of a friend who worked at Modell's Sporting Goods, my father learned of an Adidas distributor, Carlson Importers.

Carlson's was located in Manhattan's Lower East Side, on Orchard Street, a narrow and cobblestoned avenue that had its own unique thumbprint and heartbeat.

The street was part open flea market, part a bustling bazaar, part cattle-pen—hundreds of buyers and sellers crammed together, bobbing and weaving, pushing and shoving as if in a rugby scrum.

We walked past brick-faced tenements fronted with zig-zagging fire escapes; countless Kosher delicatessens exhaling a symphony of scents—pickled eggs, hot pastrami and warm bagels. We saw stout women wearing long black dresses, shawls and babushkas strolling alongside short men in dark suits and white shirts. The men all wore yarmulkes, had beards like bushy trowels and hair that hung in tendrils that reminded me of long, fuzzy earrings.

Carlson's was in an old, dilapidated warehouse held together by exhaust fumes and pigeon dung.

We entered the building through a steel door. The vestibule was dark and stank of urine and roach spray. On the right-hand wall were brass mailboxes, the fronts either torn off or badly dented. Beneath the mailboxes were doorbell buttons with name slots. One said Carlson Importers. Fifth Floor.

My father pressed the bell. A buzzer sounded. We stepped into a lobby where two elevator doors flanked a mailbox fed by a glass chute. A cardboard sign read—"Elevators Out of Order."

We trudged up five flights of stairs—turning at landings, climbing, turning, climbing. Colorful swirls of graffiti decorated the walls. Crushed beer cans sat on the steps. From somewhere came a strong scent of cigar smoke.

We knocked on Carlson's door. Seconds passed. A minute. I grew anxious. Then the door opened. Standing there was a tall, thin man, lean as a greyhound, maybe early forties, unshaven. He had a hatchet face and close-chopped blond hair. He wore black baggy pants, a gray flannel shirt and paisley suspenders.

He glared at us, his forehead wrinkling horizontally, like a venetian blind. In a German accent that was thicker than crusted glue, he said, "Vut do you vant?"

"A pair of Adidas sneakers," my father said.

"I am not retailer," he said. "I am wholesaler."

"I know," my father said, "but we took two buses and a subway ride to get here. Can you at least sell us one pair?"

The German stroked the corners of his mouth with his thumb and forefinger. "Veddy well," he said, stepping aside and ushering us in with a sweeping arm motion. "My name Heinz. I only sell you one pair."

"Fine," my father said. "That's all we want."

We entered a loft the size of a tennis court. Swords of sunlight filtered in through large grimy windows reinforced with wire mesh. Sneaker boxes were piled on metal shelves, wall-to-wall and floor-to-ceiling. An old Victrola sat on a corner table, playing German music.

Heinz squatted down like a baseball catcher. "Vut size?" he said, his face close to mine, his breath eggy.

"Twelve," I said.

"Not sure I have," he said. "But I check."

Heinz climbed a tall, railed ladder that reached up about twenty feet. He rolled along a wall until he stopped and pushed aside some boxes. Twitching with impatience, I hopped up and down as if my white Converse All Stars were burning my feet.

Heinz descended backwards down the ladder, holding a blue-and-white sneaker box. He handed it to me as if it were a chalice. I took the box with cupped hands, quickly ripped the top off, then sat on a folding chair and tried on the sneakers.

They fit perfectly.

My father and I left Carlson's. Outside, it was a beautiful afternoon, the air cool and crisp, not a cloud in the sky.

"Thanks, Big Tom," I said.

He smiled. "My pleasure."

"No," I said, giving him a hug. "Mine."

Chapter Three

I've often thought about why I became so addicted to basketball. Why not football or baseball? I was, after all, the much-heralded quarterback on my grammar school team. And in 1963, I was the best pitcher on the Union City all-star team that played in the Pony League World Series in Rockford, Illinois.

I didn't watch games on television or follow my brother to schoolyards or idolize some local hero.

All I know is the narcotic of basketball entered my system at age five.

My parents threw me a birthday party. After blowing out candles atop a vanilla cake and then eating a slice, my father presented me with a square box wrapped in brown wrapping paper.

I ripped the paper off. Feverishly. Inside the box was another box and inside that a red and white biddy basketball, like the real thing, only smaller. I took it out of the box and immediately started dribbling around the living room. Around tables and chairs. Around my mother and father. Even my brother.

I couldn't have expressed my feelings then, but I can now: I had an out of body experience, a sense, even at that young age, of surrendering to something enormous.

The basketball became my constant companion. I took it everywhere. To church. To school. To the bathroom. I even slept with it the way other kids my age slept with teddy bears.

As I got older, what captivated me even more about basketball was that I could play by myself. Unlike football or baseball, I didn't need anyone to catch with or throw to. All I needed was a ball, a basket and my imagination—the fantasy of hitting the game winning shot with the clock counting down.

By age eight, I was practicing every day in Hudson schoolyard—metal backboards, bent rims, potholed asphalt. I choreographed my moves over and over, breaking them down to the tiniest detail. I practiced the through-the-legs dribble. The spin dribbled. The crossover dribble. I worked on different shots. Bank shots. Hook shots. Jump shots. From ten feet. Twenty feet. My objective always was to keep improving, to outwork and outsmart my opponents. To play chess when they were playing checkers.

I was in the schoolyard before school. After school. On rainy days. Sweltering days. I remember once a snowstorm hit. The temperature was well below the freezing mark and the swirling winds were so fierce that the wind-chill factor had to be thirty below. Or so it seemed.

My friends bolted. I stayed and kept shooting as the snow fell, drilling down from the sky like fat feathers. Once inch. Three inches. Calf-high.

The world became pure white. Soundless. There were no people, no cars, no cats, no dogs. My face was frozen. My hands were numb. I could barely see the rim. I finally stopped when my feet felt like blocks of ice.

I even practiced basketball at night in the apartment. While my parents were in the living room, my father watching The Jackie Gleason Show, my mother reading Vogue magazine, I dribbled a soccer-sized ball around like a madman. It drove my mother nuts. Not only because of the annoying thump thump thump of the ball, because I would occasionally toss the ball through a make-shift wire hoop attached to the living room door and break picture frames, religious statues and decorative bowls. Once, after attempting a hook shot, I missed and shattered a Waterford vase.

My mother looked up at me with exasperated eyes and said, "What's wrong with you?"

"I dunno."

"Maybe you should spend less time on basketball and more time on schoolwork."

"You mean study?"

She put the magazine aside. "If you want to give it a name, alright. Study!"

I almost never studied, was barely getting passing grades. It frustrated my mother to no end.

She could never figure out how I could calculate all sorts of arcane basketball statistics yet be failing math.

"Who cares about arithmetic?" I'd say.

She flipped her hands in the air. "You should. You'll need to know it someday."

"I doubt that."

To help me improve my grades, my mother purchased a twelve-set volume of Encyclopedia Britannica. Nice leather bindings with gold-edged pages. She placed them ever so nicely on a bookshelf.

I remember taking a volume off the shelf only one time. It was at the exact same moment, my mother arrived home from work. Seeing me with the book, she lifted her arms up as if signaling a field goal. "Praise the Lord!" she exclaimed. "You're actually reading an encyclopedia."

"You betcha."

"What are you looking for?"

"Something about James Naismith."

Her eyebrows knitted together.

"Who's James Naismith?"

"The man who invented basketball."

She lowered her arms.

"Basketball," she said. "That's all you ever think about."

I shrugged. "What else is there to think about?"

"Maybe you should try reading a book."

"I just read one."

Her eyes narrowed. Her hands on her hips. "When?"

"Last night."

She flashed a Pepsodent smile. My mother LOVED books. She bought them as often as most people purchased toilet tissue. She felt they percolated a person's mind and as such badgered me— no, ordered me—to read, saying "No matter how much money a person makes, having plenty of books makes them even richer."

I, of course, rolled my eyes.

"So you read a book," she said, her voice a flare of excitement. "That's wonderful. What kind of book? History? Science?"

"No. Hoop Crazy by Clair Bee. It's about a basketball player named Chip Hilton."

Her smile collapsed. "What am I going to do with you?"

"Buy me a new basketball?"

She smirked. "How about this?" she said. "How about I get you a subscription to National Geographic magazine?"

"I'd rather have one to Sport Magazine."

She shook her head and gazed up at the ceiling. "You know, Mr. Smarty Pants, one of my greatest hopes is that someday you'll become an avid reader."

I snorted. "Fat chance."

My mother tousled my hair as if kneading pizza dough. "Don't know what I'm gonna do with you," she said. "Why don't you get ready for dinner."

Ten minutes later, she was yelling at me to get out of our bathroom, which reeked of Ajax. I wasn't washing up before supper. I was pantomiming my jump shot in front of the medicine-cabinet mirror when I accidently hit the door. The door flew open, depositing all sorts of medicines and toiletries on the floor. My mother wasn't pleased.

I started playing organized basketball at eight. "The biddies," as they were called, was an organized league for kids under twelve played on a smaller court with a smaller ball.

The games were held at Robert Waters gym, a cockpit with walls only inches from the court, rickety bleachers and poor lighting. It was apparent from the get-go that I wasn't the biggest nor the fastest player, which didn't bother me. My goal was to be more workhorse than racehorse. Even as a young boy I played with such intensity it sometimes unnerved me.

Because of this intensity, I was often injured: bloody noses, scraped knees, jammed fingers, sprained ankles and pulled muscles.

My bruises ranged in color from yellow to black. I had so many floor burns it looked like I'd been scorched. Some teammates began to call me Ben, since I always smelled like Ben-Gay.

Coach Mastorelli was nicknamed "Wiz." He was the Frank Lloyd Wright of young talent. A short, curly-haired character with a deeply tanned face and alert dark eyes, Wiz had the snaggled underbite of a bulldog. Though short in stature (picture Danny Devito with curly black hair wearing shorts and sneakers) Wiz was tall in effort and energy.

While playing for the University of Vermont in the 1950s, Wiz had been named a Little All-American for players under six feet. He knew and cared a lot about the game. Getting a compliment from him was as rare as getting the truth from a politician.

When he once told me I was the hardest working, most dedicated kid he had ever seen I felt like I'd been given a papal blessing. "I've seen a lot of kids come and go," he said, "but you… you take the cake. You never stop hustling. You think basketball is guerilla warfare. You're a goddamn kamikaze."

I wanted to win so badly that once, in a meaningless game, I dove after a ball going out of bounds like a swimmer starting the 100-meter freestyle. I crashed head first into a wall. I stood and started walking—wobbling, really—like a drunken sailor. Someone suggested taking me to the hospital for an X-ray. Wiz said, "Maybe we should take the wall instead."

Another time a random elbow chipped my front tooth. Blood stained my shirt and lips. Wiz suggested I take a seat. I said no way.

"God!" he said. "You're a stubborn kid!"

"Thank you," I said.

"It's not a compliment."

I handed him a piece of tooth and hustled back onto the court.

That night Wiz called my father and told him that I should "defuse my intensity."

My father, sitting in a lounge chair in the living room and sipping a can of Ballantine beer said, "What do you think about that?"

"About what?"

"Defusing your intensity," he said.

Trying to spin a basketball on my index finger, I said, "Why? If you're considered a blue-collar worker why can't I be considered a blue-collar player?"

Big Tom's reply? "Ooookay."

As I got older and I wasn't playing, my father sometimes took me to see games at local colleges—Princeton, Rutgers, Seton Hall, St. Peter's College or to pro games at the old Madison Square Garden on 8th Avenue between 49th and 50th Streets. We always went to doubleheaders because my father said it was a bargain to see two games for the price of one.

I still remember walking under the marquee at the old Garden, the crowds pushing and shoving, the hawkers selling pictures and pennants, the smell of hot dogs and sauerkraut emanating from Nedick's.

We always sat in the "nosebleed" section of the stands that was fogged with cigarette and cigar smoke. We ate popcorn until the first game began, the cheers rising, the lights glowing, the court shining.

We saw the New York Knickerbockers play the St. Louis Hawks. The Syracuse Nationals play the Boston Celtics. The teams didn't matter to me as much as the individual players like "Jumpin" Johnny Green. Richie Guerin. Willie Naulls. Bob Cousy. Bob Pettit. Cliff Hagen. Oscar Robertson. Jerry West. To me, these guys were gods. Mythical figures. They enchanted me. Motivated me. I became so emotionally jazzed watching them, it was as if I had walked into a magnetic field and got electrically charged. I looked at the court and dreamed, promising myself that someday I would be a pro and play in Madison Square Garden.

My goal, as a youngster, was to have a game like my idol, Jerry West. I did read a bit by then, but only books and magazines about basketball, fingering the pages with the exactness of a blind man reading braille.

Skill-wise, my game was improving.

The only problem was my temper.

Once, when I was ten years old, I stormed into the locker room after my team had lost a game. I thought my teammate, Eddie, was loafing. I chewed him out. Eddie told me to fuck off. I shoved him against a wall. He pushed me away. I was just about to punch him when Wiz arrived and pulled me aside.

Outside the locker room, Wiz stood before me, his arms folded across his chest like an Indian chief.

"You don't hit teammates," he yelled.

"But he deserved it."

"He did, huh?" Wiz shook his head. His eyeballs smoked. "Why? Because he missed a few shots?"

"Because he wasn't hustling."

"That's for me to decide, not you." His words weren't spoken. They were detonated.

"Look, Rich," he said. "I'm only trying to do what's best for you. That includes not only improving your game but also your behavior." He palmed my shoulder. "Do me a favor. Apologize to Eddie."

"But…"

He tick-tocked an index finger. "No buts. Do as I say."

When I told my father about the incident, he said Wiz was right: I should apologize. I asked if I could think about it. Okay, he said, think about it.

Instead of thinking about it, I went to see my maternal grandfather, John Barrett, who I thought was a longshoreman but who had been a gangster, alongside Bugsy Siegel and Meyer Lansky, before taking a job at a corner candy store in Union City.

I worshipped the man, the strength and the scent of him, the Old Spice cologne and Dutch Masters cigars. He seemed larger than life even before I knew what larger than life meant.

From childhood, my grandfather always treated me like an adult. He told me straight. No bullshit. He rarely, if ever, sprinkled his lectures with herbs and spices, condiments or sauces.

His favorite word was "moxie." It was his chant, his mantra. His second favorite word was "bellyaching," as in "stop your bellyaching." I soaked in his words as if I was a sponge.

The day I went to see him at the store on Bergenline Avenue, he was standing behind a counter, smoking a smelly stogie and reading the Daily Racing Form.

A tall, thin man with a high forehead and a strong nose, he wore a starched white shirt, red suspenders and a black onyx ring on his left pinkie.

He took a puff of his stogie and expelled a thin trumpet of smoke. "What can I do you, kid?" His voice was pure Jimmy

Durante.

"Need some advice."

He waggled his eyebrows like Groucho Marx.

"If it's about sex," he said, "just keep your pecker in your pants."

I told him what happened with Eddie and how Wiz wanted me to apologize.

He took another puff, wreathing himself in cigar smoke. Then he pointed a finger at me stained yellow by his alternative smoking addiction: Chesterfields.

"This Eddie kid sounds like a real beaut," he said. "He didn't do what he's supposed to and you did what you were supposed to. You set him straight. If it was up to me I would have given the weak sister a knuckle sandwich." A beat. "Trust me, he got the message. Don't apologize."

"Okay," I said.

He put a hand on my shoulder.

"Need any salad?" Salad was his word for money. Nothing cheered him more than giving it away to family members.

Before I could respond, he slipped a folded-up dollar into my palm. Or, as he called it, a "bone."

"Thanks," I said.

He winked. "Don't spend it all it in one place."

I nodded and started to walk away.

Then I heard his ear-splitting whistle, the one where he spread two fingers in his mouth and blew, as if hailing a cab that would inevitably stop in its tracks, leaving rubber on the pavement.

I turned.

He shouted: "You have two feet, right?"

I cocked my head. "What?"

"Fucking stand on them."

When I got home after speaking with my grandfather I told my father what he had said. My father lifted his eyes toward the ceiling.

"Look, Rich," he said. "You decide what you want to do. But remember there is no wrong time to do the right thing."

The two men couldn't have been more different. My grandfather was aggressively pugnacious where my father was pugnaciously unaggressive. My grandfather wanted to strike the first blow; my father preferred to absorb it. A typical conversation between them went something like this: My father: "Cream rises to the top." My grandfather: "Yeah, and so does scum." My father: "I love Irish whisky." My grandfather: "I wouldn't drink that Paddy piss if you paid me." Yet the two, somehow, always got along if for no other reason than they both loved my mother.

After some debate with my father, I called Eddie. I said I was sorry. It was the first time I ever humbled myself. It wouldn't be the last.

The next day I went to see Wiz and told him I apologized. He put his hand on my shoulder and said, "Good. Now start behaving yourself."

"I'll try."

Wiz pressed his lips together. He had Yoda beat by three decades. "No trying. Do."

A few weeks later, Wiz took me to Linderman's, a popular ice cream parlor that had a counter on one side with swivel stools, tubs of ice cream beneath it and soda fountains above. On the other side, a large glass case was filled with penny candies. The place always smelled like licorice.

Both of us dressed in shorts and T-shirts sat in a back booth. Nestled against my right leg was a basketball.

Wiz pointed to it and said, "Did you really have to bring that?"

"Would Zorro go anywhere without his sword?"

Wiz shook his head and massaged his temples.

A waitress came and took our order. Burgers, fries and Cokes.

"It never hurts to apologize," Wiz said. "We all make mistakes in life. The key is to learn from them."

I nodded and said, "I just hate losing."

"Losing hurts and stays with you longer than winning," he said, in a soft voice. "But losing teaches you more. It helps you deal with heartbreak and heartache. Makes you tougher, more resilient."

I nodded again. A nearby table was full of kids my age, girls in white blouses and boys in black tees. They were wadding up paper cups and tossing them back and forth at each other, laughing hysterically. I envied their tomfoolery.

"You have all the tools to be a great basketball player," Wiz said, fiddling with a salt container. "The only thing that can stop you from reaching your goal of becoming a pro someday is you."

I had no idea what he was talking about.

"You're different than any kid I've ever coached," he said. "You're so focused, so determined. But I'm concerned that that determination might become too much for you."

I said nothing.

"The point is," he said in tones a kindly priest might use to console someone in need, "keep basketball in perspective."

"Okay," I said, not aware that self-knowledge was a wide-ranging thing, constantly changing, its elasticity part of its potency, and that it can only be achieved through observation, contemplation and introspection. It's the proven formula for how one discovers themselves. For me, that recognition was many years away.

The food arrived. The burgers were juicy and the fries crispy.

"I will admit," Wiz said. "You've been acting with decorum."

"What's 'decorum?'"

"Appropriateness."

"Meaning?"

"Your behavior on the court has improved greatly."

I grinned. "I'm glad."

Wiz's grin was even wider. "Me, too."

Wiz then paid the check and we stepped outside. The sun was bright and there was a slight breeze.

Wiz moved within inches of my face and put his hands on my shoulders.

"One last thing," he said.

"What's that?" I said, dribbling the ball from my right hand to my left.

"Don't think by me taking you to lunch I won't stop getting on you."

I smiled and said, "I wouldn't expect anything less."

Chapter Four

By age twelve, I was arguably the best biddy basketball player in the state.

I should have been satisfied. But I wasn't. Wasn't happy with my game. To improve, I walked the streets, looking straight ahead, straining to see things on my left and right to master my peripheral vision. I enlisted the help of a dance instructor to better my footwork. He had me stand on one leg like a flamingo to gain better balance and hopscotch through speed ladders for quickness. I used ankle weights to help me jump higher. I lifted barbells to pump my biceps. I practiced juggling to better my hand eye coordination. I dribbled constantly with my left hand so it would be as effective as my right.

I ended almost every day by sprinting around the block. Ten times. Stopping and starting. Accelerating. Zig-zagging. I wanted to have extraordinary stamina, to be a player of perpetual motion, always moving without the ball which would free me for shots and exhaust my opponents. A neighbor once called me "the mechanical man," adding "that you run so much you must have a super-charged battery up your ass."

The downside to all this running was that I regularly got blood blisters on my feet.

My last game as a biddy basketballer was for the league championship. My team was playing an opponent who had a player, Bobby Tatano, that many thought was as good, if not better, than me.

I couldn't wait to face him. We'd be playing before many coaches from private high schools who, I was told, were ready to offer me or Bobby a scholarship.

The morning of the game I woke early and dressed quickly. My mother offered to make me a big breakfast, eggs and bacon, but I had no appetite. I just gulped a big glass of orange juice.

As was my pre-game custom, I went to my bedroom and blasted the song "Chantilly Lace" by The Big Bopper. I danced around like an electrified monkey.

I got to Robert Waters gym two hours before game time. I put on my uniform and hit the court. Alone. I began a series of dribble moves—around my back and through my legs—followed by shooting jumpers from around the key. I ended the session only after hitting ten free throws in a row.

Fifteen minutes before the tip-off both teams took the floor and began layup lines. I looked over and saw Tatano. He saw me. I blitzed him with a stare. He shot me the finger.

Tatano was an Italian kid who at twelve looked twenty. He had a dark complexion, dark eyes and thick, curly black hair. His hands were the size of saddles and his forearms resembled overinflated footballs.

His team won the opening tap. Bobby immediately got the ball and dribbled at me, his head down, his eyes like two high beams. He performed a cross-over dribble, the ball exploding down from his left hand up into his right. My legs got tangled. I fell on my ass. I attempted to get up quickly, but I was like a splayed horse, trying to get to its feet and flailing about helplessly. I rose just as Bobby stopped at the top of the key and buried a jumper. My face burned with embarrassment.

Running back down court, Bobby blew on his knuckles and said, "Nice defense. What are you a matador?" His smile was so wide he could have eaten a Hershey bar sideways. It took all my willpower not to chase after him and punch his lights out.

Minutes later, he was leading a fast break. He looked right, then floated a pass, less thrown than conjured, right to an open man for an easy layup.

I demanded the ball and drove to the hoop, Bobby on me like shrink wrap. I went in for a layup. Bobby trampolined high and blocked my shot. I never before had a shot blocked. I clench my fists so tight, my forearms spasmed. What the fuck?

Okay, enough's enough. Calm down. Play your game. You're a better player than Tatano. Show it.

My team had the ball. We passed it around, setting screens and making cuts. I received the ball on the left wing and dribbled right, Bobby shadowing me. I quickly did a reverse dribble and caught him off balance. I elevated into the air and released a high parabola jump shot that fell perfectly through the net.

Bobby shouted, "Lucky shot."

"Get lost," I said.

The game seesawed back and forth, Bobby's team leading, my team leading. Bobby scoring, me scoring, both of us playing as if to music only we could hear. At halftime, Bobby's team led by five.

Wiz gave a rousing halftime speech that would've made Phil Jackson envious. He ended it by telling us to "go out there and play your hearts out."

We started the second half not playing much better than the first. Too many turnovers. Too many missed layups.

Bobby's team, on the other hand, played precision basketball. He scored almost at will, hitting jumper after jumper and driving to the basket like a man possessed. He was Atlas, carrying four players on his shoulders.

With six minutes left in the game, my team down by nine, I drove hard to the basket. Trying to block my shot, Bobby missed the ball and instead whacked me hard in the face. I fell to the floor. I quickly got up and went after him. Yelling and screaming, spittle flying from my mouth. Teammates and coaches had to hold me back. I was dragged off the court.

The referee called for a timeout. Blood dripped from my nose. A trainer checked me out and said nothing was broken. He stuffed cotton into both my nostrils. I returned to the court and hit both free throws.

Bobby's team took the ball out. I stole the inbound pass and went in for a layup. A minute later I hit a jump shot along the baseline. Two minutes later, I drove the lane and got fouled hitting a floater. I buried the free throw. My team now trailed by one.

We full-court pressed. One of Bobby's teammates threw a bad pass that I intercepted. I glanced at the clock. Seven seconds left. I dribbled into the lane, Bobby defending me. I pump-faked a shot. Bobby rose... descended. I ascended. Tossed up a ten-footer. The ball rolled around and around the rim like a globe on its axis. I watched and leaned back like a bowler trying to will a ball away from the gutter. After a few seconds, the ball shimmered through the net. The buzzer sounded. Cheers erupted. Game over. We won.

My teammates rushed the court and put me on their shoulders. I cut down the net like they did in a big game on TV and was given a trophy taller than a giraffe's neck. I looked over at my smiling father and gave him the thumbs up sign. He mimicked the gesture.

I then glanced at Tatano. He was shaking his head.

As I left the court, he headed in my direction, looking pissed. His muscular arms were held out from his sides, as if he were carrying two heavy buckets. I made a fist, feeling like a convict about to be shanked.

When he got within inches of my face, Bobby said, "Your nose is bleeding."

I wiped the blood on my shirt.

Just as I was about to call Bobby an asshole, his face brightened and he extended his hand. "No hard feelings, right?"

I looked at his hand for a few seconds. Then, slowly, I unclenched my fist and shook it.

"Right," I said.

He grinned. "You don't give an inch, do you?" he said.

"Neither do you."

"But we're different."

"How's that?"

"For me, basketball is fun. For you it's war."

After the game, my family and I went to the Hearth, a small intimate place that smelled of beer. It had a curved mahogany bar, dark wood tables and leather banquettes.

The owner had been at the game and offered to comp our meal. My father wouldn't hear of it. Neither would the owner. After some discussion, my father waved a white napkin.

"Did I suck or what?" I asked my father.

"You played fine," he said.

"Not by my standards."

"Maybe your standards are too high."

"Maybe they're not high enough."

My father rubbed the back of my neck. "I know how much you love basketball," he said, "but it's not healthy to be so obsessive."

Before I could respond, my mother said, "I'm so happy you work hard to develop your game, but it might be better if you worked harder on developing yourself."

"What does that mean?" I said, angrily.

"It means that there's more to life than shooting a basketball."

"Well, if there is, I haven't found it."

The Hearth was crowded. At one table sat two middle-aged, thin men in white shirts, black suits and skinny black ties. Both wore yarmulkes. Sitting next to them was a young, well-dressed black couple. She had high cheekbones and smooth skin; he had a bluish complexion and wide eyes. Not far from them was a trio of forty-something Chinese women, wearing chiffon dresses, sapphire earrings and high heels. They smoked cigarettes and drank martinis.

My parents and I ordered steak sandwiches, the house specialty. I ate mine quickly but I was still hungry. I was always hungry.

After dinner, as we headed out, we stopped by a table where one of my teammates and his parents and his sister were having dessert.

His parents complimented me on the game and said I had a great future ahead of me.

At some point I went to the bathroom. When I came out, my teammate's sister, Maureen, materialized like some glorious genie.

She wore a white skirt and a tight blue crewneck sweater. Tall for her age, she had wild red hair and green eyes. Only twelve, she was one of those girls who skipped cute and went right to pretty.

"You played great today," she said, moving close to me and smelling of baby powder.

"Thanks. But not really."

She tilted her head and squinted at me, her eyes narrow and her lips pursed. "My brother says all you care about is basketball."

"He's right."

"I bet someday you're gonna be a pro."

"I think so."

Maureen then stood on her tippy-toes, brushed a lock of hair from my forehead and gave me a kiss on the mouth. Her lips tasted like spearmint.

All I could say was, "Thanks."

Maureen smiled.

"You have a girlfriend?" she said.

I didn't answer. In the background, I could hear people chattering and silverware clinking, the radio behind the bar crackled out the song "Chances Are" by Johnny Mathis.

"Well," she said, "do you?"

"Do I what?"

"Have a girlfriend."

"Yes," I lied. "Of course."

Her smile faded.

"What's her name?"

"Spalding."

"I don't know any girl named Spalding."

"You should," I said. "She's a ball."

Maureen pursed her lips.

"I'll still root for you," she said.

I nodded.

She then turned and walked back to her family's table.

My parents and I left the restaurant and went home. I took Spalding to Hudson Schoolyard and shot jumpers for hours and hours, thinking of Maureen's kiss.

Chapter Five

The next evening, around six o'clock, I hurried out of our apartment. Dusk was coming on, and the air was cool. I dribbled over to Hudson Schoolyard. At that hour, the playground was usually empty, but on this day a teenage couple was sitting on a bench, making out. It annoyed me that they'd intrude on my practice.

Wearing my blue-and-gold Jerry West jersey with "Los Angeles Lakers" on the front and the number 44 on the back, I began shooting free throws, then jump shots from around the key.

As I moved to the right baseline, I noticed the guy swagger in my direction. Built like a tight end, he had a shiny, black pompadour and long bushy sideburns. His eyes were dark circles. He wore high black Cons, tight blue jeans and a white cotton V-neck tee shirt under a black leather jacket.

He stood before me, four inches taller, twenty pounds heavier and maybe three years older.

"You're making too much fucking noise, hot shot," he said, a cigarette in his lips.

The word "hot shot" pissed me off. He knew who I was and didn't like, I suppose, that my success on the court made me stand out in a way he didn't. So he wanted to fight with me and go brag about it to his buddies.

"What can I say?" I said, holding the basketball against my right side.

He exhaled an angry cloud of smoke that came out of his mouth like a claw opening. "You can say you're sorry," he said. "Your dribbling is disturbing my girlfriend."

I looked over at his girlfriend. Sitting with her legs crossed, she was pale with long blonde hair. Her cut-off blue jeans barely covered her butt and her white lace blouse was too tight over her large breasts.

"I'm sure you disturb her even more," I said, tossing my ball aside.

He flicked his cigarette away and stood with his hands at his side like a gunslinger.

"You think you're hot shit because you can throw a ball through a hoop, huh, mutha fucker?" His mouth curled into a smirk. He took a step forward, cracked his knuckles and moved within inches of my face. I took a step backwards.

He looked amused. "What's the matter?" he said. "You afraid to fight?"

Actually, I wasn't. My grandfather, my mother's father, the gangster, had taught me, almost from the time I left the crib, how to box. So, too, had my Irish born grandfather who was well-known in the neighborhood for yanking sassy bartenders over counters. He had schooled me on the basic mechanics of boxing: the proper footwork, the combination punches. He always said to "Hit the fookin' eejits quick and hard."

The guy turned to his girlfriend, tossing his head like a horse. "Get a load of this scumbag," he shouted. "He's scared shitless."

"Then kick his ass, Frankie, why don'cha?" his girlfriend said, standing. "Then let's get the fuck outta here."

Frankie's nose almost touched mine.

We began circling each other. Then he stopped moving and stood with his feet spread, flat-footed in a slight crouch. I shuffled toward him. The asphalt was dry and firm. I had room to maneuver.

He swung at me with his right hand. I side-stepped it and drove a hard and quick punch into his stomach. He grunted, then threw a wild left hook. I ducked, straightened up and rammed my right fist to his neck. His head jolted back and he gasped, his legs wobbly.

I circled him counterclockwise, shuffling and keeping my fists up. Sweat rolled down my face and arms. I felt loose, confident.

Frankie lunged at me. I hit him with a combination left jab, right hook. He doubled-over, coughing. I stepped back, bouncing on my toes.

"Had enough?" I said.

Breathing heavy, the wind knocked out of him, he started to rise, but quickly dropped down on one knee, like a batter in the on-deck circle.

Looking down at him, I said, "Guess you have."

I picked up my ball, turned and started to walk away. Then I felt a tap on my shoulder. I spun around and got punched in the face by his girlfriend's fist.

I wobbled down the street, listening to her laughing behind me. Not wanting to show any emotion, I dribbled the ball as if trying to pound it into the pavement.

With each step, the throbbing behind my right eye intensified, my eye closing, my cheek swelling.

When I got home, my mother was standing before the kitchen sink, scrubbing clothes on an angled washboard.

"Hi, Mom," I said, casually.

She turned and put a hand over her mouth. "Oh, my god, what happened to your eye? It's swollen," she said.

I lied. "A guy sucker punched me,"

"Why?" she said, wiping her hands on a dish towel.

I lied again. "I don't know."

"You don't know?"

"I think he thought I was making too much noise."

"Sit, sit, please sit," she said, gesturing to one of the four metal chairs set tightly around a tiny table with a marbleized blue Formica top.

I sat and put a finger to my cheek. It felt tender.

"Let me get you some ice," she said, opening the refrigerator. "You're gonna have one heck of a shiner."

She wrapped ice cubes in a tiny towel, handed it to me and I applied it to my eye.

"Just relax," my mother said. "You'll be fine."

I leaned back in the chair and looked out the window. A clothesline, dangling underpants and undershirts, ran from our windowsill to a tall creosote pole. Behind the pole was an old, abandoned factory with a pigeon coop on the roof; it resembled a wired prison cell.

Twenty minutes later, my father arrived, wearing his milkman's uniform. Dirt on his shirt and wet stains under his armpits.

He looked at my eye and said, "What the heck happened to

you?"

"I got in a fight."

His eyes widened. Unlike me, my father wasn't quick with his fists. He was more a talker than a fighter. Still, he often reminded me that cowardice was unmanly, undesirable, and probably unforgivable in heaven. He said, "You win?"

I continued lying. "Yeah."

He smiled. "Good. Let's celebrate."

My mother was leaning against the stove and holding one hand on her hip. "What about dinner?"

"Don't worry about it," my father said. "We'll get a bite at The Spot."

I loved going to The Spot with Big Tom the way other kids my age loved going to the circus.

The Spot was the local "gin mill"—a boozy fraternity house that was, is, and shall always be the place that introduced me to the world of men. It's where I learned at a very young age how to shoot pool, throw darts, toss dice and read the Daily Racing Form—lessons certainly not taught by the Sisters of Charity at St. Michael's grammar school.

It was only a few blocks from our apartment on 1711 Manhattan Avenue; The Spot served cheap grub and draft beer. It had grimy linoleum floors, dirty tin ceilings and metal signs advertising different beers: Schaeffer, Ballantine, Pabst Blue Ribbon. There were wooden tables carved with initials and obscenities, a dartboard, pool tables, pinball machines and an old jukebox that pumped out oldies but goodies.

The guys at The Spot were, for the most part, big and muscular men who liked to arm wrestle, laugh loud and spout profanities.

They were truck drivers and factory workers and gas station attendants who wore soiled uniforms and steel-tipped boots. They had crew cuts, dirty fingernails and unshaven faces. Some wore hard hats and some smelled of sweat. Others reeked of booze. They stood two-deep at the warped bar and ordered shots and beers. Empty glasses quickly piled up. Cigarette butts overloaded the tin ashtrays.

Often there were bookies. They wore rumpled suits, smoked tiny cigars and parted their shiny black locks straight down the middle, like singers in a Gay Nineties barbershop quartet.

I loved watching them hustle back and forth like nervous squirrels to the payphone. One minute their smile would be brighter than a glacier; a half hour later, their mugs would be so red and sweaty it seemed a cardiac moment was inevitable.

I remember one time a bookie was watching the television behind the bar. He had bet big on the Yankees. But in the top of the ninth, Yankee shortstop, Tony Kubek, made a throwing error that cost the Yankees the game. The bookie pulled out a gun from his waistband, ready to blast the TV. The bartender stopped him. Just in time.

Occasionally, one of the guys brought in his big-breasted, peroxide blonde girlfriend. She stood by the jukebox, smoking a cigarette. She wore a tight black cocktail dress and four-inch spiked high-heels. She spoke in a voice smokier than the bar.

She'd throw coins into the jukebox, play Sinatra and start tick-tocking her head from shoulder to shoulder, while twitching her caboose like a rumba dancer. Some of the guys watching looked like they were in need of smelling salt. I, too, stared wide-eyed.

Most nights, a lean, young Irish bartender with a thick brogue and reddish complexion worked behind the bar. His hair was the color of bronze. He wore a plaid bowtie and a white shirt rolled up to his elbows, a claddagh ring on his index finger.

When not pouring beer, he instigated bets: What "babe" would win the Miss Rheingold contest or what horse would win the Kentucky Derby? Who was better? Willie Mays or Mickey Mantle? The debates were hotly contested and inevitably the loser had to buy a round of drinks.

On the whole, these bar guys weren't highly educated but they had a colorful way with words. Making a phone call was "dropping a dime." Bosses were "big shots." A shapely woman was "built like a brick shit-house." A gay person was "a fruit." A big drinker was a "lush." Money was "scratch." An Italian was a "ginney." A German was a "Kraut." A black person was a "shine." Even though he used those derogatory terms my father was far from a racist. His best friend, Marvin, was also a milkman. And black. My father called him "Ebony." Marvin called my father "Ivory."

They also dispensed more advice than Dear Abby. Sometimes it revolved around basketball—"A good player creates shots for himself. A great player creates shots for his teammates." Other times, their counsel was more pragmatic. "Never worry about where you escape from. Worry about where you escape to." Or: "There's a big difference between having talent and being a winner. Just like there's a huge difference between having intelligence and being successful."

Some of the best moments I had at The Spot revolve around the hilarious conversations. I remember one time Butch, who was half in the bag, told Big Tom he was getting a divorce.

"It got to the point where we just hit an implant," Butch said, in a voice so 'Joisey' he made Andrew Dice Clay sound like King Charles.

"I think you mean 'impasse,'" Big Tom said.

Butch, who had a nose like a pitted potato, wiggled his fingers. "Whatever."

"Sorry about the divorce," my father said.

Butch burped. "I fucked up."

My father patted his shoulder. "Don't be hard on yourself," he said. "It takes two to ruin a marriage."

Butch shook the patterned glass he held in his hand. The ice cubes rattled. "In my case, three…if you could Jim Beam."

My father nodded.

"So I'm fuckin' movin,'" Butch said.

"Where to?"

"I'm buying a condom in Arizona."

My father coughed into a fist. "It's condo, Butch. Condo."

"Fuck's the difference?"

If there was one thing these "hooligans," as the bartender often called them, impressed upon me it was that I never—never ever— under any circumstance smoke cigarettes or drink alcohol as a teenager.

I was only allowed to drink Ginger Ale or a Shirley Temple. The reason they gave, usually at a high decibel level, was because of the number of talented local athletes whose athletic careers had been detoured by "booze and butts."

So strict were they about this rule that once when a non-regular offered to buy me a beer, Chet, who had bulging biceps, pinned the culprit against the wall and told him if he ever did that again he'd "rip out his esophagus."

Chet then put me in a headlock and said, "Here's the scoop, Betty Boop. I ever see you take a sip of scotch or smoke a stick before you turn eighteen, I'll have you talking like a soprano."

"Okay."

"Not okay. Promise me."

"I promise."

"Good," he said, releasing me, then giving me a noogie.

I've never smoked a cigarette and only started drinking alcohol, mostly wine, after college.

At some point in the evening, after "hitting the bottle," my father would step to the jukebox, drop a dime in a slot, press some buttons on the keypad and seconds later out would come his favorite song: "Give Me The Simple Life" by Rosemary Clooney.

"You always have to play that song?" I asked once.

"Better believe it."

He then broke into a Fred Astaire-like series of kicks and taps, moving from the jukebox to the pinball machine.

With a cocky-ass grin on his face, he turned and said "You ready?"

"Better believe it."

"Okay," he said, blowing into cupped hands. "Let's do it."

My father was a whiz at pinball. He stepped to the machine and moved his fingers up and down as if he were playing the clarinet. He dropped a coin in the slot and then snapped a silver ball into action. It shot to the top of the playfield, ricocheting around before beginning its descent, striking bumpers and setting off gongs and rings, hitting sunburst caps and hole kickers. My father, his stomach up against the machine, his body tilted forward, his head down, aggressively worked the flippers, smacking the steel ball back up again and again until finally it fell into the long chute down the left side. He regularly and inevitably racked up thousands of points.

He stepped away. "Okay, Rich," he'd say, "let's see what you got."

"I got a great game," I said.

My father gave me a rare, harsh stare. He hated bragging or anything close to it. "Never tell people how good you are," he often told me, "let your performance speak for itself."

I stepped to the machine, my body steeply inclined. I snapped a ball into play. It bounced around the board, flew downward. I hit the flippers, redirecting the ball toward the ellipse at the top of the playfield. It ricocheted around, hitting bumpers and sending up dings and pings, the scoreboard a storm of light. My score was almost identical to my father's.

His turn. My turn. His turn. My turn. Both of us pummeling the board and working the flippers. My father played to win. So did I.

More times than not he beat me. Which always pissed me off. Once, after losing, I threw a cue ball against the wall of the bar and broke a framed picture of Marilyn Monroe.

"Jesus, Tom, what's Rich's problem?" the bartender asked my father.

"Losing," my father said. "He can't accept it."

"What's he do in the morning?" the bartender said, "Brush his teeth and spit out lava?"

"No," my father said. "Some days he doesn't even brush his teeth."

The fact that my father never let me "just win" distinguished him from the many other fathers who let their sons win because they felt it "gave their kid confidence." On the other hand, there were also fathers who often embarrassed their sons during or after a game.

Once when my biddy basketball team won a big game, I got a ride home from my teammate Joey and his parents.

Joey's father, a man with a face like a sick frog, was driving. Out of nowhere, he did a half-head turn and yelled, "Dammit, Joey, what's wrong with you? How in Heaven's name could you miss so many goddamn free throws?" I cringed. "If you don't wanna play the right way," his father added, "then why don't you quit and become a cheerleader." Joey fumed. "Maybe I will." His father stopped the car, whipped his head around and yelled: "Just try it, mister, and I'll slap the shit outta ya." Joey said nothing. His father resumed driving. The three of us rode the rest of the way in silence, except for the hissing sounds that came from the cigarettes his father chain smoked until he dropped me off.

Aside from pinball, my father was an ace handicapper who loved "playing the ponies." One day when I was thirteen, he took me to Monmouth Racetrack in Oceanport, New Jersey. It was a warm afternoon, maybe eighty degrees, the sky a bright blue.

The track was crowded, hundreds of bettors, almost all men wearing short-sleeve white Banlon shirts, black baggy pants and straw fedoras. They leaned against the railing, reading The Racing Form and chomping fat cigars. My father, who wasn't a big bettor, introduced me to some of his "rail-bird" friends.

One in particular amused me. His name was Freddy. Freddy had slicked-back oily black hair and a pencil-thin mustache. He wore shiny shark-skin suits, black shirts and skinny white ties. He chewed toothpicks and used binoculars. Speaking out of the corner of his mouth like Sylvester Stallone and rolling a silver half-dollar from knuckle to knuckle across the back of his hand, he'd say things like, "Listen, kid, the only thing better than a good piece of advice is a good piece of ass." Or: "Remember, kid, it doesn't matter if a team wins or loses. All that matters is that they cover the spread."

Occasionally, he offered something touching, almost profound. Holding a glass of Calvert Whiskey, his pinkie raised, he'd say, "Understand, kid, everyone who touches you changes you. They can make you a better version of yourself." He'd then pinch my cheek and flip me the half-dollar.

One day my father won a "shitload of money" (maybe a few hundred bucks) on an exacta. I was so excited I jumped up and down, shouting, "We're rich, we're rich!"

"You like the money, huh?" my father said.

"I love money."

"Means that much to you?"

"The money?! Heck, yeah! There's nothing more important!"

My father took his winning ticket to the cashier window and had the cashier break the money down into five, tens and ones.

"Let's celebrate," my father said. "Whaddya say we go to The Spot and have a great meal?"

I was ecstatic. "Yeah!"

"But first I wanna go home and take a quick snooze, okay?"

"Okay."

When we got home, my father told me to separate the money into piles. Fives, tens, ones. Excited, I said sure. I turned on the radio and started shaking my shoulders and boogieing to the sound of Sam Cooke singing "Twistin' the Night Away."

My father went to sleep. I stacked the money. When I finished, I woke him.

He came into the living room, rubbing sleep from his eyes. He looked at the stack of bills and, to my utter amazement, took the money and flung it into the air. Dollars fluttered like falling snowflakes.

"Count it again," he said, smiling.

"Why?"

"Just to make sure you didn't put any dollars in the wrong pile." He then left the living room and headed toward the kitchen.

I scratched my head and started gathering the money. Jay and the Americans were now singing "She Cried." I wasn't crying but I wasn't happy. I was hungry and wanted to eat.

After restacking the money, I called my father who returned, sipping a can of Schlitz beer.

He looked at the stacks and said, "Good job." I smiled. He smiled. Then once again he grabbed the money and tossed it in the air. I looked at him as if he'd lost his mind.

"Whaddya doing?!" I shouted.

He took a gulp of beer and said, "You don't mind stacking the money again, do you?"

"Yeah, I do mind."

"You do?!" He sounded surprised. "Why?"

"Because I've already done it twice and I don't wanna do it anymore."

"You mean you're tired of counting money?"

"Darn right, I am."

"How about that," he said, satisfied he'd made his point, then crushed the beer can.

"Can we go to dinner now?" I asked, my voice a whine.

"Sure," he said, quickly gathering up the money.

We went to The Spot and had burgers and fries. My father brought "drinks for the house."

"You have any money left?" I said, between bites of cheesecake.

He held up his hands in a papal gesture. "Not a dime."

"So you wasted it."

"I didn't waste it," he said. "Look around. Everybody's having such a good time."

And everyone was—smiling, laughing, joking. Tossing darts and shooting pool. One couple slow danced to Sinatra's "Come Fly With Me."

"Didn't you wanna save some money?" I said.

He smiled, showing the tip of his tongue between his teeth. "For what?"

"A rainy day?"

"Nah. I prefer to spend it when the sun's shining."

I shook my head incredulously.

Many years after that day, I took my father to The Palm, a fancy steak restaurant in Manhattan. There were caricatures of famous people on the walls. The floor was covered in sawdust. Waiters wore white aprons.

I was wearing gray pants and a navy-blue blazer with shiny brass buttons. My father wore jeans and a plaid shirt.

"Nice spot," my father said, grabbing his napkin, whipping it out and laying it on his lap, "although a corner hot dog stand would have suited me just fine."

A waiter appeared and handed us menus. They were leather

bound and larger than a billboard.

Holding it up, my father said, "This thing is heavier than a brick."

Sitting around us were people who looked as if they just jumped out of the pages of Town & Country magazine. The men sported three-piece pin-striped bespoke suits, starched shirts, Windsor knots and Rolex watches. Cuddled up next to them were magnificently coiffed women in Chanel dresses wearing gold necklaces and diamond earrings. One puffed on a cigarette fitted into a long, ivory holder. Another sipped a cocktail decorated with a tiny paper parasol.

The waiter returned and took our order. Shortly thereafter he returned with a bottle of expensive Cabernet. He showed me the wine label for inspection. I nodded. He unscrewed the cork and tipped a drop of wine into my glass. Before I could taste it, my father said, "Go ahead, pour it."

The wine was poured. The waiter backpedaled away. My father and I clicked glasses. It made a tiny chime.

My father sipped his wine.

"Mmmm," he said.

My eyes widened. "What did you say?"

"I said, mmmm."

"That's what I thought you said."

He grinned.

"You gonna start drinking wine now?" I said.

He smirked. "And give up beer?! Not on your Irish life."

Our meal arrived. The waiter uncovered our plates with a magician's flourish. I had filet mignon; my father had a cheeseburger.

"You should have ordered a steak," I said. "Steaks here are big and juicy."

"Nothing beats a cheeseburger."

"Not even corn beef and cabbage?"

"Everything beats corn beef and cabbage."

We finished dinner and crossed silverware on our plates. My father wiped his mouth with his napkin.

I signaled the waiter and he brought the check. We both reached for it. I got it first.

"My treat," I said.

"I'd like to contribute."

I shook my head. "Save your money."

"For what?" He flashed a mischievous grin. "A rainy day?"

"Very funny," I said, remembering the afternoon at Monmouth Racetrack.

"You still get tired of counting money?" my father said.

"I don't count money anymore."

"How about that." He smiled like a learned leprechaun. "So whaddya do with it?"

"I spend it."

"On what?"

"A good time."

"A good time, huh?"

"Yep."

His face brightened. "That's my boy."

I can honestly say I have never taken a job because of money. In fact, I have at times turned down jobs that would have paid me a lot more. This isn't to imply that making money wasn't and isn't important. It was. And is. It's just that it's never been the be-all and end-all. Whatever money I make, I spend almost as fast as I make it. Just like my father back in the day.

When my father was in his mid-eighties and dying of heart failure, I went to visit him at the Jersey Shore Medical Center. He was in a private room, dimly lit. The curtains were closed. He was lying in bed, wearing a hospital dressing grown and sleeping soundly. Looking at him, I remembered the many times he drove me long distances to games, the many nights he stayed up with me when I was sick, the days we talked about my life and my goals. I gently touched his face, something I had never done as an adult. I wanted his image to stay with me.

I looked at my mother. Her face was pale and drawn. She was holding my father's hand, tenderly rubbing her fingers in his palm. It was, for me, the greatest gesture of love I had ever seen.

My father died the next day. His death crushed me. Looking at him in bed, his head square on a pillow, his body immobile, tears flowed down my face. I couldn't move. Couldn't speak.

Not long ago, I drove past the place where The Spot used to be. It's now called Manhattan Bar & Grill. Yet I could still see my father stepping out of the tavern, swaying in invisible breezes on the sidewalk, his uniform soiled, his hair mussed, his smile wide. I can still hear his voice, so soft and warm, and envision myself as a young kid, running into his arms, being lifted high into the air, getting hugged and tickled and giggling.

All that remains of him is stored in my heart.

Chapter Six

In 1964, a few weeks after my father took me to the track, we got a visit from Hank Morano, the basketball coach at Emerson High School.

Emerson was Union City's public high school, populated mostly by tough kids from the neighborhood. They went there because Emerson had a reputation for good teachers and strong athletic programs. Its football field, Roosevelt Stadium, was the largest in the county.

Some of the Emerson guys (Ant'ny or Jo-wee) sported duck tails and leather jackets. They smoked cigarettes. Some of the girls (Duh-neese or Mart-a) wore tight lycra pants and pink rayon blouses, their jaws working furiously on Bazooka bubblegum.

Hank was an imposing man: tall, handsome with black hair and blue eyes. He wore a blue blazer, a white shirt and a striped tie. His gray pants were perfectly pressed. Despite his accountant-like appearance, Hank was known as a strict disciplinarian who took no shit, a Bobby Knight without the antics. His well-coached teams frequently won state championships.

Hank wanted me to attend Emerson. He began his pitch by

rhapsodizing about my game.

"You're a terrific basketball player," he said, in a deep voice like James Earl Jones. "I think Emerson is the perfect school for you. We play a tough schedule and I'm committed to making every player reach their potential."

I nodded. My father nodded. My mother nodded.

"Let me ask you this," Hank said, "What do you hope to accomplish as a player?"

"I wanna be a pro."

"Think you can?"

"I know I can." Even at that young age, I was very confident of my abilities.

Hank flashed a smile. "You keep playing and improving like you are there's no doubt, no doubt whatsoever, you'll be a pro."

My heart skipped beats.

"What I especially like about your game," Hank said, "is less your scoring ability and more your passing ability, especially on the break. You see patterns where others see chaos."

I almost jumped up and hugged him. As much as I enjoyed scoring, and that's what I was always praised for, I wanted to be appreciated more for my assists.

Passing out assists, you see, makes the game more interesting. At any moment the geometry of action on the court offers all kinds of options and possibilities. A player with the ball who can see different alternatives and make different choices, especially when leading the fast break, is invaluable.

Since I enjoyed dishing out assists, I worked hard to improve my passing skills. I read everything I could about the Boston Celtics ball-handling wizard, Bob Cousy—called "The Mobile

Magician" and "Houdini of the Hardwood." I studied all his moves and techniques. The best compliment I ever received in grammar school was once after I performed a "no-look pass" an angry opponent shouted: "Who do you think you are—fucking Cousy?"

My goal wasn't just to play the game. I wanted to choreograph it.

"Way I figure it, Rich," Hank said, "I could see you, at times, playing point guard. Would you like that?"

"I'd love it!" I shouted.

"Okay," he said. "Sounds like a plan."

Hank stood, flexed his right knee and winced. Probably an old basketball injury from his playing days at St. Peter's College.

"One last question," Hank said, looking at me. "Who's going to decide what high school you attend? You or your parents?"

"Me." I said, confidently.

Hank looked at my father. "Pretty autonomous kid."

"To a pathological degree," my father said.

"He always been like that?" Hank said,

My mother smiled. "Since the day he left the womb."

Hank shook my hand. It was a bone crusher. He thanked my parents for their time and left.

A few weeks later, I was invited to a tryout at Power Memorial High School in New York City.

Power had, arguably, the best high school hoops program in America. A four-year Christian Brother's Academy, it also had, at the time, the country's best player, Lew Alcindor.

Alcindor had led Power to three straight New York City Catholic championships, a 71-game winning streak, and a 79-2 overall record. At 7 foot 2 inches, he was nicknamed "The Tower from Power." He would, of course, go on to UCLA, and turn the Bruins into a college powerhouse, change his name to Kareem Abdul Jabbar and then become an all-time NBA great.

The Power tryouts were for the best players in the New York Metropolitan area. Those who did well would be offered a full scholarship. The tryout was by invitation only. I was the only kid invited from New Jersey.

I couldn't wait to test my skills against some of the city's best players whose basketball wizardry was second to none.

The gym at Power was small and old. It reeked of sweat and liniment. When I arrived, twenty players were on the court, running sprints, doing stretches and shooting baskets. The majority were black, taller and more muscular than my six-two, one hundred and sixty pound frame.

Most of the black players wore tight tank tops, white tube socks and hi-black Cons. Some had faint mustaches, huge afros and arms like gasoline hoses. I sported a loose, white T-shirt, floppy, white socks and Adidas sneakers. My cheeks were pink, my hair short and my arms barely reached below my waist.

Playing against black players was nothing new to me. I had competed against them when I played for the Union City all-star team in the 13th annual International Biddy Basketball championships, held in Jersey City.

In the first round, we played against a mostly black team from Chester, Pennsylvania. They had a small guard named Eddie Swain who simply dazzled the fans—and me—with his basketball brilliance. He was a blur leading the fast break, driving hard to the hoop and finishing with acrobatic layups. He hit jumpers from around the perimeter, often over the outstretched arms of two defenders. Indeed, he was so unstoppable he was named the tournament MVP and given the Merit Cup Award by Sports Illustrated as Mr. Biddy Basketball.

After seeing Swain play I made it a point to seek out other black players, since they were beginning to dominate the sport. I'd have my father drive me twenty miles to playgrounds in Newark, New Jersey, where I was often the only white kid on the court.

Locally, I sought out the best black player in my county, Ron Dabney, who had the size and game of Charles Barkley and later played for St. Louis University. Dabney, six inches taller, dazzled me with his quick moves around the basket and long-range shooting. We'd play one-on-one for hours. Once, after I made an around-the-back dribble and blew by him for a layup he yelled, "Yo, bro, that move damn near straightened my afro."

Many of the players at the tryout reminded me of Ron. They carried themselves with assurance, jumping and leaping and spinning in the air like circus performers. They also engaged in serious trash talk, verbal spit balls. They all had nicknames like Cadillac, Mercury, Eraser, Terminator. One player wore a shirt that read: "I will play you/J you/slay you."

"Yo, bro," one player shouted to another, "You bring your shit to me, I be givin' you a Spalding facial."

The addressed player stood 6'8, probably weighed 250. Holding the ball like a chalice, he looked at the rim as if to frighten it. Then taking two quick steps he performed a tomahawk dunk, damn near shattering the backboard. He eyeballed his tormentor. "Take that, muthafucker."

Despite the comic banter, there was a real seriousness surrounding the tryout. We all knew we were competing against each other, not only to win a scholarship but to prove who had the goods.

After the warmups and a recitation of instructions, we were randomly broken up into four teams and began scrimmaging. Power's coach Jack Donohue—rimless glasses, gray haired, stomach like a beer keg—walked up and down the sidelines like an army sergeant inspecting his troops

"Pass the ball, pass the ball," Donohue yelled at a player who was dribbling too much.

The player didn't stop. Donohue grabbed the whistle hanging from his neck and blew it.

"Hold it, hold it," he shouted, walking onto the court, his face tomato red. "I don't want any solo acts, you hear me. Basketball's a team game." He clapped his hands. "So, c'mon, let's move the ball."

He walked off the court. Play resumed.

Immediately a kid grabbed a rebound and headed down court, a three on two fast break. At the top of the key, he looked right and passed the ball around his back to a player cutting on the left. The ball sailed into the bleachers.

Donohue called time out and made substitutions.

As the errant passing player left the court, Donohue whispered in his ear. His face dropped. He grabbed his gear and left.

It went like that all day—players getting dismissed for dumb mistakes or showboating—until only ten players remained.

The remaining players began putting on an encore performance, hitting long-range jump shots and grabbing rebounds above the rim.

By late afternoon, the competition was fierce. I was whacked with so many elbows I felt like a human pinata. Once driving the lane a player elbowed my head so hard it caused my eyes to blur. Another player with a tattoo of a knife on his bicep slapped me, intentionally, in the privates when he felt I was guarding him too closely. I left the court for a few minutes to catch my breath. But when I returned I was like an angry bull coming out of a chute.

Toward the end of the scrimmage, I found my zone. I caught the ball on the right wing. A teammate moved over to set a screen. I waved him away. I wanted to take my defender one-on-one. I dribbled from my right hand to my left, then back, making a quick crossover move and banked in a twenty-footer. Minutes later, I grabbed a rebound and leading the break dished a bounce pass between two defenders to a trailing teammate for an assist. And not long after that, I dribbled straight at a defender, lifted my body slightly as if I was going to pull up for a jumper. My defender rushed toward me. But I didn't pull up. I kept my dribble and blew past him for a layup.

When the scrimmaging ended, Donohue thanked everyone for participating. He asked four of us to "stick around."

Tension was palpable. Some players paced, rubbing their hands together anxiously. Others sat on chairs, biting their fingernails. I stayed on the court, shooting jumpers.

Donohue talked to each player one at a time, his hands flapping in the air. One player left crying. Another cursed loudly and kicked a ball against a wall.

There were only two players left, me and a six-nine kid.

Donohue waved him over and the two talked quietly. At the end of their discussion, the player leaped in the air and shouted "yes."

He then hugged Donohue, sprinted from the gym, raising his fists in triumph.

Donohue called me over.

"Well, son," he said, grinning and putting a hand on my shoulder, "we're offering you a scholarship to Power Memorial."

His words thrilled me—this certification of my talent. I thought I had played well, but other guys could jump higher, shoot better, were stronger and faster. Indeed, there were moments when I felt like a tortoise compared to hares.

"You have an all-around game," Donohue said, standing close to me. "That's the kind of player that appeals to me." A 100-kilowatt smile. "Are you interested in coming to Power?"

"Maybe," I said.

Donohue reared back. He swallowed hard. His Adam's apple bobbed.

"Maybe?!" he said in a resentful tone.

"Power is a long commute from Jersey," I said. "I'd have to take a bus and two trains."

"Look," he said, speaking through gritted teeth, "You don't wanna come to Power, then don't. There's a helluva lot of players who'd be honored to get a scholarship to Power. So think long and hard about your decision."

I went home and talked with my parents about the tryout.

"How'd it go?" my father asked.

"Went well," I said. "I was offered a scholarship."

"Congratulations. Whaddya think?"

"I think it's too far. I wanna go to a school nearby."

My father made an exaggerated swipe of imaginary sweat off his forehead.

"Whew!" he said. "Good decision. Commuting to Power would have been tough."

The next day I called Donohue and said thanks but no thanks. He damn near hung up on me.

A week after that tryout, Mike Rubbinaccio, the coach of St. Michael's High School in Union City, stopped by our apartment. Mike was a very Italian guy, stocky and balding; he could have easily played a cohort of Tony Soprano, except Mike was an easy-going, gregarious man who unfolded his personality like a toreador's cape.

He told us how he had played at St. Michael's with Tommy Heinsohn, who was then starring for the Boston Celtics. (I would eventually break all of Heinsohn's scoring records.)

"Maybe someday you could play for the Celtics," Mike said, crossing his legs and placing an arm over the back of the couch.

"I'd like that," I said, envisioning myself playing for the Celtics in the Boston Garden, the Taj Mahal of basketball. How sweet!

"Well," Mike said, clasping his hands, "I'm offering you a full scholarship."

I glanced at Big Tom. He beamed. My mother wrapped her arms around my shoulders and kissed my cheek.

I looked at Mike and said, "I accept your offer."

Mike grinned like a Buddha. He stood and hugged my mother, shook hands with my father and patted me on the back.

"We're gonna achieve great things together," Mike said.

I swung a fist in the air. "You better believe it."

Chapter Seven

St. Michael's High School was located on Eighteenth Street in Union City, a three-story, brick building with big windows, cramped classrooms and no football field or baseball diamond. Just a small gym for basketball, the only game that mattered.

There were four hundred and twenty-four students, seventy-nine of which were freshmen. The boys wore blue blazers and gray pants. The girls wore green blazers and plaid skirts. Even though St. Michael's nickname was "the Fighting Irish" and had a majority of students who were Irish, there were a fair number of Italians, Polish and Cubans.

My family's apartment was only three blocks from St. Michael's. I could sleep late, take my time getting dressed, eat a leisurely breakfast and still make it in time for school.

On my first day at St. Michael's, the homeroom teacher, sixty-year old Grace Squire—bouffant hairdo, double chin and sweet smile—read each student's name out loud, alphabetically. When she got to the V's, she said, "Romualdas Vyzas."

I looked at Romualdas. "You Spanish?"

He shook his head. "No. Lithuanian."

Tall and lanky, Ray, as he was called, became not only my best friend but also a treasured teammate, a fearless and ferocious rebounder who I later dubbed Chairman of the Boards.

Once against a very good Lincoln High team from inner city Jersey City, Ray exchanged body blows and vicious elbows with their star player Vinnie Roundtree, who later played for Rutgers. Roundtree was built like a railroad car and had great leaping ability; he inhaled rebounds. If it wasn't for Ray keeping him off the boards, we would never have won, no matter how many points I scored.

Thanks to Ray and Pat Clark, St. Michael's prowess on the courts was only matched by its eccentric teachers.

Sister Ruth watered artificial plants. Sister Elise spoke to invisible saints. And Sister Gertrude literally choked kids who didn't button the top button of their shirt.

The Latin teacher, Mr. O'Neil, a lean, watery-eyed guy in his late sixties had hair like a gray Brillo pad. His breath reeked of bad coffee and he spoke like a tipsy Daffy Duck, honking his vowels and spitting out his consonants. When he conjugated Latin words beginning with the letter "P" students in the front rows were greeted with sprays of spittle.

Despite a cast of characters right out of a Frank McCourt novel, I was focused on basketball.

After a few preseason scrimmages in which I played well, I was named a starter my freshmen year. The team captain was Bob Kellert, a senior with a deadly left-handed jump shot. Even though he was the star player, I had no intention of being a side dish to his entrée. I worked out early before school started and after school ended. No drill was undeserving of my full attention and concentration. I'd set up chairs in a straight line on the court and dribble around them, followed by shooting countless jumpers from around the perimeter. Getting me to leave the court was damn near impossible.

One night when I was practicing, alone, the school's janitor, Harry—short and bald, sideburns like cobwebs—said, "Gotta lock up."

"Fifteen more minutes," I pleaded.

Harry looked at his watch. "It's after ten o'clock, for god sakes."

"Please."

"Okay. Fifteen minutes. No more."

A half hour later, I was still shooting jumpers, my shirt and shorts soaking wet.

Harry approached me, holding a broom. "You're a pain in the ass," he said. "Now go the hell home, will ya?"

"Just a little longer."

He swatted me on the butt with his broom. "Get out," he shouted. "Now!"

I took one last jumper. Swish.

Throughout my high school career, I was always the first player in the locker room. I wanted to get my head right. Focused. I sat by my locker thinking about the other team and what I needed to do. As other players arrived, I wanted no noise, no music, no laughter—nothing that would break my concentration.

To me, the locker room wasn't a social club. It was a business office.

I only missed one day of work my entire high school career, a game against Memorial High School. The night before the game I was in bed wrapped in blankets, sweating, shivering and vomiting.

My mother called our family doctor, Max Miller, a short, thin, jowly man with grey hair who still made house calls.

Dr. Miller took out a thermometer, shook it and put it in my mouth. After a few minutes, he took the thermometer out and looked at it.

"A hundred and one," he said. "Not good."

I looked at him through half-open eyes.

"I'm going to prescribe an antibiotic," he said. "Otherwise, stay in bed and drink plenty of water."

"But I have a game tomorrow," I said.

"Forget it."

"I can't forget it," I said, coughing.

"You have no choice."

He then closed his small black medical bag and left.

The next day I could barely get out of bed.

I urged my parents to let me play.

"Absolutely not," my mother said.

That night my parents went to the game. When they left, I called a friend of mine and told him to phone me and let me know how the game was going.

He called me from a payphone just before halftime.

"Your team isn't doing well."

"Come get me," I shouted.

"You're sick. I can't…"

"COME FUCKING GET ME!"

I slipped out of bed, dressed into my uniform and struggled into my friend's car.

We arrived at Memorial's gym just as the second half was about to start. Seeing me enter the gym, St. Michael's fans cheered wildly.

My parents, on the other hand, did not cheer.

I played the entire second half, drenched in sweat, my ears ringing, my head pounding. Twice, running down court, I felt so dizzy I thought I would faint.

Despite my good intentions, I barely scored ten points and had more turnovers than assists. We lost.

On the car ride home, my father said, "That was a stupid thing to do."

I didn't respond. I just sat in the backseat, moaning.

The next day Dr. Miller returned.

"What were you thinking?" he said, his voice cold and solemn.

"I just wanted to help my team."

"Well, you didn't. Now stay in bed and get some rest."

"For how long?"

"For as long as it takes."

I coughed and said, "But I have practice tomorrow."

He drew his head back and gave me a withering stare.

"For God sakes, will you listen to me?"

"Can't," I joked. "My ears are clogged."

"So's your head. Go to sleep before I knock you out."

Dr. Miller left.

Despite my parents' objections, I made it to practice.

As my game improved and I scored more points in my

sophomore year, I started getting lots and lots of publicity. Articles and pictures of me were often in The Jersey Journal and the Hudson Dispatch.

The publicity had its pluses and minuses. People I didn't even know knew me, or thought they did.

One cold February morning, I was sitting on a bus next to my teammate, Ray. We were headed to school. The bus was crowded, overheated, faintly smelling of diesel fuel and cheap perfume. Seated around us are a buffet of commuters, various ages, colors and nationalities: Blacks, Whites, Asians, Cubans, Dominicans. Even a Jewish guy sporting a navy-blue yarmulke emblazoned with a New York Yankee logo.

Almost all the passengers were adults puffing cigarettes, discharging scarfs of smoke from flared nostrils that fogged the air. There was lots of sneezing, coughing and hacking. Outside the window, it was raining and trees were shivering in a wind so strong branches bounced along the pavements, like so many pick-up sticks.

Sitting in front of Ray and me were two girls in blue blazers and plaid skirts. One was a shapely blond with high cheekbones and a creamy complexion. Her companion was a thin brunette with long eyelashes and nose freckles. Both smelled like ripe apples and both were drinking cans of chocolate Yoo-hoo, while talking about an upcoming, highly publicized basketball game between their high school…and mine.

Blondie asked her girlfriend, "You going to the game tomorrow?" Her voice had an artificial, actress quality.

"Wouldn't dare miss it," the brunette said excitedly. "It's the biggest game of the year."

"Think we'll win?" Blondie said, languidly brushing hair back from her high forehead.

"It'll be tough," Brunette said. "St. Michael's has O'Connor. Some say he's the best player in the state."

Blondie pushed the air with her hand as if tossing something into a trash can.

"He may be a great player," Blondie said, "but as a person he's a real douchebag."

Ray looked at me and whispered, "You know her?"

I shook my head.

"I didn't know you knew him?!" Brunette said, excitedly.

"Of course I know…him."

"How?"

"I dated him," Blondie said, winding a lock of hair around a finger.

"Really?!" Brunette said.

Blondie nodded. Rain pelted the windows. A fierce wind rocked the bus. It teetered past a cluster of businesses: Pizza parlors, liquor stores, laundromats, bars and bodegas.

"I dated him only once," Blondie said, smirking. "Trust me, once was enough."

I tapped Blondie on the shoulder and said, "Excuse me, but I couldn't help but overhear your conversation. I go to St. Michael's."

She turned and gave me a quick glance. "Good for you."

"I know O'Connor," I said.

Her mouth twisted and she snorted.

"I think he's a nice guy," I said.

"Yeah, well, I think he's a jerk," Blondie said.

Reaching over her shoulder, I extended my hand and said, "I'd like to introduce myself." A beat. "I'm Rich O'Connor."

Blondie's head swiveled around. She waved her hands in front of herself, crossing them back and forth rapidly as if trying to erase me.

"Nice to meet you," I said. A theatrical pause. "…for the first time."

Blondie's face reddened. Her companion, mouth agape, eyeballed Blondie as if she was an imposter. Blondie said, "You're a fucking liar."

"I'm not the liar," I said.

"Yes…yes, you are!" Her voice was a broken stutter. She stood and pulled the overhead cord. The bus braked and sighed to a stop. Blondie looked at me and shouted, "I hate you! I really hate you!"

"Hate me," I said, bewildered. "You don't even know me."

With red-faced ferocity, she unleashed an ear-spitting shout, her chin trembling with an effort not to cry, "Yeah, well, you fucking disgust me!"

Heads turned, eyes widened, mouths dropped. I felt illuminated as if by a gigantic flashlight.

Blondie grabbed her companion's forearm and yanked her from her seat. The two girls stumbled down the aisle like two drunken sailors.

The bus driver pulled a lever. A hiss sounded and the bus door opened. The girls quickly exited.

I turned to Ray. "You believe that shit?"

Ray cocked his head. "The downside of being you."

The bus restarted and lurched forward. Glancing out the rainy, rattling window, I saw my image waver in the watery glass.

Ray and I, drenched from the rain, arrived at school. A male teacher—bald with bifocals—greeted us. He gave an ominous look and said, "Sister Therese wants to see both of you." A beat. "NOW!"

We walked to her office, moving with gallows-bound footsteps, as if heading for the inevitable executioner.

On the way, I noticed classmates staring at us. Strangely. Gravely. They said nothing. They seem to know something we don't. But what?

Ray and I took a seat in the principal's anteroom. It reeked of damp carpeting and musty books.

I looked at Ray. "Whaddya think she wants?"

Ray, his knees fanning back and forth, said, "Whatever it is, it ain't good." Five, ten minutes passed. The silence in the room congealed.

An office door suddenly swung open and Sister Therese Alma appeared. She was wearing a black habit, a white wimple and small, wire-rimmed glasses.

She stood for a moment, framed in the doorway, one hand on her right hip. Short and stocky, she had sharp, strong features.

Sister Therese turned her eyes slowly from me to Ray, like a spectator watching a tennis match. She then zoomed in on Ray and pointed to her office. "Get in there, Raymond."

Ray was with her for almost a half hour. When her door reopened and Ray reappeared, his face was the color of uncooked chicken. He made a slashing gesture across his throat and mouthed, "Suspended."

I didn't have a clue why.

Ray left. The anteroom was quiet. I squirmed in my seat, crossing my leg first one way and then the other.

Sister Therese soon beckoned me into her office with a crooked index finger. I unwound from my seat and brushed past her. She smelled like Clorox.

Her office was dimly lit from above, like a boxing ring. It was meticulous and had a strong scent of furniture polish and floor wax.

She pointed to a chair. "Be seated."

I sat.

Sister Therese stood behind her desk for a moment. Then she paced, back and forth, back and forth. After about thirty seconds, she sat and leaned forward with her elbows on the desk, her fingers clasped.

"You know why you're here?" she asked.

"No idea."

She glared at me. "Well, mister, it seems you and Raymond stole some goodies from the corner deli." We had stolen some Ring Dings and Devil Dogs.

"I…"

"Don't try and deny it," she said. "There were witnesses." She paused, then, "And just so you know, I have suspended Raymond."

I swallowed hard and assumed I, too, would be suspended and miss the next game.

"But," Sister Therese said, lifting an index finger, "I'm just going to give you a warning this time. Don't do it again." She pointed to the door. "You can leave now."

I was flabbergasted. As much as I didn't want to miss playing, I also didn't want to be granted immunity. Ray was important to me. We were teammates, brothers. Not getting suspended would be unfair to him.

"Sister," I said, "You can't do this."

Her eyes flickered like a lightbulb going bad. "What can't I do?"

"You gotta suspend me."

She took off her glasses and squeezed the bridge of her nose. "I already told you," she said. "I'm not going to do that."

"This is unfair to Ray," I said.

"Look," she said, "you've given this school a lot of prestige. A lot of positive publicity. You're being recruited by major colleges. I don't wish to tarnish your reputation nor the school's reputation." A pause. "You're dismissed."

"But…"

She made a gesture like an umpire signaling safe. "No buts. Now. Please. Leave. I have work to do."

I left.

Outside in the hallway, I stood still for a moment, not believing what just happened.

I looked up and saw Ray walking in my direction.

"You get suspended?" he said.

I swallowed a hit of embarrassment. "No," I said.

Ray cocked his head. "The upside of being you." (As it turned out, I had my father accompany me back to school later that day, and he convinced Sister Therese not to suspend Ray.)

Looking back on high school, the best thing to happen to me my freshman year occurred off the court. I had been in school just a few weeks when, walking a hallway with Ray, I saw this girl who was tall and slender, blonde hair and blue eyed. I did a double take worthy of Oliver Hardy.

"That girl is stunning," I said to Ray.

"No shit."

"I'm gonna ask her out." I said.

"Whaddya nuts?! She's a fucking sophomore."

"So?"

"So there's no way she's gonna date a freshman."

Ray then put both his hands on my shoulders, leaned in toward me and stared deeply into my eyes. "Look," he said, as if talking to an idiot, "Just because you're a star basketball player doesn't mean she's gonna faint in your fucking presence. Granted, you're a confident dude, but…forget about it."

"She probably doesn't even know I play basketball."

"Doesn't matter. Trust me, you got no shot."

I grinned. "You know me," I said. "I'm willing to take one."

The next day, I was leaning on a car outside school waiting for Carol. It was a beautiful fall afternoon, cool and sunny, the leaves on the trees turning red and yellow.

Around three-thirty, Carol and two friends appeared, all holding books. The girls started walking. I followed at a safe distance. They strolled past a Dairy Queen, a grocery store, a pizzeria. I caught the zesty smell of pepperoni.

After seven blocks, Carol separated from her buddies.

I quickly increased my pace, spun before her and said, "Hi."

She narrowed her eyes.

I cleared my throat, gave a stupid little wave and said, "Hi. I'm Rich O'Connor."

"Do I know you?" she said, pulling her books close to her chest.

"Ah…no. I…I go to St. Michael's. I'm a freshman."

She nodded. "I'm Carol."

"I know."

"You do?"

"Yeah."

She lowered her books.

"Mind if I walk you home?" I said.

She smiled. "Sure. Why not."

We walked and talked. About St. Michael's. The nuns and the priests. Where she lived. Where I lived.

When we got to her house in Weehawken, I said, "How…how would you like to go to Christina's some night and get pizza?"

She thought a moment.

"If you go I promise to shower," I said.

She threw her head back and laughed. "In that case," she said. "It's a date."

I damn near jumped up as if leaping for a game's opening tap.

"Awesome, great, even terrific," I said. "How's Friday?"

"Friday's good."

I smiled. "I'm…I'm going out for the basketball team."

"I hope you make it."

"I should. I'm on scholar…yeah, I hope so."

I then shook her hand and said, "Well, have a nice day."

Carol said bye. I watched her walk toward her house and disappear behind the front door.

A block away I actually did jump up and punch the air. YES!

I got home and called Ray.

"I did it," I said.

"Did what?"

"Got a date with Carol."

"Don't bullshit a bullshitter."

"I'm not kidding."

"What? You bragged to her about what a great player you are."

"She knew nothing about me being a basketball player."

"Seriously?"

"Serious as Red Auerbach."

Carol, it turned out, was as nice as she was smart. She helped me with geometry. She rewrote my English compositions. In her senior year, she graduated class valedictorian. We dated all through high school and my first year at Duke. We broke up because, like most adolescent relationships, we simply grew apart.

For all the publicity my performances generated for St. Michael's, the school received as much, if not more attention, when it was announced at the end of my freshman year that St. Michael's would be closing. The reason? Financial mismanagement. The parish needed money to pay off big debts. How those debts accumulated nobody knew for sure. Or, if they did, they weren't saying.

The uproar in the community was considerable. How in Heaven's name could they close the school down when it had, arguably, one of the best players and best teams in the state? It was insane.

Alumni and parents pushed hard to keep the school open. There were meetings and fundraisers. But it appeared inevitable St. Michael's would close before the start of my sophomore year.

And so once again I was being recruited by dozens of high

schools--some as far away as Worcester Academy in Massachusetts.

I was all set to attend another Catholic school, Holy Family in Union City, but then a miracle happened, or maybe it wasn't a miracle.

At one of the meetings, Father Matthew Martin, the school's director, stood and argued that "keeping the school open one more year to let the seniors graduate would only be fair."

Coach Rubbinaccio offered to ask his former high school teammate and current Boston Celtics star, Tommy Heinsohn, to return to St. Michael's and support keeping the school open.

Heinsohn accepted the invitation. He even agreed to participate in a short scrimmage.

After the game, he took me aside and said, "You got all the tools, kid. I look forward to seeing another St. Mike's player in the NBA."

Thanks to all the objections, it was decided that the school would remain open but it would no longer accept boys—only girls. There would be no sophomores or juniors. Just 27 senior boys and 31 senior girls. And 110 freshmen girls.

Almost immediately, many competent teachers quit. They were replaced by knucklehead instructors with questionable credentials and loose morals. One male teacher, known for smoking things other than menthols, spent much of his time making passes at girls with cute asses. And still another instructor showed up more often than not with his breath smelling of booze.

In retrospect, keeping St. Michael's open because of our team seems like perverse logic—as if the adults had their priorities out of whack. But hey, to me, it sounded swell—if for no other reason then my basketball career was flourishing.

By my junior year, Parade magazine, among many other magazines, had named me a unanimous high school All-American. My senior year I finished scoring 2025 points, ranking me in the top five scorers in New Jersey scholastic history.

Even more rewarding was that Howard Garfinkel, who ran the legendary Five-Star Basketball Camp in Honesdale, Pennsylvania, which I attended twice for free, wrote in his national scouting report—subscribed to by every major college coach—that I was a "can't miss prospect."

Thus, began the avalanche of letters and visits and phone calls from over fifty college coaches, offering me full scholarships.

Chapter Eight

The coaches appeared at my school, my games, my practices and my hangouts. They called our apartment all hours of the day. Almost everyday. We had to change our phone number five times.

They all had different personalities, approaches and offers. But the one thing they shared in common, with rare exceptions, was the ability to sell insincerity sincerely.

To this day, the words and images of all those coaches, over fifty of them, still flicker through my mind like an old newsreel.

The first time Al McGuire, then the head coach at Marquette University and later a color man on network basketball games, phoned my house, he talked faster than an auctioneer. After a torrent of turbo-charged compliments, he said he'd like to visit.

"Great," I said, excitedly. "When?"

"How's tonight?"

I said ordinarily that would be fine but my parents and I had plans to visit my grandfather.

"Want me to come along?" Al asked, his voice softer than

cashmere. "I have a way with the old-timers."

"Ah…well…maybe another time."

"No problem," Al said. "How's tomorrow?"

"A…a…sure."

"Great," he said. "Looking forward." A beat, then: "Tell Grandpa I wish him well. Grandfathers have more warmth than freshly baked bread."

The next night, my father and I met Al at The Camelot restaurant in Union City, owned by my coach's brother, Blackie Rubbinaccio.

Al—dark, wavy hair, mischievous eyes, uncommonly handsome—came into the place chuffing like a steam engine. He wore a navy blue blazer, white golf shirt and black jeans. With him was a tall, thin three-piece suit guy in his fifties who could have been a model for GQ—everything starched and wrinkle free. Al introduced him as a bigwig in the dairy industry.

"I thought your father, being a milkman, might enjoy speaking with him," Al said.

Al then suggested he and I sit at one table while my father and Al's friend sit at another. Seemed weird. But okay.

Al was energetic, a human dynamo, a 100-mph talker who spoke about riding his Kawasaki motorcycle, collecting toy soldiers and growing up in Queens.

"But enough about me," McGuire said. "Let's talk about Marquette. Without question, it's the premiere basketball program in the country. Bar none."

He gulped a glass of his water.

"I only recruit the most talented kids in the country," he added. "And almost all of my starters go on to have great careers in the pros."

I smiled. Then asked Al why my father wasn't sitting with us.

"My friend is talking to him about a job," he said.

"What kind of job?"

"In the dairy industry."

"Where?"

"Wisconsin."

"Doing what?"

"Keeping the cows happy."

Al's eyes twinkled.

On the way home, I asked my father what he thought of GQ man.

"Guy was a blowhard," my father said.

A few days later—at my father's urging—I called Coach McGuire (which I hated to do because I so enjoyed him) and told him I wasn't interested in Marquette. I said Wisconsin was too far from home, even though the real reason was my father didn't dig GQ man's offer.

Following Al's visit, there was one from La Salle's coach, Tom Gola, a former New York Knick great who resembled a young Tom Selleck, minus the mustache. He stood six-foot-six and spoke elegantly—which, in retrospect wasn't surprising for a Philadelphia icon, who would one day get elected to the Pennsylvania State House.

The night he visited, he dropped anchor on the couch and spent most of the evening talking about how he hated recruiting. He said too many kids or their parents wanted money or a car. It was disgraceful. La Salle, he said, would never stoop that low. Never. Under any circumstance.

"It's just not how we operate," he said, turning his palms over like a man showing he had nothing to hide.

He then proceeded to talk about his days playing for the Knicks. His rap put a headlock on my affections.

Not long after his visit, a La Salle alum called and invited me to dinner at the Old Homestead Steakhouse in downtown New York. A big stretch limousine picked me up. I wore a suit and tie.

The Homestead was impressive: tin ceilings and linen tablecloths, friendly waiters and huge portions. I had a steak the size of a hubcap.

Mr. Alumni was a nice guy. Courteous and persuasive. He lavished praise on La Salle and Gola, calling him "a tower of integrity."

Toward the end of the meal, he slid a napkin across the table. For a moment, I thought I might have some spinach lodged in my front teeth.

"Look underneath," he said.

I did.

There was a wad of twenty-dollar bills.

"It's yours," he said. "Every month. If you choose La Salle."

I didn't know how to respond.

He lifted an index finger. "Just don't tell Coach Gola about this," he said. He winked. "He's too much of an honest man for something like this."

He extended his hand. We shook. I didn't take the money.

Later that night, I told my parents what happened. They were shocked. My mother, who was enamored with Gola, said there was no way he would have known. My father disagreed. I didn't know what to think. Still don't.

The decision not to attend La Salle was made easy when Gola

announced his retirement from coaching after leading La Salle to a 23-1 record during the 1968-69 season. The following year, the team was barred from the NCAA tournament because an alumnus had offered some players "no-show" jobs.

Following Gola was another NBA great: Bob Cousy, formerly of the Boston Celtics. The Cooz, as he was known, had been the ultimate playmaker, a ball-handling magician who could dribble through his legs and throw passes around his back—Houdini in hi-black cons. He was now the head coach at Boston College.

I remember the night Cousy called my house.

I answered the phone and said, "Hello?

"Hello. This is Bob Cousy."

"Ray?" I said, thinking it was my high school teammate playing a joke.

"No, this is Bob Cousy."

"Okay. Ray. You're hilarious. Cut it out."

"No, this isn't Way. It weally is Bob Cousy."

Cousy was of French-Canadian heritage and had a very distinctive voice. His r's came out as w's.

"Yeah, okay."

"I weally am Bob Cousy."

I gulped hard. "Really?"

"Weally."

It took some time, but Cousy finally convinced me he was the real deal. I was suffused with embarrassment. I couldn't stop apologizing. "Forget it," he said.

"B.C.," he then said, matter-of-factly "is a great school in a great town. You'll get a good education and not be very far from home. Your parents will be able to see you play often."

He never once talked about his playing career. He never once used fancy rhetoric, lavish praise or grandiose promises. He was pure straight talk. Without even visiting Boston College, I was ready to sign a letter of intent.

But then, not long after, Cousy called and said he was resigning. He hinted that the emphasis at B.C. was on hockey and football. This was before the advent of the Big East Basketball Conference.

I thanked him for his honesty and said I was disappointed. I would find out years later he quit because he found recruiting to be a "rat race."

At the same time Cousy was recruiting me, so were Duke assistant coaches Chuck Daly and Hubie Brown. Daly, who would later coach the Detroit Pistons to the NBA championship and the U.S. team to an Olympic gold medal, visited several times. He was the Beau Brummell of coaches, always sporting custom-made suits, alligator shoes, starched shirts and fancy ties. His hair was always perfectly coiffed. His fingernails were always perfectly manicured. He wore a ring so flashy even the Pope would have kissed it.

Chuck enjoyed talking to my mother because she worked in the fashion industry. The two of them talked about different styles of clothes, different kinds of fabrics. Chuck would show my mother the silk lining of his newest sports coat. "Snazzy, huh?" he'd say, adding, "It's very expensive."

When he turned his attention to me, he said, "You have to sign with Duke. It's a great school with great academics. The campus is beautiful. The basketball program is first class." A big, winning smile. "Trust me, Duke is, without question, the perfect place for you."

Then after his last visit, Chuck called and said he was leaving Duke for...Boston College. Would I want to visit? I said, of course.

After touring the campus, Chuck took me to dinner and in a quick pivot, said, "Listen, nothing against Duke, it's a terrific school, although it's not all that it's cracked up to be. It's a very southern school and you're a very northern guy. It wouldn't be a good fit. So you should stay in the Northeast. Near your family. B.C.'s a great school with great academics. The campus is beautiful. The basketball program is first class. Trust me, B C., without question, is the perfect place for you."

I decided against Boston College, but not because I didn't like Chuck, I really did, but somehow without Cousy the campus just didn't seem the same.

I also felt, fairly or unfairly, that Chuck did a dirty dance by waltzing away from Duke and then boogieing to B.C. I understood why coaches changed jobs, but some of the anti-Duke lines Chuck was feeding me were, shall we say, artificial sweeteners.

With Chuck gone at Duke, Hubie Brown picked up the baton for Duke. Hubie—lean, full-faced, brown curly hair—was a one-man cavalry.

His pitch was upbeat and positive. Truthful. Genuine. He talked about his father, Charlie, the way I talked about my father: with affection and admiration. I very much respected that. Respected Hubie.

When Hubie spoke about basketball, he became a player whisperer, a basketball genius who understood the X's and O's the way Einstein understood mathematics.

One night in 1968, after visiting our apartment, Hubie and I were standing outside on the street. It was late and a cold wind blew. I was wearing a heavy coat, Hubie a light sweater. I asked Hubie, who had seen me play the day before, if I was correctly executing a reverse dribble. He told me to get a basketball. I did. He took it from me, and performed the move, the spin precisely executed. Watching him was almost hallucinogenic. He was Balanchine in brogues.

After a time, he handed me the ball. "Let's see you try." I attempted the move. He watched me closely, his eyes like periscopes. "No, no, no," Hubie said, his voice echoing in the night. He stood behind me and adjusted my move. "Try again," he said. I tried again. Not good enough. I tried still again. No dice. "If you wanna be a great player," Hubie said, "you gotta focus. You gotta do things right."

After a number of tries I finally got the move down pat. Hubie put his hand on my head like a faith healer. "You did good," he said. "But there's always room for improvement."

I smiled, proud of myself. Then Hubie said, "Choosing Duke, you'd be playing against some of the best college players in the country. Either you want the challenge of testing your abilities against the best or you don't." He gave me a Dirty Harry/Josey Wales squint. Only thing missing was the poncho and cigarillo, and him blowing smoke off his index finger.

But his challenge was effective. It made me want to show him what I was made of. Even more, his words resonated with me. Inspired me. Years later, whenever I faced a challenging task or was confronted with opposition or resistance I thought of Hubie. He was my reference point for putting my head down, forging ahead and proving my worth.

The antithesis of Hubie was University of North Carolina

coach Dean Smith. Smith had a craggy face and a prominent nose. He was soft-spoken, genteel—Mr. Rogers. Though he wasn't wearing a sweater or removing his shoes, he somehow, in his nasally Kansas accent, bounced me on his knee like an avuncular uncle. Without using lofty rhetoric, he pigeon-cooed me with stories about UNC—its glorious tradition and beautiful campus. He convinced me to visit Chapel Hill.

I liked everything about UNC. I especially liked Smith and his assistant coach Bill Guthridge, but I told Smith I was leaning toward Duke.

"Sorry to hear that," Dean said. "You're the player we most want. There's not another player in the country who can match your skill set. Believe me. You're our number-one choice."

I was flattered to hear Smith, a man of integrity, call me his first choice. It was quite the compliment.

A few weeks later, I played in an all-star tournament against teams from around the country: Pennsylvania, Ohio, Massachusetts, Washington. I spoke with a number of players who were also being heavily recruited by UNC. More than a few said Smith told them they were his "number one choice."

I was disappointed to hear that but not entirely surprised.

I wanted, at that point, to stop the coaching carousel and decide on a college, but my father said I should visit more schools and listen to more coaches.

And so I did. I listened to Maryland's Lefty Driesell who talked so fast I ran out of breath listening; to Kentucky's Adolph Rupp who spoke with such syrup I could almost taste molasses coming through the phone; to Wake Forest's Billy Packer who yapped so convincingly he could have charmed the socks off a rooster; and to Billy Raftery, a La Salle alumn who waxed so complimentary about his alma mater you would have thought it was the Kingdom of Heaven.

I also listened to a coach from the Atlantic 10 who offered me not only a full scholarship, but also one for my girlfriend, Carol. I listened to a coach from the Atlantic Coast Conference who said I would never have to pay for meals or clothing. I even had a coach promise me the use of a sports car whenever I needed it.

On a recruiting trip to the University of Florida, I was introduced to a buxom blonde cheerleader with a seductive sing-song voice. She strongly suggested we make sexual music together. When I said no because I had a girlfriend at home, she made a sad face and said, "Does that mean you won't be coming to the U?"

I also visited Columbia University. On the campus tour I saw the Students for a Democratic Society, led by Mark Rudd, chant and riot against the Vietnam war. There were smoke bombs and rocks thrown and buildings on fire. When I saw a helmeted cop clubbing protestors, I figured Columbia wasn't the place for me.

Chapter Nine

My first visit to Duke occurred in the fall of 1969. I flew to Durham, North Carolina with my father.

At the time, I didn't know much about Duke except that it had one of the finest college basketball programs in the country.

On the flight down to Durham, I read some brochures the school had sent me.

Founded by Methodists in 1838 under the name Brown School, it later became known as Duke in 1924 when the founder's son, James B. Duke, established the Duke Endowment with a $40 million trust fund. From day one under Mr. Duke, the priority was academic achievement with a small enrollment. (Today, Duke has only 6, 789 undergraduates and 9,991 postgraduates.)

The school covers over 8,600 acres and is divided by the East and West campuses. It has a law school, a medical school and a world renowned research center. According to most publications— Forbes, The Wall Street Journal, U.S. News & World Report— who rank colleges by academic standards, Duke is always in the top five.

As is its basketball team, which came into national prominence in 1952 when guard Dick Groat (who would become a star shortstop with the Pittsburgh Pirates) was the first Duke player to be named National Player of the Year. Since then, Duke has had many more players given that distinction, including Art Heyman, Johnny Dawkins, Danny Ferry, Christian Laettner, Grant Hill, Elton Brand, Jason Williams, J.J. Redick and Zion Williamson.

The day I arrived on the Duke campus, my father and I were driven directly to Cameron Indoor Stadium where we met Duke's head coach, Vic Bubas, who in 1964 had coached Duke to the NCAA finals, where they lost to UCLA.

Back then, the NCAA tournament only included 16 teams and when Duke didn't make it, they played well in the National Invitational Tournament, which was just as prestigious.

Bubas was a handsome man with a high forehead, aquiline nose and quick smile. He wore a dark suit, white shirt and striped tie, perfectly knotted. He looked more like a corporate attorney than a coach.

He didn't talk like a coach, either. He wasn't loud or animated. His voice was soft, honey sweet and milk warm.

His office was large and well-lit. There was a big, fancy desk and a blue and white carpet with a big "D" in the middle. On the walls were action pictures of past Duke stars: Jeff Mullins, Jack Marin, Mike Lewis, and Art Heyman.

Leaning forward in his chair, hands clasped on the desk, Bubas said, "I see using you as I did Heyman." Heyman was a swingman who was voted the College Player of the Year in 1963. He was my exact height and weight: six-five, two-ten. "You can play forward against the slower forwards and guard against the smaller guards. You have good range on your jump shot and your ability to penetrate the lane and dish is amazing." A big, winning smile. "Bottom line: you're my kind of versatile player. You come to Duke and you'll achieve greatness."

His words made my body tingle.

The next day, Hubie gave me a tour of the campus. Cameron Indoor Stadium. Wallace Wade football field. The gothic stone chapel. The Sarah P. Duke Gardens. The place was more magical than Disneyland.

"As beautiful as this campus is," Hubie said, "what's even more impressive is the atmosphere in Cameron. It's unlike any college gym in the world. Once you experience it, you never forget it."

Hubie handed me off to Dick DeVenzio, the team's starting point guard. Barely five nine and 150 pounds, Dick had short blonde hair and inquisitive eyes. He played at Ambridge High School in Pennsylvania, averaging 30 points a game his senior year while leading the school to an undefeated state championship. In 1967, Parade magazine named him the best high school point guard in America.

Dick took me to the Duke Gardens. Lush, green and flower-fragrant, it was packed with students: Shirtless guys smoking joints or throwing Frisbees. Mini-skirted girls wearing headphones and reading books. Music blared from cassette players: Crosby, Stills & Nash, Three Dog Night, The Doors and Creedence Clearwater Revival. This wasn't college. It was Coney Island.

Dick pointed to a pretty, shapely co-ed and said, "Nice, huh?"

I mentioned how on my University of Florida recruiting trip a few weeks before, a player had said, "Listen, man, you see a hot babe on campus you better run over and introduce yourself. You could be here for four years and never see her again."

Dick laughed. "Not the case here," he said. "Florida's got, what? Over 30,000 undergrads. Duke has only 5,000, of which only 1,500 are girls. So don't sweat it. If you see a beautiful girl, you'll see her probably every week."

Dick paused, watching a pretty co-ed stand and stretch.

"Trust me," he said. "You can't miss here. Here Duke basketball players are gods. Getting laid is easier than getting grits."

Later that night, my father and I went to a game at Cameron. The gym was small, old, intimate, a tiny bandbox that is the college basketball equivalent of Boston's Fenway Park. Still in use today, it's one of the last arenas in college basketball where the crowd feels as if it's sitting in your lap.

Students stood shoulder-to-shoulder, waving banners, signs and pennants. Behind one basket, a band blared. On the court, a dozen beautiful cheerleaders tumbled. There was clapping, cheering, yelling, whistling, deafening chants of "Let's go Duke!" "Let's go Duke!" Foot stomping had the stands shaking. Cameron rocked. Cameron rolled.

Within minutes after the start of the game, I saw six-eleven center Randy Denton score in the paint; small forward Rick Katherman hit long-range jumpers; DeVenzio triggered a fast break and fired a no-look pass to Brad Evans for a layup. At his best, DeVenzio was as indefensible as a riptide.

Watching the players perform made my mouth drop and my eyes bulge. I felt as if I wasn't witnessing a team but rather a highly choreographed dance routine.

Orchestrating this performance was, of course, Bubas. He was

Bob Fosse and Alvin Ailey rolled into one. He had the players moving in perfect harmony: cutting, screening, passing, gyrating to the basket, pirouetting around defenders and spinning through double-teams. The crowd was continually brought to a crescendo.

After the game, I told my father I was going to sign with Duke.

My father smiled. "Good choice," he said. "Duke's a great academic school with a great basketball program." His eyes got misty. He cleared his throat. "I'm so proud of you," he said.

"Thanks," I said.

"No," my father said. "Thank you."

A week later Hubie came to Union City and I signed my letter of intent.

But then, shortly thereafter, the unimaginable happened. Vic Bubas phoned and said he was retiring. The news hit me hard. It felt as if a monarch had abdicated his throne.

He said his replacement would be Raymond "Bucky" Waters, his former assistant and the coach of West Virginia.

"Bucky's a great coach and a great guy," Bubas said. "He'll be coming to see you in a day or two," A brief pause, then: "Hope this doesn't change your mind about attending Duke."

I didn't respond.

I revisited Duke and met with Bucky. He had a pock-marked face, a crew cut and large teeth. He seemed personable enough, but I wasn't overly impressed.

After our meeting I thought about calling Dean Smith and professing my desire to attend Carolina.

Hubie Brown, who would remain as an assistant, sensed my discomfort. Trust me, he said, it'll all work out. I trusted him—

because as far as I was concerned Hubie walked on water.

And so I became a "Dookie."

My first few weeks at Duke were eye-opening. It was culture shock. At orientation, students introduced themselves and quickly said, "Where you from?"

Instead of answering, I volleyed the question back.

The answers were Boston, Chicago, D.C, L.A., even Palm Springs. When I said Union City, New Jersey, I got a blank stare.

I was placed in Taylor dormitory. My roommate was Gary Melchionni, an All-American guard from Bishop Eustace High School in Pennsauken, New Jersey. He had a brother, Billy, who was then a star with the New Jersey Nets.

Gary and I were like Oscar Madison and Felix Unger, him being the neater and quieter one. But unlike The Odd Couple, we never had disagreements or fights.

Our dormmates were mostly wealthy, white kids who had attended fancy prep schools and whose family backgrounds—culturally and economically—couldn't have been further from mine.

I was, as the expression goes, a duck out of water.

The Duke freshmen grew up, for the most part, in large suburban homes with dishwashers, hot showers and two cars in the driveway. They had nice monthly allowances, and their dorm rooms were filled with books, designer sheets and high-end stereo equipment.

All I had was fifty bucks in my pocket, an old cassette player, worn bedding and magazines about basketball.

The students made it clear that they were at Duke for the education. Some wanted to study theology or geology, physics or linguistics, sociology or psychology. A few preferred medicine and law.

Me? I had no course of study in mind. I simply aspired to make All-American, have some fun and get my ass into the NBA.

My first week two students approached me in the elevator. One was short and chubby. The other was slim and hawklike.

"What's your major?" The short one asked.

"Basketball," I said, smiling.

The guys glanced at each other. I got the impression they didn't care for my answer. But I didn't care. Secure in the armor of my talents, I figured it'd just be a matter of time before I had the entire student body in my corner, cheering me on.

The slim guy said, "Yeah, well. I did hear you're gonna have a helluva freshmen team."

Still smiling, I said, "Damn right."

My freshmen team (freshmen couldn't play varsity back then) consisted of all high school All-Americans: center Allan Shaw from Millville, New Jersey; forward Jim Fitzsimmons from Fairfield, Connecticut; guard Jeff Dawson from Downers Grove, Illinois; Melchionni and me. Our coach was Jack Schalow.

Jack—blonde and blue-eyed—was a former marine instructor who was built like a championship bodybuilder. He was constantly doing chin-ups and one-handed push-ups.

He ran practice the way I imagine Patton ran his brigade. He always stood at halfcourt, his shirt tight against his body, his biceps bulging.

A player would make a stupid pass and Jack would immediately grab the whistle dangling around his neck and blow it.

"What kind of pass was that?" he'd yell, his face turning fire-engine red. "You don't float the damn ball. You zip it." A pause. "You gotta do the fundamentals right. It's all about fundamentals, fundamentals, fundamentals." He tapped the side of his head. "Concentrate, guys, concentrate."

He'd blow his whistle and practice resumed.

Jack never accepted excuses or laziness. Make a mistake and his face would inflate. Yet he made playing a pleasure, taking five guys with big egos and making them understand the difference between the interests of the team versus the interest of the individual. He stressed that winning required subordinating our selfish impulses for the team. We all bought into his philosophy.

"A great team, a really great team," he'd exhort, pacing the sidelines, "is like a jazz group that allows for improvisation and variation without breaking the rhythm."

And God help us if we broke that rhythm.

"Jesus H. Christ," he'd shout, waving his arms as if warding off a swarm of bees. "I don't want anyone over-dribbling the ball for a shot. I want the ball passed around. I want movement, goddamnit. Movement. I don't want guys standing around watching each make flights of fancy. This isn't goddamn tennis or golf. It's a team sport. Team, team, team."

Our team was—and still is—the only freshmen team in the history of the ACC to go undefeated. We were, in a word, spectacular, not only beating opponents but trampling them. On nights when all cylinders were firing we couldn't do anything wrong. We moved so fast our sneakers squeaked. We perfectly executed pick-and-rolls, back-door cuts, screens. We expertly switched on defense, creating steals and turnovers. In transition we ran the break as if running from the bulls at Pamplona.

We ran like that because Jack had us in peak condition. His favorite drill at the end of practice was "suicides."

In a suicide you stand at the baseline, sprint to the foul line, touch it with your hand, then sprint back to the baseline, touch it with your hand, then sprint to the half court line, touch it, sprint back to the baseline, then sprint to the far foul line touch it and then sprint back to the original baseline.

"Okay," Jack shouted. "Line up."

We all lined up along the baseline. Jack looked at his stopwatch.

"At the whistle," he said. "Start running."

Jack blew his whistle. We ran the suicides. Once, twice, even three times.

As we ran, Jack yelled, "You're gonna run till you drop."

When we finished running some players had their hands on their knees, gulping for air.

Jack looked at his stopwatch and said, "Some of you guys were a tad slow." A diabolical smile. "Let's do one more."

Moans and groans. We lined up again.

Jack blew his whistle. We ran as fast as possible.

"A team might outshoot us," Jack hollered. "But I'll be goddamn if a team will outrun us."

We were in such good shape and so fundamentally sound that for the first time in Duke history a freshmen team beat the varsity in a preseason scrimmage.

Because of our success, we were treated with the reverence of pros in a state which, at the time, lacked any professional sports teams. We were on television regularly. We were in the newspapers daily. Alumni wanted to host us. Fans wanted to know us. We were, in a word, celebrities.

All of which I detested, but I found no way to plug the dike from the ever-surging sea of fans.

I remember one night after a big game (which we won) I went to a Sigma Chi fraternity party. The frat reeked of beer and booze, menthols and marijuana. People danced. Music blared. From an eight-track music player, The Rolling Stones sang "Honky Tonk Women."

I noticed a gorgeous girl chomping gum, blowing a large pink bubble, popping it with her teeth and chewing it back into her mouth.

She waved. I waved back. She smiled then took a small compact from her purse, powdered her nose and walked toward me.

Wearing a tight white Duke T-shirt over a navy-blue miniskirt, she had shoulder-length blonde hair, a slim waist and lips smeared with fiery red lipstick.

"Great game," she said, her Southern drawl thicker and richer than barbecue sauce.

"Thank you," I said.

She extended her hand. I shook it. Her hand was warm and moist, as if she were in the grip of a fever. "My name's Belle."

"Nice to meet you. I'm Rich."

"I know who you are."

I smiled. "What dorm you in?"

"Oh, I'm not a student here. I go to Durham Tech. I'm a freshman." Durham Tech was a public community college.

"I'm a freshman, too."

"I know," she said, grinning, the slightest tip of her pink tongue showing between her fire-engine red lips. "I know all about you."

"You do?"

"Of course. My grandfather, father and brother are huge Duke fans." A dazzling smile. "But I'm the biggest fan of all of them."

"Awesome."

"You mind getting me something to drink?" she said.

"Sure. What would you like?"

"A beer."

I headed over to a makeshift bar, slaloming through a throng of celebrating students. Hi-fives and backslaps. I turned and grinned at Belle who was chewing on her fingernails as if she was starving. I got her beer.

"Thanks," she said. She looked at my cup. "What are you drinking?"

"Coke."

"No alcohol?"

"I don't drink."

Her eyebrows rose. "Wow! An athlete who doesn't drink!" She lifted her cup. "Oh, well. Cheers!"

I clicked her cup. "Cheers!"

She looked around the room and said, "A lot of gorgeous girls here."

I nodded.

Belle moved close to me and whispered, "Can I ask you a personal question?"

"Sure."

"How many of these girls here have you screwed?"

"Excuse me?" I said, almost spilling my drink.

She flashed a playful grin. "Okay. You don't have to answer.

I'll just assume you screwed many. Being a big man on campus and all."

"Well, for your information, I haven't slept with any of them."

"Why's that?"

"I have a girlfriend in New Jersey," I said, referring to my high school sweetheart, Carol.

"And you're loyal?"

"Yes."

Belle stared at me, completely baffled. "Wow!"

"Look," I said, "It's been a pleasure meeting you, but I really got to go."

She grabbed my forearm tightly and said, "Oh no, you can't leave yet."

I looked at my watch. "It's late."

"C'mon. Stay. Pleeeease." She put out her arms, like a child asking to be lifted from the high-chair. "Pleeeease. Just a while longer."

"Okay. Just another minute."

She patted my hand. In the background The Rolling Stones were now singing "Sympathy for the Devil."

"I got an idea," Belle said. "Let's go someplace where we can be alone."

"That's not gonna happen."

She stiffened.

"I don't do this, you know?" she said.

"Do what?"

"Pick-up basketball players. I don't want you to think I'm some kind of groupie or anything."

"I'd never think that." I lied.

"Because that's not who I am. I like you. You're a great player."

"I'm flattered…but…"

Tears brimmed in her eyes and trembled on the lower lids.

I tried to think of something to say, something comforting, but for a moment I couldn't.

"Why are you being such an asshole?" she said, two tiny tears rolling down both cheeks.

"Look, I don't mean to be hurtful…"

"Well, you are," she said, sniffling.

"I'm sorry you feel…"

Belle then tossed what was left of her beer in my face and stormed out of the frat house.

As I was wiping the beer off my face, a friend came over and said, "I see you've made quite the impression."

"Yeah, right."

He snorted. "Oh, well, you win some, you lose some."

"And sometimes," I said, "You wish to hell you didn't even have to play the game."

The encounter with Belle was unusual, but it was just one of many strange fan experiences.

Often, I, along with my teammates, was invited to the home of some prominent doctor from the renowned Duke Hospital who lived in some fancy palace outside Durham.

Wearing an apron and chef's hat, the doctor, a surgeon, stood behind the grill, barbecuing burgers and dogs.

We—the players—sat nearby in big, comfy lounge chairs. Beneath our feet was a lawn as manicured as the courts at Wimbledon. Above us were tall magnolia trees filled with mockingbirds.

Stepping out of the kitchen, holding a large tray, was the Doc's wife. Tall and thin, stately as a heron, she wore a flowered dress, rose-colored sunglasses and a giant floppy hat.

"Y'all comfortable?" she said, her voice sweeter than mint jelly.

A collective "Yes, ma'am."

She reverentially bowed down, her shoulder blades sticking out like wings.

"You boys care for some chips and dips?" she said, extending the tray.

Another collective "Yes, ma'am."

"Good. I made the dip 'specially for you fellas since you are"—a spotlight smile—"so special."

We tried the dip and said, "Delicious."

"I'm so happy you like it. I was so afraid you wouldn't."

She rushed inside and returned minutes later holding another tray, this one filled with tall glasses of ice tea. Made, of course, 'specially for us.

"Chow time," the doctor yelled.

We stood and sat at a large wooden table covered with bone china, silver cutlery and vases filled with so many flowers as if to suggest a funeral.

"May we give thanks," the doc's wife said.

We lowered our heads, closed our eyes and clasped our hands.

"Thank you God for all our blessings," the Doc's wife said. "And please, Lord, let Duke win all its games."

A player next to me whispered, "Think God will help us?"

"Only if he hates Carolina."

Sometimes neighbors—always bombed from drinking cocktails in glasses the size of bird baths—stopped by.

One night a big-time lawyer, who wore a Duke-blue Nehru jacket, white pants and shiny white patent leather shoes sidled up to me. Short with a low forehead and a toupee that was slightly askew, he had metallic blue eyes and skin like baked-chicken.

He shook my hand, working my arm up and down as if it was the handle of a water pump.

"You have some game," he said, now patting me on the back. "Gets me excited watching you throw some amazing passes."

"Glad to hear it."

"You're a great player," he said. "That's who you are. A great, great player."

"Thank you."

"You know what I loved," he said. "I loved it when you hit that baseline jumper in the Carolina game! Wow! What a shot!" He took a big gulp of his drink. "I think it was over George Karl. Am I right?"

"Right as rain," I said, not remembering the shot.

He put his hand on my shoulder and started rubbing my collarbone.

"You ever need anything, anything at all, a ride, a meal, anything, y'all call me, hear?"

"Appreciate it."

"Least I can do for ya."

I nodded.

"I mean, it. I really, really mean it. Your wish, my command."

"Good to know."

He drained his drink and shook his glass. "Think I need some more Wheaties," he said. "Can I get you anything?"

"No, I'm good."

He then stuck out his hand to be slapped. I tapped it softly.

"Well, gotta go get myself fortified." He saluted me. "Keep up the good work."

I saluted him back. "Aye, aye."

At night's end, the lawyer's very tipsy wife, a towering temptress who wore a white dress tighter than a mermaid's skin, approached me.

"Just wanted to say, I had a great time tonight," she said, her blue eyes unfocused, her voice a hot whisper.

"We did, too," I said.

With her long, pink fingernails she excavated an olive from her Bloody Mary and nibbled it. "I soooooo enjoy watching you play," she said.

"Thanks."

Swaying slightly, she put a hand on my forearm. "You're a very nische person," she said, slurring her words. "And so cute I could eat you up."

"I wouldn't suggest it," I said. "You might get indigestion."

She laughed hysterically and spilled some "bloody" on her dress.

"Oopsie daisy," she said, brushing the stain off her right breast. "And I just brought this darn dress especially for tonight. Rats."

She then grinned, turned and sashayed away, shaking her rear end like Tina Turner. As I watched her, it hit me: You can get a hangover from things other than booze. I had one from fans.

Chapter Ten

Early in my freshmen year, my teammates and I were asked to pledge by almost every fraternity.

But none of us had any interest.

Why? We all had different reasons, but for me fraternities seemed like places of conformity, animal houses where guys guzzled beer and exchanged silly handshakes.

I also didn't like what pledges had to go through—bizarre initiation rituals (not that we would have had to, of course, being star athletes) like being insulted and ridiculed, being pissed on or, worse, having your head plunged into a toilet.

In the almost three years I was at Duke, I only attended two fraternity parties, where some guys dropped "trou," blew farts and groped women.

At one of the parties, a "rush chairman" pulled me aside. He was a short, chubby guy with hair like an Afghan dog.

"How can you not join?" he said. The rye on his breath was so heavily aromatic it smelled like a slice of pumpernickel. "Every basketball player in the history of Duke belonged to a fraternity." He smiled. "Don't you get it! Fraternities are where the action is.

It's what campus life is all about. It's where the girls are." An even louder burp, then: "Plus, don't you realize what a coup it is for us to have a basketball jock in our fraternity?"

To abort the conversation, I said I would rethink my position. He said "awesome" and patted on the back, as if trying to burp me. He then excused himself because he thought he was "about to barf."

I found it interesting that the rush chairman called me a "jock." Until I got to Duke, I had never heard that term. And certainly had never been referred to as one.

At first, I thought the word was a compliment, but later discovered it was a term of disparagement.

Once, while showering in my dorm, I overheard one student say to another "Fucking basketball players think they're hot shit."

The other replied, "They are hot shit."

"Yeah, well, they're still no more than dumb jocks."

The point was later driven home to me when my theology teacher, Professor James Charlesworth, pulled me aside one day after class.

A studious-looking man with dark hair across his narrow forehead, he sported thick-rimmed black glasses that he kept pushing up the bridge of his nose with a tap of a fingertip.

"Do me a favor," he said. "Raise your hand and talk more in class. You can't just sit there and let the other students think you don't know anything. You have brains. Use them. Otherwise, you'll get cheered on the court and jeered off it."

I nodded, doubting I would change my act, which was to sit in the back of class, hardly listening and never saying a word—if for no other reason than I had nothing intelligent to say.

"Trust me when I tell you," Charlesworth continued, "There are a lot of smart, rich, talented kids at Duke. They're here primarily for an education. They love basketball, but they enjoy personal success more."

The majority of students I interacted with came from private schools. They were scholastic high-achievers who spoke better and read better than me. Coming from my whacky, instructor-deficient high school, there was no escaping my ineptitude. At times I felt intimidated.

I mean, here were guys and gals my age debating and swapping intellectual theories and interpretations on religions and philosophers and politicians. All I debated was whether Oscar Robertson had a better jump shot than Jerry West. (West, of course, did.)

Indeed, I was so educationally unaware that once when I heard two dormmates discussing the Marxists, I thought they were talking about the Marx Brothers—Groucho, Harpo, Chico, Gummo and Zeppo.

I remember calling my grandfather and saying, "I think I'm the dumbest kid at Duke."

My grandfather snickered.

"Listen, kid," he said. "Whatever it is you think they know, you can learn. What you know they'll never fucking learn."

"What's that?"

"Moxie."

My sophomore year I hardly ever went to class.

And outside of class, I rarely read a book, except for basketball biographies. Indeed, I was so uneducated in English literature I wouldn't have known E. B. White from Snow White or Thomas Wolfe from the Big Bad Wolf.

When tests came, I didn't bother studying. Somehow I still got C's. It made my day when Duke went to a Pass-Fail system and grading didn't really matter.

Away from the classroom there was basketball and only basketball, the practices and the games. Yet there was a strange dynamic surrounding the team. The players were all really great talents, but we weren't really great friends.

The thing that many people don't understand about big-time college basketball is that for all the talk of how teams are close-knit families who defend and protect each other, the fact is it's not always true. It's exaggerated and overblown. At least, it was when I was at Duke.

It should go without saying that the Duke players were highly competitive. As a result, the competition for playing time was fierce, especially in practice. That's where you earned your minutes.

My first game as a varsity player came in 1972, against Princeton in the Greensboro Coliseum. Princeton's star was Brian Taylor, also a sophomore who came from Perth Amboy High School in New Jersey. Brian played the same years I did. For my money, he was the best player in the state—a truly gifted athlete who would later play twelve years in the NBA.

Starting the game against him was my goal. In the weeks leading up to it, my competition at small forward was Rick Katherman, a junior who had been a starter the previous year.

Rick was the team's best shooter, a sprinter who raced up the court and quickly got off what today would be three-pointers.

He and I went at it pretty good in practice. Pushing, shoving, elbowing. But no matter how good my defense was, Rick still got open and buried his jumpers.

I had no choice but to refine my game, becoming a maestro of maneuvers, a Swiss Army knife of versatility.

I worked hard on mastering the back-door play, executing the give-and-go, the pick and roll, passing off the dribble. I wanted every move to have a purpose. I wanted to know where my teammates were on the court at all times and what each would do when I had the ball so that I could make the necessary pass when they sprang free from an opponent.

I worked, too, on my jump shot, extending my range way beyond the free throw line. I spent many a morning alone in Cameron taking as many as a hundred shots, each shot launched precisely as the one before it.

Mostly, though, I worked on dribbling.

I wrapped my right hand in thick tape and dribbled everywhere with my left. I snuck into Cameron Indoor Stadium at night and dribbled around chairs. I went to Wallace Wade Stadium early mornings and dribbled on grass. I even dribbled in my dorm room until a neighbor asked me to "stop the racket."

A teammate, forward Chris Redding, kidded me that all I wanted to do "was grab a rebound and dribble fast downcourt."

He was spot on. I luxuriated in engineering the fast-break, pounding the ball and seeing the kaleidoscope of action before me, teammates on the wings, defenders back-pedaling. I looked right. The defense shifted. Then I'd make a "blind pass" to a teammate on my left for a wide open layup.

No other play excited me more. Perhaps the best compliment I ever received as a player was when my freshman coach, Jack Schalow, told me, "From now on, I'm gonna call you Kodak since you so clearly photograph the floor."

I also had one more thing going for me—stamina. I ran up the steps at Wallace Wade Stadium. I sprinted around the court at Cameron. I hightailed it around campus as if something hairy and howling was chasing me.

Still, despite all my efforts, I thought Katherman would start. It would be the first time in my life I would not be on the court for the opening tap.

The thought infuriated me so much I thought about buying a voodoo doll, naming it Katherman and sticking pins into it.

I called my grandfather.

"Practice is like hand-to-hand combat," I told him. "Guys play with steam coming out of their ears."

"Isn't that why you choose Duke… so you could compete against the best?"

"Yeah, but I didn't think the competition would be my teammates. I thought it would be the guys from UNC or Maryland."

"Do me a favor," he said. "Put your hand over your heart."

"What?!"

"You heard me."

I did as instructed.

"Is it beating?"

"Yeah."

"Good. Now stop the bellyaching and go play your game."

On the bus ride to Greensboro, I sat by myself, looking out the window at fast-food restaurants, gas stations, furniture stores and car dealerships, while seeing in my reflection the look of someone watching a frightening movie and trying not to scream.

Max Crowder, the team trainer, stopped by my seat.

"You okay?" he said. "You're awfully quiet. Usually, we can't shut you up."

"Just thinking about the game," I said, swallowing hard.

We got to the Coliseum and went to the locker room. Guys started undressing and putting on their uniforms. I slowly put on mine. I was number 12.

Ten minutes before game time, Bucky entered the locker room and stepped to a black board. The room was quiet, players sitting on three-legged stools rubbing their hands together or circling their necks.

Bucky gave us a pep talk, saying "don't underestimate this Princeton team because they play in the Ivy League. This kid Taylor is the real deal. He alone can carry a team."

He then began writing down the names on the board. My stomach roller-coastered. He scribbled Denton…DeVenzio… Saunders…Melchionni and…me. At small forward.

I was shocked. Couldn't believe it. I tried to show no emotion, but inside I was vibrating.

I looked over at Katherman. He sat motionless, his face crimson, his jaw tight, his eyes staring daggers at Bucky.

I played well. Scored only six points, but had seven rebounds and a handful of assists. Our team won, 79-75.

I started every game for the rest of the season. Katherman and I rarely spoke.

My sophomore year was a good one. I finished the season as the team's second leading scorer (12.7ppg) and second leading assist man (2.4). I should have been ecstatic, but I wasn't.

Problems within the program were festering. There was discontent with Bucky, his rules—mandatory early breakfasts, nightly study halls, long practices and dress codes.

Many players were unhappy. Don Blackman transferred to Rhode Island. Two of my freshman teammates, Jim Fitzsimmons and Jeff Dawson, transferred—Jim to Harvard where he became the team's leading scorer, Jeff to the University of Illinois where he led the Big Ten in scoring.

Our team ended the year 20-10 and 9-5, 3rd in the ACC. That wasn't enough for the NCAA tournament, but we were invited to the National Invitational Tournament, which, at the time, was a big deal.

In the first game of the NIT, I scored 20 points in leading the team to an opening round upset over Dayton. In the second round, we beat Tennessee, which got us into its NIT semifinals for the first time in Duke history. Our next opponent was North Carolina. We had beaten them once during the regular season and lost to them twice. They beat us in the semis, 73-67. I had a solid game, scoring 18 points. In the consolation match against St. Bonaventure, I had a team high of 30 points and 9 rebounds. In Madison Square Garden, "The World's Most Famous Arena." It was one of the best games I ever played.

A few days later, Bucky named Gary Melchionni and me co-captains for the 1971-1972 season. A photo of us was taken outside Madison Square Garden and used for the following season's media guide cover. By all accounts, I was expected to be an ACC all-conference player my junior year.

The Seventies were an interesting time to be in college. There were pot smokers. Casual sex. Carlos Castaneda. Watergate. The Vietnam War. Protests. Rallies. The shooting at Kent State. The movie Deep Throat. Gay Liberation Day. The hostage crisis at the

Summer Olympics. Bell-bottoms. Tie-dye T-shirts. Make love not war.

It is—and was—reasonable to say that student rebellion was germinating like a magical seed, and I was witnessing it in full flower.

To steal a lyric from the late singer David Crosby, I started to let "my freak flag fly." I grew my hair long. (Or at least as much as Bucky allowed.) I wore ripped jeans and tie-dyed shirts. Listened less to the Beach Boys and more to Led Zeppelin, Pink Floyd and Bob Dylan.

I also became friends with students who weren't athletes, who had different perspectives, different backgrounds.

One such person was John.

I saw John one day when I was sitting in the Duke lunchroom with a cluster of football and basketball players. John came out of the cafeteria, carrying a tray waist-high and walking as if on tippy-toes. Thin and built like a dancer, he had soft features and long, shaggy blonde hair. He wore blue short shorts and a white tank top. He went to a table and sat by himself.

One of the football players said, "Look at that pansy motherfucker."

I knew John. We lived in the same dorm and had briefly spoken a few times.

"Cocksucker's more queer than Truman Capote," another player said.

"He's not a bad guy," I said.

"How do you know?" the player said. "What? He suck your weenie?"

I ignored him.

"You know what," I said. "I'm going to join him." I did this because in high school there was an obviously gay kid who was regularly tormented. Rarely, if ever, had I come to his defense. Years later, my indifference and inaction bothered and humiliated me. Going to sit with John was, I suppose, my attempt at a make-good gesture.

"Just protect your sausage," another player said.

Laughter and snickers.

I picked up my tray and walked over and took a seat across from John.

"Mind if I join you?" I said.

He didn't respond.

I put my tray down on the table and sat.

"How you doing?" I said, friendly-like

John looked at me with darkened eyes.

"Why are you doing this?" His voice was soft, modulated.

"Doing what?"

"Sitting with me?"

"You seem lonely."

"Well, I'm not," he said, tightening his lips and moving his teeth as if he were nibbling on a small hard seed.

"Look…"

"I appreciate your grand gesture," he added, "but I know damn well you wouldn't do this if you weren't a jock." He said the word 'jock' as if it was an obscenity.

I smirked. "What's that supposed to mean?"

"It means don't do me any favors."

"I'm just trying to be nice."

"Well, don't."

"Fuck's with you?" I said.

"Whyn't you get lost."

I stood, gave him the finger and walked back to the jock table.

"What happened?" a player said. "Johnny Boy didn't find you attractive?"

I smirked. "He's a scumbag."

That night I thought about my exchange with John. He was right. There was no way in hell I would have sat with him had I not had the protective armor of being a star athlete. I was just trying to show off, for all the wrong reasons.

The episode made me wonder. Am I a good guy or a bad guy? Or am I just some idiot fuck caught in the misty middle.

Weeks passed after my "lunch" with John. Then one day I saw him in the dorm, sitting alone in a chair and reading a book.

I approached him. He glanced up at me, smirked, and looked down quickly.

"I'm sorry," I said.

"About?"

"You were right. I wouldn't have had the balls to sit with you if I wasn't an athlete." A beat. "So, again, I apologize."

He closed his book, cleared his throat and looked at me like an artist sizing someone up for a portrait.

"Okay," he said, with some trepidation. "I accept your apology."

I extended my hand. He extended his. We shook.

I said, "Maybe we could try having lunch again."

We had lunch a few weeks later in the Student Union building. I was wearing basketball shorts and a Duke basketball T-shirt. John wore tight green shorts and a bright yellow tank top. A fire-engine red silk kerchief was knotted around his throat.

"Nice outfit," I said.

He put a hand behind his head and looked to the side, smiling. "You like?" he said.

"Let's just say I wish I had my sunglasses."

John nibbled on his salad. I wolfed my burger. John said, "Does it bother you that I'm queer?" (The word gay was rarely used back then.)

"Not particularly."

Athletes walked by our table. One football player passed John, turned and blew me a kiss.

John told me how, as a young kid, he tried to hide and cover up his feelings. A shrink told him that his homosexual desires were nothing more than unresolved emotional issues. When he did finally come "out of the closet" his athletic-obsessed father beat him. Disowned him. Kids in high school bullied him. He felt alone. Rejected. He spent much of his adolescence by himself, painting and singing, playing the piano. He loved music, especially classical music. He found it unfathomable that I knew nothing about Beethoven and Mozart, Cole Porter or George Gershwin. He gave me cassettes of their music so I'd stop listening to that "boring shit by Crosby, Stills, Nash & Young." He gave me books on art and history and talked about "individuation," a term I never heard before. It meant developing an understanding of yourself.

Looking back, I see how John not only enlightened me on the arts, he also gave me insight and appreciation for a lifestyle I knew nothing about and probably had no respect for. John altered my mindset. He was my flashlight into the darkness.

John wasn't the only student to broaden my perspectives.

One day, while sitting in the Duke Library reading, as usual,

Sports Illustrated, a girl walked over and looked down on me.

"Can I help you?" I said.

"No," she said. Tall and brunette, with a sprinkling of freckles on the bridge of her nose, she had cornflower blue eyes, high cheekbones and a shapely body. "Maybe I can help you."

"What are you, a social worker?"

"I think you're acting like a dumb jock," she said. Despite the insult, I liked her voice. It had the sweetness of a sun-softened caramel.

"Is that right?" I said.

She nodded. She was wearing faded bell bottom jeans and a white, flimsy peasant blouse embroidered with daffodils. As far as I could tell, she sported no bra, jewelry, make-up or lipstick. She smelled like lavender.

"I sometimes see you in the library, but you're either flirting with some girl or sleeping," she said. "You seem like a bright guy, yet I've never seen you reading a book."

"That's 'cause I have someone who reads to me."

She smirked and handed me Hugh Prather's book: Notes to Myself.

"What's this?"

"It's a book, birdbrain."

"I know that. What's it about?"

"It's about one man's personal struggles and his ability to transform them into opportunities for growth and understanding."

"Wow."

"Read it," she said. "You might actually dig it."

I winked. "I'm more than happy to read it in your dorm room."

She snorted. "Don't be such an asshole, okay?"

Students walked by sipping coffee from Styrofoam containers and wearing headphones. Bearded professors with horn-rimmed glasses sat at desks reading books. The place was quieter than a funeral parlor.

"I'm in your Psyche class," she said.

"Are you?"

"Guess you wouldn't know since you never come to class."

I narrowed my eyes. "By the way," I said, "what's your name?"

"Karen."

"I'm..."

"...I know who you are," she said. "Read the book. It might enlighten you."

She turned and strolled away, a large leather bag slung over her shoulder. On it were pinned buttons: Ban The Bra. Flower Power. We Shall Overcome.

A few nights later I got around to reading the book. There were a number of passages underlined. One in particular fascinated me: "As I look back on my life, one of the most constant and powerful things I've experienced is the desire to be more than I am at the moment—an unwillingness to let my mind remain in the pettiness where it idles—a desire to increase the boundaries of myself—a desire to feel more, learn more—a desire to grow, improve, purify, expand."

Heavy shit, I thought. Intriguing.

The next day, I visited Karen in her dorm. She was wearing a tie-dyed T-shirt and short shorts. Her legs were long and tanned. Her toenails were painted red. Just being in the same room with her set my libido on an absolute tidal wave of desire. I was sure I could jimmy the lock off her affections and have some acrobatic athletic amour. At the very least, a smoochy détente.

"You like the book?" she said. She was sitting on a waterbed, her legs drawn up to her chest and her arms clasped around her shins. The room reeked of incense.

"I did. It made me think."

"That must have been a novel experience."

"Ha-ha."

Her room had beaded curtains, bean bag chairs, lava lamps, totem poles of books and posters of Albert Camus and Martin Luther, Janis Joplin and Bob Dylan—a far cry from my room, which had no books and posters of Jerry West.

"I'm going to start giving you books to read," she said.

"I don't read."

"Books by Kierkegaard, Emerson, Camus, Thoreau, and Sartre."

I looked at her cross-eyed. "Who?"

"You know what Sartre wrote."

"Haven't a clue."

"He wrote 'Man is nothing more than what he makes himself.'"

"Wow!" I said, not knowing the appropriate response.

Karen put a cassette into her recorder. Grateful Dead sang "Truckin'."

"You get high?" she said.

"Only on basketball."

"Some of your teammates get high."

"I know."

"But you don't."

"No."

"Far out."

She rolled a joint that resembled a snake that swallowed a beach ball. She lit it, closed her eyes and inhaled as if she was about to jump off a huge cliff. She then exhaled. The room reeked of marijuana.

"Shit's dynamite," she said, extending the roach.

I waved it off. My resistance had less to do with dope and more to do with conformity. Some teammates often pushed, even insisted, I "toke up." When I said no, they gave me a strange, almost sinister look which intensified when I also refused to drink alcohol. At times, I felt almost ostracized. Uncertain if I fit in with the athletes or the aesthetics. Perhaps neither.

Karen took another hit.

"Whaddya think of Werner Erhard."

"Never heard of him."

"He has a philosophy of transformation, personal responsibility, accountability and possibility."

I tried hard not to roll my eyes.

Karen said, "I'm going to take one of his seminars. Wanna go?"

"Ah...well...ah..." I immediately pictured a ballroom packed with hand-holding crazies, free-associating, primal screaming and having tearful catharsis while hugging teddy bears.

"C'mon," she persisted. "Whaddya got to lose?"

I refrained from saying, "My mind."

We went to Erhard's seminar. The place was packed, filled with guys in jeans and plaid shirts, girls in mini-skirts and leather vests. In the wake of the 1960s, Werner Erhard's seminars and speaking engagement drew huge crowds, eager for answers.

Erhard was entertaining, charismatic and commanded the stage. I liked what he said about self-improvement and self-actualization, the need to discover who you are and what you want. He said, "Create your future from your future and not your past." His words resonated.

On the drive back to Duke, Karen said, "Just so you know, I don't fuck basketball players."

"Neither do I."

"I only date guys with brains."

"Leaves me out."

"Oh, I think there's some hope for you."

"Maybe if I go to Lourdes."

As we neared Durham, Karen put her head on my shoulder and fell asleep. The windows were open and a slight breeze blew strands of hair from her forehead. On the radio, Jefferson Airplane sang "Somebody to Love."

I looked over at Karen and recalled something she once said to me: "Seeing yourself for who you truly are is a necessary condition for changing who you want to be."

As I drove through the darkness, I thought about that, and asked myself a difficult question. Who 'did' I want to be? The answer came quickly.

I wanted to be more than just a basketball player. I wanted to have all the freedoms of my fellow students.

Raindrops started hitting the windshield. I took a glance out my window. Looking at the rain, I traveled backward in time to a rainy afternoon when I was sitting on a bus with my high school teammate, Ray, listening to a girl I didn't know badmouth me simply because I was a star basketball player.

Her words hurt me. They were cruel and cutting. But she was right about one thing: I was nothing more than a basketball player.

I pondered that for a while, and it hit me that because of my youthful obsession with basketball, I was unacquainted with culture and all but a stranger to the world outside the perimeter of a court.

Twenty minutes later, we arrived back at Duke.

"We're here," I said to Karen.

She shifted in her seat and rubbed sleep from her eyes.

"Sorry I dozed off," she said.

"Not to worry."

"You tired?"

I took a moment to answer.

"No," I said, smiling. "In fact, I think I just woke up."

Chapter Eleven

By the end of 1971, things within the basketball program were getting worse. Brad Evans, the starting guard the previous year and a local legend from Durham High School (he was the state's athlete of the year) quit the team. Six-ten center Dave Elmer transferred to Miami of Ohio, where he led the team to an upset victory of UNC in Chapel Hill. And six-seven forward Ron Righter transferred to St. Joseph's in Philadelphia where he averaged thirteen points a game.

With so many talented players gone, we had a hard time not only recruiting the country's top talent, but we also struggled to play .500 basketball.

Why did so many players leave? The reasons varied from not enough playing time, to grueling practices, too many rules, little opportunity for self-expression, or just a flat-out dislike of Duke.

After he transferred, Jim Fitzsimmons told The Harvard Crimson that "the jock atmosphere (at Duke) had a lot to do with it. Sports are a big thing down in Durham and academics as opposed to the rest of the student body are grossly underplayed for athletes, which I just couldn't understand."

Other players never did go into great detail about their displeasure. Some simply packed up their bags and left, while others just didn't return after summer vacation.

I began putting in less time on basketball and more time listening to music, going to movies, attending rallies and even reading some of the books Karen had given me.

One day Bucky summoned me to his office. I arrived and was greeted by his pretty and pleasant secretary, Judy Coble.

"Hi, Richie," she said in a sweeter voice than Dolly Parton.

I genuflected slightly and extended my arms toward her. "Good afternoon," I said, pretending not to be nervous.

She smiled. "Have a seat, Coach Waters will be with you shortly."

I sat and shifted uneasily in my chair. Being called to Bucky's office was never fun.

A buzzer sounded. Judy picked up her phone, then quickly put it down.

"Coach Waters will see you now."

I entered his office. He was sitting behind his big desk wearing a navy-blue polo shirt with Duke Basketball scripted over his right breast.

He pointed to a chair. "Sit."

I sat straighter than a marine.

"As co-captain, you need to exhibit a more positive attitude," he said, his words measured. "You have to be a leader. Give the team pep talks."

"Okay,' I said, even though I was more about setting an example and less about giving Gipper speeches.

"And get a haircut," he said.

My hair was far from long. It barely covered my ears.

"Okay."

"Another thing," he said, holding up one finger. "I don't like some of the things I'm hearing."

"Like?"

"Like you're skipping study hall."

"Ah…well…"

"I also hear you're not going to class. Is that true?"

"Somewhat."

"Well, you can't play basketball forever. You better start developing some other talent."

The sad fact was, he was spot on. Outside of basketball I didn't have any talent. None. Zero. Nada.

I wasn't a good student and I never thought seriously about what I would do for a living except play in the NBA. And even though I was still on track to accomplish that goal, I was beginning to fully realize my scholarly deficiencies.

I hid those deficiencies behind "Cliff Notes" and the kindness of others who helped me write my English compositions.

Even with their help, the results weren't great.

Once, after turning in a term paper, my English professor said, "It's bad enough you misspell words, but you also dangled a few participles."

I hadn't a fucking clue what he was talking about.

After leaving Bucky's office, I decided to talk with my freshman coach, Jack Schalow. I said I wasn't happy with so many players leaving and Bucky not digging my act.

He said he, too, wasn't happy. I asked why. But being the

honorable man he was, he wouldn't tell me. (He left Duke a few years later.)

Jack and I were more than just player/coach. We were great friends. He often said, "No matter what the future holds, we should never lose touch."

And we never did. Years later, when he was an assistant coach with the Portland Trail Blazers, we would talk often on the phone and always meet for drinks after the Trail Blazers played the Knicks.

One night we went to P.J. Clarke's, a famous bar in Manhattan.

After some chit-chat about the Trail Blazers, I asked Jack why he left Duke. Even after so many years he was hesitant to answer.

"C'mon," I said. "You can tell me."

He fell silent, looked down and stared into his beer glass.

"Remember the first time we scrimmaged against the varsity?" he said, turning the glass slowly in his hands.

"Yeah. We beat them."

"That's right…we did."

Jack took a long sip of beer, staring straight ahead.

"After that game, Bucky told me he didn't appreciate us winning." He ate a few nuts from the bowl in front of him. "He told me not to do it again."

"But we did."

"Precisely."

"And?"

"And he and I barely had much of a relationship after that." A pause. "Can't say whose fault it was. Mine or his. Either way, we didn't have much communication."

A long, awkward silence.

Then Jack pounded the bar top. "Goddammit," he said, his voice startling me with its mingled tone of anger and lament. "I loved Duke. Loved our freshmen team. There was no way in hell I was going to put the brakes on our team. No fucking way."

To this day, and I'll never be dissuaded, I firmly believe that had Fitzsimmons, Dawson and I stayed at Duke we would have been, under a different coach, one of the ten best teams in the country by our senior year.

"We did have some good times though," Jack said, after calming down.

"For sure," I said, remembering the many afternoons we went to lunch and spent the entire time talking basketball and telling stories. I remembered, too, one morning when he came over to my dorm and helped me move furniture—heavy stuff, like a couch and a desk. For a big-time college coach to do that would be like the Pope showing up at a local church Bingo night to help set up chairs.

Jack finished his beer. We left Clarke's and went outside. It was cold and noisy, cars honking, trucks backfiring, a police car wailing.

Jack flagged a cab. Just as he was about to duck inside, he put his arms around me, held me tight and said, his voice cracking, "Thanks."

"For what?"

"For being part of something so special it will never be forgotten. The only undefeated freshman team in ACC history."

"Thanks to you," I said.

Jack stepped into the cab and rolled the window down. "I'll be in touch," he said, smiling.

And he did stay in touch, phoning regularly. He called me one day in 2005 and said he was sick. Had cancer and was dying. He just wanted me to know, one more time, how special our team was.

"You guys," he said, in a weak voice, "made my life a success."

I swallowed hard. Tears rolled down my cheeks.

I still can remember the last thing he said: "Don't forget me."

"Not a chance," I said.

He died a year later. He was only 67.

With Bucky and I not getting along and my interest in things—books, music, movies—increasing and my desire to play decreasing, I still felt committed to playing the best I could. I led the team in scoring with 15.5 points per game.

January 22, 1972. Duke versus the University of North Carolina at Cameron Indoor Stadium.

Just before leaving my dorm to head over to Cameron, I read Hugh Prather's book Notes to Myself. I focused on the line "Don't discard yourself, be more of it."

As I walked toward Cameron, whispering those lines to myself over and over, I passed hordes of students, shouting "Good Luck." "Fuck Carolina." I got back slaps, handshakes, hugs and kisses. I felt enormous energy welling up inside me.

Carolina's record was 12-1. They were undefeated in conference play and ranked No. 3 in the country. We were 7-6 and 1-2 in the ACC standings. They were a heavy favorite, largely because their best player, Bob McAdoo, was having a sensational season. (He would go on to become a huge star with the New York Knicks and the Los Angeles Lakers, leading the NBA in scoring three times.)

The key to us winning was stopping Bob, which was a big

ask since he could instantly turn a game into a one-man shooting show. Although he played center, the six-ten McAdoo had not only the perfect basketball body—long arms, muscular body, big hands, quick feet—but he was, at the time, one of the few big men who could run the court like a deer and shoot from anywhere around the perimeter.

Game time. Drums pounded, trumpets blared, students chanted. The roar was so deafening and so protracted the court seemed to shake.

The teams took the court. Besides McAdoo, Carolina had supremely talented players who would go on to ABA and NBA careers: Dennis Wuycik, George Karl and Bobby Jones. Nicknamed "the Secretary of Defense," Jones was a four-time NBA All-Star and an eight-time member of the NBA All-Defensive team. In 1983, he was voted the Sixth Man of the Year. Thirty-six years later, he was elected to the Naismith Memorial Basketball Hall of Fame.

The game was close the entire way. With a minute left, the score tied, my teammate Robby West, a reserve guard, got fouled scrambling for a loose ball. He stepped to the line and hit a free throw that put us up 74-72. The crowd went nuts, shouting so loud it seemed to spread around Cameron like one huge gust of wind.

But Carolina came right back and scored: 74-74.

Bucky signaled for a time-out. There were eight seconds on the clock. We huddled around him. He took out his chalkboard and diagramed a play. He designated Gary Melchionni to take the ball out and get it to me so I could dribble into the lane and either score, get fouled or dish to forward Chris Redding.

We took the court. The crowd was standing, whipped into

a frenzy. The referee gave the ball to Melchionni and blew his whistle. We did a lot of screening and cutting. Karl was guarding me so close, I couldn't get open. With no other option, Melchionni passed the ball in-bounds to West.

Robby got the ball at midcourt, dribbled left, then right. The clock was ticking down. Seven seconds, five seconds. With three seconds left, Robby stopped at the top of key and fired up a J, a defender all over him. The ball nestled into the net.

Pandemonium. Duke 76-Carolina 74.

Carolina called time-out. In his huddle, Dean Smith diagrammed a play. Even though he wasn't having a great night, we expected the ball to go to McAdoo.

The buzzer sounded. Both teams took the floor. Carolina passed the ball in bounds. We double-teamed McAdoo. The ball went from Karl to Jones to Wuycik. A shot was taken. The ball bounced off the front of the rim. Game over. Duke won. Fans flooded the court.

In the locker room after the game, we were all jumping around shouting and yelling. Everybody was congratulating Robby on his heroics. Someone shouted that his shot "was heard all around North Carolina."

A reporter from the Durham Morning Herald, Frank Dascenzo, approached me and said, "Great game. You and Redding both scored 24 points."

"Really?" I said, having no idea.

"And McAdoo only had three," Frank said, handing me a stat sheet.

"Holy shit!" I said, looking at it and seeing McAdoo was only 1-12 from the field, no doubt the worst game of his collegiate career.

Poised with pen and pad, Frank said, "You do anything different to prepare for the game?"

"We just executed our game plan."

"I meant you personally. I mean, you played all forty minutes and you seemed so confident on the court."

"Can't say that I..." I hesitated: Should I mention Hugh Prather? Nah. He'd probably think me odd.

Before Frank could ask me another question, Robby West walked by. I stood and hugged him. Even though Robby never had much of a career during his time at Duke, in this game he rose to the occasion.

But the best thing about that night was that my father had driven straight from work, ten hours, to be at the game. When I came out of the locker room, he was waiting for me.

He hugged me so hard he lifted me off the ground.

When we disengaged, he said: "You made me so proud tonight."

"Thanks, Big Tom," I said. "Glad you were here."

We walked toward my dorm. Once again, I got a lot of high-fives and hugs.

"What party you going to?" my father asked as we passed a number of fraternities where students were drawing beer from kegs and music was blaring.

"A private one," I said.

"Where?"

"Wherever you wanna go."

He squinted. "Are you kidding? Go out with the guys. Have fun. Celebrate. Don't waste your time hanging around with an old fart like me."

"Sorry. Nobody else I'd rather be with."

His voice broke as he said, "Okay."

We went to the Angus Barn restaurant in Raleigh.

Throughout the evening, Duke fans stopped by the table and bestowed congratulations. One couple even offered to pay for our dinner. My father declined.

When we drove back to Durham, my father dropped me off outside my dorm.

"You sure you don't want to stay overnight?" I said.

"Can't. I have work tomorrow."

"Can you take the day off?"

"Nope."

"Why?"

"Gotta take care of business."

He then drove off, ten hours and went straight to work.

I walked back to my dorm, not realizing I had just played the last great game of my college career.

Chapter Twelve

I can still remember how not long after the Carolina game, I was sitting inside a phone booth, unable to dial.

My mind was focused on the previous week, a week that had been full of sleepless nights spent lying on my back on the bed in my dorm room, staring at the ceiling with glazed eyes. When morning came and the sun burst through the window, it illuminated a framed photo of me in my Duke uniform. I looked at it for almost a half hour, then got up and turned the picture over.

Now, in the phone booth, my hand shaking, I grabbed the receiver and dialed O.

An operator answered. "May I help you?"

"I'd…I'd like to place a collect call," I said.

"What number, please?"

I gave it.

"And your name?"

I gave that, too.

"Hold, please."

The line rang…and rang.

"C'mon," I whispered. "Somebody answer."

After ten rings, my mother answered the phone. The operator asked if she'd accept the call.

"Of course," my mother said.

"Go ahead, sir," the operator said.

"Mom."

"Richard," she said, in her typical effusive way, "How are you?"

"I'm…I'm okay. You?"

"I'm good." She paused. "But you…you don't sound okay. What's wrong?"

I swallowed hard. "I'm…I'm thinking of quitting the team."

Her voice suddenly shaky, she said, "Quitting the team? But… but you love Duke."

"I do love Duke. I just don't like the basketball program."

"Is it Bucky?"

"Partly."

I heard a sniffle "Maybe…maybe you could talk to Bucky. Work something out."

"It's beyond talk."

My mother got quiet. I imagined her sitting at the kitchen table, dressed stylishly as always, crossing her leg one way, then the other way, her free hand clenching and unclenching.

"Let me put your father on the line," she said. "He's in the living room."

I pictured him lying on the couch in his filthy work clothes, holding a can of Schlitz and watching CBS News.

"Hey, Rich," he said, getting on the line. "What's going on?"

I told him about wanting to quit.

"You sure you want to do this?" he said, his voice calm.

"I've given it a lot of thought…so yes."

"This is a big decision," he said.

"I know."

My father fell silent.

"I've lost my desire," I said.

"You mean you don't want to play anymore?"

"It's not that I hate the game. I love the game. And I want to still play. But I just hate all the bullshit. All the guys leaving. All the dissension. It's drained me. I want something more."

"Like what?"

"That's it," I said, my voice cracking. "I don't know."

My father took a deep breath. "Okay," he said, "You've always had a mind of your own. I trust and support whatever decision you make."

I'm not surprised to hear him say that. Throughout my life, I never felt the absence of his support. It was because of him, and, of course, my mother and grandfather, that I tried to reciprocate their trust by not getting into any serious trouble. I never had run-ins with teachers or cops. I never did anything that embarrassed or shamed them.

Now talking with them on the phone, I had a glimpse of my childhood as it was, as good as it was, and as safe it was, when we did not lack for anything, when love was unasked. It was simply a given.

My mother got back on the phone.

"You gonna be okay?" she said, her voice thick, as if she'd been crying.

"I'll be fine."

"I want you better than fine," she said, sniffling. "I want you happy and content."

"I'm working on it."

After I hung up, I called my grandfather.

"Look," he said, "I hope I taught you to have the courage of your convictions. You make a decision, you stick to it. Never look back, always look forward. Never have regrets. You understand?"

"I do."

"Good."

A moment of silence.

"I wish things were better," I said.

"Forget wishing. Life's about doing." A pause. "So whaddya gonna do?"

"I'm gonna quit."

"Fine. When you telling Bucky?"

"Tomorrow."

"Keep me posted."

The next day, after practice, I drove to Bucky's house outside Durham. It was cold. The sky was black. No moon and no stars. I gripped the steering wheel so hard I nearly broke it.

I sped through winding roads, thinking about what to say. I got so deep in thought I ran two red lights and narrowly missed hitting a deer. I concocted different speeches in my mind. None worked. Finally, I determined to make my case short and sweet: "Coach, I quit."

I rang Bucky's doorbell. He answered it, dressed smartly in black pants and an argyle sweater. I was wearing jeans and a hooded sweatshirt.

Surprised to see me, he gave me a strange look, then stepped aside and ushered me into the living room.

We took seats across from each other. Bucky sat ramrod straight, one leg crossed over the other.

For a moment we fell into a prolonged silence that made me even more nervous than I already was. I shifted in my seat, as if the cushion was red hot.

"What can I do for you?" he said, his voice stern.

"I'm quitting," I said, my heart galloping.

He uncrossed his leg and his brow furrowed. He gave his head a quick shake, as if he had not heard me right. "Quitting what?"

"The team."

Bucky pressed bunched fingers to the bridge of his nose. His eyes blitzed me. "Why?"

Still squirming in my seat, I said, "I don't enjoy playing anymore."

Bucky shook his head and leaned back in his seat. "You're kidding me, right?"

"No," I said, rubbing my hands together.

Bucky inflated his cheeks and released the air in them with a tiny, plosive sound.

For a long moment we locked eyes. From an unforeseen room I could hear faint voices. Perhaps Bucky's wife, Dorothea, was talking on the phone. Or maybe his children were playing.

"I don't believe this," Bucky said.

Again silence. The pause was intense, as if all the air was sucked out of the room.

Bucky shut one eye and focused the other one on me as if he were aiming the barrel of a gun. "This is a very selfish and immature act on your part," he said.

I said nothing. My mouth was dry. My hands were clasped tight, my knees fanning back and forth like bat wings.

"Do you realize you're throwing away a promising career?" he said.

Blood pounded at my temples. I licked my lips. "I…"

"And you don't care that you're letting down not only the school but your teammates?"

"I'm…I'm…sorry about that…but…but…"

"There are no buts," he said. "What you're doing is wrong."

Bucky paused and gave me a long, piercing look.

"You will regret this, you know," Bucky said.

I sat there numb, my heart doing a dizzying tour of my chest.

Bucky abruptly stood. "Is that all you have to say?"

I coughed into my fist and rose shakily. "Yes."

Bucky shook his head and said, "You can leave now."

We didn't shake hands.

I stood and walked tentatively and cautiously to the front door, as if stepping through a land mine. My hand shook when I grabbed the doorknob. I turned it and stepped outside.

I went back to my car and sat behind the wheel for a long time, motionless and deadened, as if I had been given a huge dose of an anesthetic.

After a few minutes, I started the car and slowly drove back to the campus, feeling an odd sense of relief, as if I had risen up from murky waters just in time to take a delicious draft of fresh air.

It was the end of my Duke run. The final sprint. There'd be no more curtain calls, standing ovations, fawning adulation. Only a short stay with long memories.

I wanted to go home, back to Union City. I didn't care about attending any more classes or getting any more credits. Academics were the furthest thing from my mind.

I went to my dorm room and started to pack. A toothbrush and toothpaste. Sneakers and sweatshirts. Record and cassettes. After a few minutes, I stopped and sat on the edge of my bed. Suddenly it hit me: What had I done?! My God? What had I done?! Had I really tossed away my career? Thrown away everything I had ever worked for? Ever wanted? Ever dreamt of? I started panting heavily, followed by tears that spilled forth at an alarming rate. Was I a quitter? A coward? A fool? All I can say for sure is this: I had never before understood what depression meant, but I understood it that day.

I was so exhausted I fell asleep.

I woke up late the next morning and finished packing. I walked stiffly to my car, squeezed in behind the wheel and looked one last time at the dorm I had lived in for almost three years.

Staring at it, I felt a seizure of pain because I was leaving a school I loved. But I had no choice: I simply couldn't bear staying at Duke without playing basketball. The school probably would have revoked my scholarship anyway.

As I write this, decades after leaving Duke, I have the vantage point of truly understanding why I gave up all boyhood dreams of basketball stardom. It was a combination of things. It wasn't only that I didn't get along with Bucky Waters. It wasn't the mandatory breakfasts and study halls. It wasn't the lack of culture outside the walls of Duke. It was, specifically, that I needed to restart my life, to find something else that would captivate my interest.

To this day, people still ask me how I could make the swift transition from a basketball obsessive to a disinterested athlete.

The only answer I can give, and not everyone buys it, is that I was beginning the maturing process, as pompous as that may sound. What I mean is, I found, thanks to people like John and Karen, that life offered things in rich supply: books, poetry, music, museums and movies—things I had never been exposed to.

The last thing I did before leaving campus was to drive past Cameron Indoor Stadium. I thought of the cheerleaders and the bands and the nearly ten thousand fans screaming and yelling, the noise getting louder and louder until it's so uplifting you feel as if you're being carried along on a tidal wave.

There is no better arena to play basketball than in Cameron Indoor Stadium. Every college player should have that chance—at least once—to play there. It's an experience they'd never forget.

After a while, I headed home. It was cold and getting colder. Almost from the get-go, I began to shiver and feel nauseous. Twice, once in Virginia and once in Maryland, I stopped the car and vomited.

As I drove around the Washington Beltway, the car uncharacteristically silent—no music playing—it hit me that for the first time in my life I carried inside me a huge hollowness. Basketball had been my lifelong companion, my obsession, the compass that let me navigate life. Now it was gone.

I had no idea what was ahead of me, no picture of the future. Hell, I didn't even know if I had one.

All I knew at that terrifying moment was that I was leaving a world that I had lived in for so long, a world confined and defined by the perimeter of a basketball court. Moving forward, my life would never be the same.

Chapter Thirteen

I never read what the Durham Morning Herald or The Jersey Journal or any other newspaper with regards to my quitting because I quite frankly wasn't interested.

I did, however, hear from friends that both papers headlined stories about my decision.

The stories focused on how shocking it was that I would quit when it seemed I had such a glorious basketball future ahead of me. Both mentioned that my leaving would surely get Bucky fired.

It didn't. In fact, Bucky requested a contract extension. It was denied by Athletic Director Carl James. After Duke finished 12-14 in 1972-73, its first losing season since 1939, Bucky quit.

My only concern now was to find a place that would restore my spirit while furthering my college education.

The coach of Fairfield University, Freddy Barakat, was from Union City. We were more than just acquaintances. We were good friends.

I had called Freddy a few times during my junior year and told him of my displeasure with Bucky.

He listened, empathized and told me "If there's anything I can ever do for you, don't hesitate to let me know."

A few weeks before I decided to quit, I had called Freddy and asked about the possibility of transferring to Fairfield, a Division One program that, at the time, played an independent schedule, one that wasn't nearly as rigorous as Duke's.

I did tell Freddy I wasn't sure how much I still loved basketball.

"G'wan," he said. "You're a basketball junkie."

"Not anymore."

"Don't worry," he said. "I'll get you motivated."

"We'll see."

Freddy then said not to worry about Fairfield accepting all my Duke credits. He'd take care of it, and he did.

And so, I transferred to Fairfield, a school as different from Duke as fish cakes are from caviar. It had a nice campus but nothing like the gothic grandeur and magnificent gardens of Duke. It was, however, situated in an affluent Connecticut community, located roughly an hour's car ride from New York City.

Aside from Freddy, I chose Fairfield for other reasons. One, it's proximity to Manhattan, which I wanted to explore. Two, if I agreed to play basketball I would be given a full scholarship, which made my father happy since he wouldn't have had the money to pay for my education.

I remember the day I drove to Fairfield to begin taking classes. Fred—dark-skinned, large nosed, rimless glasses—met me outside the Fairfield University gymnasium. He was wearing red shorts and a white polo shirt emblazoned with Fairfield over his breast.

"Good to see ya, good to see ya," he said, bouncing up and down several times on the balls of his feet.

"Good to see you, too, Freddy," I said, suddenly realizing I now had to call him coach.

"C'mon inside," he said, putting his arm around my shoulders and escorting me into his office.

His office wasn't big or ornate like Bucky's but it had a good sized desk, some chairs and a large white chalkboard.

"I'm excited you chose Fairfield," he said, taking a seat behind his desk. "I'm going to name you a co-captain."

"Thanks. But as I told you I think I've lost some or all of my desire for basketball."

Freddy leaned forward, his hands flat on his desk. "Look, Rich, I've known you a long time. Knowing you as well as I do, I doubt that."

"Don't."

He leaned back and his nostrils twitched as if stifling a laugh. "Okay, I accept what you're saying. But half of you is better than none of you."

Because I couldn't play right away (transfers back then had to sit out a year) Freddy got me a job working in a print shop in Bridgeport owned by Dom Monaco, a short Italian guy with an easy-going disposition. Since Fairfield accepted all my Duke credits, I carried a very light class schedule.

My job was to clean the floors. The thing was, there was hardly ever anything on the floors. But I would still hang out for a few hours and get paid maybe fifty bucks on the nights I worked.

With money in my pocket, I spent a lot of time in Manhattan. Since I was not, according to NCAA rules, allowed to practice with the team, I played in a league at the New York Athletic Club, located on Central Park South.

The competition wasn't great, but I was able to team up with a former New Jersey star player, Tom Sinnott, from St. Patrick's of Elizabeth. Tom had played at Notre Dame and was now pursuing a career in law enforcement.

When I wasn't hanging out with Tom, I was taking dates to plays and concerts. Some of my teammates thought I was crazy. Why go to New York, they'd say, when there are great bars in Fairfield, like the Nautilus.

But I had loved the pageantry and hustle of New York City ever since my parents first took me there as a kid. From my initial visit I embraced the city with the fervor of a catechist. I loved the restaurants and buildings, the bright lights and stretch limos. I enjoyed looking at the breaking news stories revolving around the Times Tower, the spectacular billboard that lit up Bond's Clothing store, and the puffs of smoke spewing from the mouth of the guy in the Camels cigarettes sign. When we went to the city my mother, ever the clothes horse, always demanded I wear a blue blazer, starched white shirt and grey slacks. She called it "Putting on the Ritz."

Of all the places my mother took me to, I enjoyed most going to the Horn & Hardart's Automat on 42nd Street. Oh, how I loved the Automat—the Art Deco design, the colorful murals, the plaster gargoyles and the chrome-plated coffee urns that dispense delicious cups of "jo."

I loved taking my nickels to the enormous wall of cabinets that had tiny rectangular glass doors. Behind the doors were baloney sandwiches, fish cakes, tomato soup, Salisbury steak, creamed spinach, mashed potatoes, coconut cream pie, even succotash. I'd slip my nickels into a slot, turn the glass knob and—viola—a door would pop open and there'd be my delicacy.

Recalling these fond boyhood memories, I often took the train from Fairfield University down to Grand Central Station. Walking leisurely, I exited the station and headed down 5th Avenue, past the Public Library, its entrance guarded by two stone lions; then past Lord & Taylor, its windows decorated with fashionable mannequins. At 34th Street, I'd stop and look up at the Empire State Building, the enormity of it. Towers of ambition rose within me. Someday, I thought, if I'm lucky, I'm going to take advantage of all the city's undeniable gifts.

Some days I rode the subway to Greenwich Village then walked to Washington Square Park and strolled under Stanford White's magnificent arch. The park was always crowded, hundreds of people smoking dope, riding bicycles, walking dogs, singing songs, playing guitars and dancing. Indeed, it was a place for celebration, for exaltation—men and women free to express themselves as they wished, unabashed and unashamed.

At lunchtime, I always brought a hot dog from a corner vendor and smothered it with mustard and sauerkraut. For dessert, I licked a cherry ice in a small pleated white paper cup. It was delicious.

After lunch, I'd watch the old-timers in the park playing chess. The games were intense. Despite all the noise surrounding the players, they looked lost in their own world, a world where everyone around me seemed to be enjoying their freedoms and their passions.

I was beyond envious. Flat out jealous. I so badly wanted to feel as liberated as them.

Some nights I went to jazz clubs. At the time, I didn't know a thing about jazz, beyond the impression that it was music for adult aficionados who liked to shut their eyes, snap their fingers and sway their shoulders as if in a trance-like state.

One night I hit The Bitter End in Greenwich Village where I met a sultry French singer, Yvette. Fortyish, with a halo of black hair and sparkling brown eyes, she wowed the audience with her tone, diction and emotional phrasing. I went back to hear her sing often and we became friends.

As we got to know each other, she explained to me why Billie Holiday's contralto voice ("She eez z best") was more arresting than Ella Fitzgerald's scat style and why Miles Davis's "Kind of Blue" was the greatest jazz album of all time. She chuckled at my lack of knowledge and naiveté. But she ultimately turned me into a jazz lover, educating me about the precision of piano, the hotness of horns, the pulse of percussion and the shards of guitars.

I met other interesting people at the club—Juan, a painter; Mitchell, a journalist; Raquel, a model; and Sophia, an actress. They were an outrageously glamorous group, all young, in their late twenties, who loved to drink wine, laugh and promote ideas. Every conversation touched upon the meaning of life, most of it went over my head. But I listened closely, like a young scholar at the feet of a bunch of Socrates. It was a far cry from the conversations I had kneeling before a basketball coach.

One night I met a drunken Welsh poet named Aidan, who looked like a red-bearded Santa Claus. He asked me if I knew of Dylan Thomas. I said I didn't know Dylan Thomas from Danny Thomas. The pupils of his brown eyes grew enormous and he started yelling things like "Do not go gentle into the good night" and "Always rage against the dying light of the day." I didn't know what the hell he was yammering about.

After he calmed down, he suggested I read Walt Whitman and William Wordsworth and William Butler Yeats. He said poetry would teach me about the expression of feelings, ideas that would ignite my imagination and emotion. He said it was all about meaning, sound and rhythm. I found myself drawn to his words as if by invisible magnets.

When the bar closed, Aidan, who by then could barely stand, reached into his back pocket and pulled out a small book by E. E. Cummings, Tulips and Chimneys. The book was torn and ceased.

"Read this," he said, handing me the book. "You might learn something."

I took the book and read it a few weeks later. I was moved, almost shaken, by the epigraph: "It takes courage to grow up and become who you really are." It's a line I have never forgotten.

Other days in Manhattan, I simply wandered Central Park or visited the Museum of Modern Art or poked around the East Village. At night, I'd roam 42nd Street, enthralled by the blazing brilliance of Times Square, the flashing lights and bubbling neon, the grungy dudes carrying ghetto blasters, the wigged hookers wearing leather miniskirts and the transvestites with five o'clock shadows. A couple of hambones were always handing out flyers for porno shops: "Live Nude Girls-25 cents." Such a deal.

I'd walk through the theatre district where the bright, bold letters on the marquees of the Shubert, the Booth and the Winter Garden advertised Equus, Gypsy and Fame. I loved it all and would sometimes catch myself silently singing "New York, New York, A Helluva Town."

Once, before taking the train back to Fairfield, I went to Scribner's bookstore, a gorgeous glass-fronted, two-storied Beaux

Arts-style building on 5th Avenue. Inside, there were brass and wrought-iron stairways leading to shelves and tables filled with thousands and thousands and thousands of books.

I'd run my hands over the books as if they were holy objects. One night, a saleswoman approached me. She had gray hair and a pair of bifocals hung off the tip of her nose.

"Can I help you?" she said, her voice soft.

"I'm looking for something to read."

"What are you interested in? Fiction? Non-fiction?"

I scratched my cheek. "Not sure."

She thought a moment. "Have you read Catcher in the Rye?"

I made a scrunchy face. "I'm not really into baseball."

She coughed into her fist, suppressing laughter.

"It's not about baseball," she said.

"What's it about?"

"A teenager who's dealing with issues like identity, belonging, loss, connection…"

I shuddered. Was she talking about me?

"…and existential angst."

Existential angst? What the fuck is that?

"What else would you suggest?" I said.

"Perhaps The Great Gatsby by F. Scott Fitzgerald. It's a wonderful book."

"Sure," I said. "Why not."

She smiled. "Trust me. You'll enjoy it."

I bought a copy and started to read it on the train going back to Fairfield. The book was a literary miracle, a short epic poem, a symphonic composition, a glamorous tour de force. Every word was a caress, every sentence an embrace. His paragraphs dizzied me. He wrote the way Jerry West played: passionately, emotionally, putting everything he had on the line.

After reading Gatsby, I found myself unable to pass a bookstore without going inside and looking for a book that would heat my hand and warm my mind.

Looking back, I realize that books had cast a spell on me. They made me hunger for knowledge, turning me into a voyeur who wanted to live through the experiences and emotions of others.

I read books by Ernest Hemingway and Miguel de Cervantes and James Joyce, fighting with Robert Jordan, riding with Don Quixote and strolling the streets of Dublin with Leonard Bloom.

I found getting lost in these characters was a good way to find myself.

One night after finishing Joyce's book, The Dubliners, I called my mother.

"I now love reading," I announced.

"Well, well, well," she said. "Miracles do happen."

"Yes, they do."

"Tell me, what brought about this epiphany?"

"I just started reading and became totally addicted."

She paused. "My greatest wish for you has now been realized. You've grown up."

I soon began carrying this new me everywhere, constantly trying to reinvent and improve myself, thus kickstarting a lifelong pilgrimage in which books would shape and change me, thus creating the man I would become.

Chapter Fourteen

By my standards, I played poorly my senior year at Fairfield, even though the competition was a lot less challenging than it was at Duke. True, I led the team in scoring, but as Gertrude Stein said on another matter, "I had the syrup but it wouldn't pour."

It didn't because I had lost my intensity and my concentration. On the court I found my mind wandering, thinking of who knows what. And I must admit there were times I thought I was superior to the weaker competition and instead of playing above it I played far below it.

The syrup especially didn't pour in a late season game against St. Peter's College, played at the Jersey City Armory.

St. Peter's was located only a half hour from Union City. It was, in a way, my homecoming.

Many high school friends and close neighbors attended the game. I got huge applause when introduced. Would I score twenty points? Perhaps thirty points like I had a few years before when Duke played St. Bonaventure in Madison Square Garden?

Game time. The crowd stirred. Exuberant chants of "Yeah,

Rich!" "Go, Rich!" echoed throughout the Armory. I felt good, confident. After all, St. Peter's was a college that, coming out of high school, I felt wasn't worthy of my talents. Hell, it didn't even have its own gym. The Peacocks, as they were called, played in the shabby Armory. Its shabbiness disheartened me. Compared to the Duke, North Carolina and Florida arenas, it was low-rent. I poo-pooed all the school's recruiting overtures.

St. Peter's played a zone defense. I kept getting open on the wing, taking my shots but my shooting motion was awkward, strained, unnatural. I didn't hit one jump shot outside the paint.

Worse, the passes that I used to make so easily and so magically went flying over the heads of teammates.

Once on an easy three-on-two fast break, I looked left and shuffled a bounce pass to a wide-open teammate cutting to the basket. The ball hit his feet and went out of bounds.

It was a play I used to make with my eyes closed. Now I couldn't even make it with my eyes wide open. I guess I was no longer the player my Duke freshman coach, Jack Schalow, had once called "Kodak" because I was so adept at photographing the floor and dishing an assist.

In a word, I sucked, scoring a measly four points on 2-13 from the field.

Nevertheless, thanks to the passing of John Ryan and the shooting of Ray Kelly, we won 51-47.

As I left the court, I heard voices around me saying variations on the same theme.

"What happened to him? He's just not the same player."

"He's lost it."

"He stunk."

Though the words hurt, and hurt deeply, they confirmed to me what I already knew: that the talent I once worked so hard to polish had lost its shine. That the one thing—and the only thing—I was good at was gone. Vanished. Lost in a fog of boyhood dreams.

I felt like crying but couldn't. Still, the pain was like a wall of fire behind my eyes. It struck sharp and hard.

I finally had to accept that somewhere along the way I had lost touch with the kind of player I had the potential to be. I needed now to effect a reconciliation with the boy who used to be me, who at age eight burned with a passionate heat for basketball so consuming with its unyielding and unforgiving high-reaching flame. Now that fire was no more than a mere pilot light, barely flickering.

Outside the armory, a St. Michael's classmate, Mike Sanchez, was waiting for me.

"Tough game," he said.

I was so embarrassed, so ashamed I could barely look him in the eyes.

"You have time for a bite?" he said.

"I don't," I said, lying. "I have to go back to Fairfield with the team."

"Maybe another time," he said.

I nodded and started to walk away, feeling absolute disgust with myself.

"Hey," Mike called out. I turned.

"Don't worry about the game," he said, his voice consoling. "I know you. You'll do great next time."

I only played one decent game after that, in the first round of the National Invitational Tournament against the University of

Hawaii. I scored 18 points. We still lost. My college career was finished.

Most of my friends back then thought I made a big mistake leaving Duke for Fairfield. They felt Fairfield ruined my career. I disagreed. I said I ruined it.

So, did I get anything out of Fairfield, aside from my many educational trips to New York?

Yes, I did, absolutely. I met two people who would have an enormous influence on my life.

One was Steve Romano. A lefty basketball player from Dumont High School in New Jersey, Steve had gone to Fairfield on a basketball scholarship but quit playing his junior year. Sound familiar?

He had quit the basketball team because he wanted to spend less time practicing and more time enjoying campus life. Playing hoops at a Division One school didn't leave much time for that.

What I found most interesting about Steve was his endless, panoptic curiosity. It was almost predatory. He had a formidable mind, and he sought out, to an extraordinary degree, information about movies and music, history and philosophy. He had a way of distinguishing what was important from what was irrelevant as swiftly as one could separate a penny from a quarter.

Steve faced life in the most direct and specific way, the most adult way—a way that made his future plans attainable: to become an FBI agent.

After graduation he attended the John Jay School of Criminal Justice and later did join the FBI—as a chief negotiator.

Steve showed me what it is to want something and how to go about getting it. Setting goals and putting in the hard work. But beyond that, our honest conversations about things that mattered helped me understand the true meaning of friendship, how indispensable it is to life. I can honestly say he would be the person I would want to be if I wasn't myself.

I met the other person who impacted my life at the graduation party for seniors and their parents held in the Student Union building. There was a live band and a dance floor, lots of balloons, cocktails and speeches.

While chatting with some friends, my father tapped me on the shoulder. I turned. Standing next to him was a short, attractive girl with thick black hair, brown eyes and alabaster skin. She wore a light-colored sleeveless dress and canvas shoes with high wedged heels.

"I'd like you to meet a nice Irish girl," my father said. "Her name's Peg Doyle."

"How you doin'?" I said.

She smiled. It was luminous, her teeth small and white.

"I'm good," she said, her voice calm and soothing.

My father saluted us, turned and left.

"How'd you meet my father?" I said.

"Just did."

"Funny how that happens." Typical Big Tom. Always looking out for me.

"He's quite the charmer," Peg said.

"That he is."

The band was now playing a shitty version of The Allman Brothers "Ramblin' Man."

Peg said, "I can't believe my college days are over."

"I'm kind of glad they are."

"Haven't you enjoyed Fairfield?"

"I have but not as much as Duke."

"Why's that?"

"I learned a lot there."

"In the classroom?"

"Outside it."

The more we talked the more I liked her. She was authentic. Niceness came off her in waves.

Not long after that night, I took her to New York to see the play A Little Night Music, starring Glynis Johns.

Afterwards as we strolled around town, Peg put her arm through mine and rested her head against my shoulder.

"You love New York, don't you?" she said.

"Enormously."

"Think you'll ever live here?"

"I hope so."

"After playing pro basketball?"

I snorted. "My chances of becoming a pro are slim and none."

"You should be more positive."

"I could be more positive than Norman Vincent Peale. Not gonna help."

We crossed 58th street and walked along Central Park South, leaves crunching under our feet. Above us the sky was berserk with stars and lights from the cast-iron lamps inside the park glowed. We listened as a horse pulling a Hansom cab clomped past.

"You're very much a loner, aren't you?" Peg said.

"Notice that, did you?"

"Sure did."

"I enjoy people."

"But not in groups."

I thought about that for a moment while looking into the park and seeing people running, biking and embracing.

"No," I said. "I don't."

"You like to read and watch movies."

"Yes. Alone."

"See what I mean? You only like to do things by yourself."

"There's exceptions."

"Like?"

"Like I like being with you."

We got to 5th Avenue. Across the street was the Plaza Hotel. The lights in the windows twinkled and well-dressed people stepped out of shiny limousines, heading toward the famous Oak Bar.

"You're wrong about one thing," I said.

"What's that?"

"I can't do everything by myself."

I put my hands on the sides of her face and gave her a kiss on the mouth.

"You always need another person if you want to give or get a kiss," I said.

"That's true."

"It's also true that it takes two to tango."

"So I've heard."

"Think we make a good dance team?"

"I do."

The night suddenly seemed to get quiet. In the enfolding

darkness under blazing stars, a soft wind blew, scattering leaves on the street and rustling trees in the park.

"In that case," I said, "shall we cha-cha to your dorm room or mine?"

"You choose."

"Yours. Mine's a dump."

"Good call," she said.

We took the train back to Fairfield.

Chapter Fifteen

The 1974 pro basketball college draft occurred a few weeks after the graduation party. That day my grandfather invited me to lunch at McSorley's Ale House at 15 East 7th Street, just off the Bowery.

Known as America's oldest and continuously operated bar, McSorley's was a drinker's Smithsonian. It had, among other rare items, a copy of the Emancipation Proclamation, an original wanted poster for Abe Lincoln's assassin and a pair of Houdini's handcuffs. McSorley's only rule was: "Be Good or Be Gone."

We sat at a table near the fireplace and ordered burgers and fries. I drank a Coke. My grandfather had a shot and beer.

"You don't think you're going to get drafted, huh?" he said.

"Don't think so," I said.

Leaning back in his chair, legs crossed, my grandfather wore a glen-plaid suit with peak lapels, a button-down blue shirt and a bright green tie. I sported jeans and a white t-shirt.

"You disappointed?" he said, after biting off the tip of a stogie, lighting it and taking a puff.

I thought a second.

"In a way, I guess I am. I mean, I always thought I'd be drafted, but...

"...you had a few great years."

"...I did."

"...and a helluva lot of trophies to show for it."

I had, at that point, 25-30 trophies, plus plaques and bowls. They were all in my parent's apartment, taking up one whole wall in my former bedroom.

I kept them, along with three thick scrapbooks, only because my father wanted me to. After he died, I threw everything away.

A waiter, who looked like Stanley Kowalski after a back-alley beating, brought our food.

After taking a bite of his burger, my grandfather said, "Don't be like so many people who live their lives regretting the past."

"I don't have any regrets," I said, thinking what if I did? Would it alter anything?

"Good," he said. "So? What's next?"

"No idea."

He blew some smoke rings, then picked a fleck of tobacco delicately from his lower lip.

"Remember, kid, the future is what you want it to be."

"I want it to be fulfilling."

"Everybody says that but few people achieve it."

"Why's that?"

"People are afraid to take chances, to challenge themselves. They're content to work the same job or in the same industry their entire lives and then complain at the end of it that they didn't accomplish anything. They whine about being dissatisfied. That's a coward's lament. A fucking copout."

He took a gulp of beer and said, "Promise me one thing."

"What's that?"

"You won't be afraid to take chances."

"I won't."

"And for God sakes, try and live an interesting life."

"Is there such a thing?"

He flashed a crooked grin. "There can be."

I would learn later my grandfather lived an interesting life. I learned it a week after he died in 1984.

I was in my thirties then, cleaning out a closet in his apartment when I noticed an old shoebox hidden beneath layers of blankets. I opened the box. Inside was a hand towel wrapped around a .38 caliber handgun.

Picking it up with my thumb and index finger as if holding a stinky diaper, I brought it out to the kitchen where my grandmother, Lillian, a tall, heavyset woman was bent over the sink, drying a dish.

"What's this?" I said.

My grandmother spun around, saw the gun and turned white. The dish in her hand fell to the floor and shards of glass surrounded her feet.

"Where'd you get that?" Her voice was harsh.

"The hall closet."

She reached over and tried to take the gun. I stepped back and refused to hand it over.

"Give it to me, goddamnit." If nothing else, my eighty-year old grandmother was a very formidable woman.

"Not till you tell me where this came from," I said.

Wearing a green cotton robe, my grandmother sat down in a

kitchen chair. With her thumb and forefinger, she massaged her temples as if trying to erase a bad memory.

"It was your grandfather's," she said softly. "It was given to him."

"By who?"

"Bugsy Siegal."

"Bugsy Siegel!" I said, incredulously. "The gangster?"

She nodded.

"C'mon," I said. "Don't kid me."

The reason I doubted her was because Siegel was, by all accounts, the most ruthless and murderous hitman in the Roaring Twenties, a founding member of "Murder Inc" and later credited with helping to bring the mob to Las Vegas. That he and my grandfather were friends seemed inconceivable.

"I'm not kidding." She rubbed a finger back and forth under her nose. "Your grandfather was a gangster. He grew up on the Lower East Side with Siegel and Meyer Lansky. They were good friends."

My grandfather a gangster? It was hard to believe. Before he worked at the candy store in Union City, I always thought he'd been a longshoreman at the Hoboken docks. Even as a high schooler, I should have suspected something was a little off about him. I mean, here was a guy supposedly not making much money as a steamfitter and yet he was always stylishly dressed. Granted, he purchased his clothes at inexpensive places like Bond's and Robert Halls. As early as grammar school, he would say to me, "Listen, kid, no matter what anyone tells ya…clothes make the man." He always straightened my tie and buttoned my sport coat. And God forbid I wore socks that showed my ankles. "What are you," he'd say. "Fucking Amish?"

After finding the gun I remembered the day he took me to Coney Island. We strolled the boardwalk, inhaling the seductive scent of fried clams, cotton candy and hot dogs from Nathan's.

I marveled at the lights from the Wonder Wheels and the mountainous scaffolding of the Cyclone. I looked googly-eyed at a sign that proclaimed "The Bearded Lady."

We stopped at a carnival stand where you took an air rifle and shot small metal tags off a spinning wheel. The carny, a big man with a potbelly and handlebar mustache, looked at my grandfather and said, "How about you, old timer. Care to give it a go?"

My grandfather raised his hands, palms out. "No, thanks."

"C'mon," the carny urged. "Whaddya got to lose?"

A smart aleck behind us shouted, "Go ahead, gramps, let's see what you got."

My grandfather turned and shot the wisenheimer a look that made him take a step backward.

"Gimme the rifle," my grandfather said.

The carny gave it to him. My grandfather licked his index finger and positioned himself, legs spread. He took aim and in quick succession knocked off eleven of the twelve tags.

"Holy crap!" I shouted. "That was unbelievable."

"Just lucky," my grandfather said.

"Looked more like skill to me," the carny said, eyeballing my grandfather through narrowed eyes.

He then offered my grandfather a prize. He rejected it, looking pissed.

"Something wrong?" I said.

He shook his head vigorously. "Can't believe I missed one."

Now, sitting in my grandmother's kitchen, I said, "You gotta tell me about grandpa."

She smirked. "Tell you what?"

"Everything."

My grandmother took a deep breath and said, "Here goes. Your grandfather, Siegel and Lanky worked together as tool-and-die makers, near the end of the first World War, but"—she hesitated a moment—"their real job was petty theft, which gradually turned to hijacking, loan-sharking and armed robbery."

She squirmed in her seat. "Back in those days, people on the Lower East Side didn't have much money, it was hard to make ends meet. So guys like your grandfather turned to crime because, well, because crime paid."

She said that the three amigos, all dressed in tuxedos, often hit the Cotton Club. My grandfather and Lansky brought their wives. Siegel escorted different floozies with small brains and big breasts. Their drinks were always top-shelf hooch or expensive champagne, never bathtub gin.

"It was all fun and games," my grandmother said, "until the robbery."

She then told me the story, which I later confirmed through newspapers, books and police reports.

On a cold night in March 1928, my grandfather, along with some other gangsters, stole a truckload of furs from a Bronx warehouse. The next day, Siegel and Lansky accused my grandfather of skimming, taking a cut larger than he was supposed to from the profits after they were fenced. My grandfather denied it. They didn't believe him.

A week later, there was a party at the Sunnyside, Queens home of mobster Louis "Lepke" Buchalter.

At the party's conclusion, Siegel offered to give my grandfather a lift back to Manhattan. Siegel was the designated driver. My grandfather was told to sit shotgun. Lansky sat in the back between two other gangsters, Samuel Levine and Joseph Benzole.

Siegel drove the speed limit until suddenly he swerved the car off the main road and detoured into a wooded area. My grandfather, realizing he was being "taken for a ride" kicked Siegel's foot off the gas pedal and leaped out of the car.

Running zig-zag through an open field, he was shot four times, twice in the head. Siegel and the others took off.

Somehow my grandfather survived and, amazingly, even flagged down a cab. The cabbie, not knowing where to find the nearest hospital, drove my grandfather to his parent's house at 523 Grand Street in the Lower East Side.

Horrified by the blood dripping down her son's face, my great-grandmother summoned an ambulance from Gouverneur Hospital.

In the hospital, my grandfather was questioned by a detective named Joseph P. Heinrich. My grandfather told Heinrich that Meyer Lansky shot him.

Heinrich left the hospital and on March 6 he appeared before Judge Benjamin Marvin in Long Island City Magistrates Court. Lansky, along with Levin and Benzole were charged with felonious assault. (Siegel, for whatever reason, was not arraigned.)

Days later, a trusted friend of my grandfather's, Daniel Francis Ahern, went to visit him. As a get-well gift, he brought a chicken dish called chobani.

Because Heinrich had left strict instructions not to let anyone admitted into my grandfather's room, Ahern gave the chicken to my grandmother who then presented it to my grandfather.

Reclining in his hospital bed, his head bandaged, my grandfather eyed the chicken and said, "Who gave you this?"

"Ahern."

My grandfather tossed the chicken out the window.

"What'd you do that for?" my grandmother asked.

"The damn bird's full of poison." A short time before, another local gangster had been whacked the same way, with chicken laced with strychnine.

My grandfather blamed Charles "Lucky" Luciano, the mob's chairman and a good friend of Lansky's.

"That's Luciano's way," my grandfather said. "He kills sneaky."

A few days after the chicken episode, a Luca Brasi look-a-like snuck into my grandfather's room. Speaking for Lansky, he told my grandfather that if he talked his brothers would be "taken out."

My grandfather told him to get lost.

The day my grandfather was released from the hospital, he was brought to court to testify against Lansky.

But at the trial, he recanted. The judge was so enraged, he threatened him with a charge of perjury.

My grandfather wouldn't budge. The angry judge then dismissed all charges against Lansky and his two cohorts.

A reporter from the Daily Star newspaper wrote: "Fully half of those present followed them (Lansky, Levin and Benzole) out. Shifty-eyed men hurrying from the courthouse and disappearing in different directions when they reached the sidewalk."

A few weeks later, my grandfather admitted to skimming money. He made restitution. Lansky forgave him. The two men shook hands. Hey, what's attempted murder between friends?

Later that same day, Siegel gave my grandfather the gun because, as my grandmother said, picking up a glass of water and taking a sip, "He felt grandpa was owned something."

My grandmother chuckled. "You would think after what happened, he'd clean up his act." She shook her head. "But, of course, he didn't."

A year later, on June 5th, he was sentenced to a two-year stretch in Sing-Sing for grand larceny. Seems he stole 16 pairs of trousers worth $760.00.

My grandmother pointed to an old, brown-tinted photograph of my grandfather stuck to the refrigerator door. A tall man, over six foot, with dark eyes and a prominent nose, he is smoking a big, fat stogie. His hair is slicked back, meticulously groomed. His three-piece suit is nicely tailored, his slack pressed to a knife-like cease, his tie perfectly squared. He looks like a foreign diplomat.

Yet he acted more like a daredevil.

One time when I was ten, my grandfather took me to a lake in the Catskill Mountains. It was a hot summer's day. My grandfather was wearing a ribbed wool tank top over a snug fitting pair of black-and-white checkered shorts. He climbed up a cliff nearly twenty feet above the water. Standing like Tarzan, he let out a yell and pounded his chest.

He then took a deep breath and launched himself into the lake. He rose smiling and triumphant.

When he got out, he dried himself off and said to me, "Now it's your turn."

I shook my head.

"Whaddya afraid?"

"Yeah."

He gripped my shoulders. "Look, Rich, you gotta learn to take risks. Being fearful is unacceptable."

"But..."

"No buts. Jump."

Knees shaking, I climbed up the cliff and looked down into the lake. It seemed miles away. Dark and fathomless. The abyss.

I made the sign of the cross and glanced at my grandfather. He gave me the thumbs up sign.

Closing my eyes, I jumped. Legs, arms, shouts. I hit the water hard. It was ice cold.

I surfaced, gulping blissful drafts of air. When I got back on land, my grandfather patted me on the back.

"Ya did good, kid."

I still can recall, after so many decades, how his compliment made me swoon, the sensation he imbibed in me. And though I couldn't have articulated my feelings then, I can now: My grandfather was teaching me how to deal with fear and failure, the need to conquer any weakness that I might possess.

And here's the thing: From that day forward, I don't think I ever worried about facing a challenge or dealing with defeat.

One funny thing about my grandfather was that he knew little, if anything, about basketball. He never once played the game. Yet he was adamant when giving me suggestions. Almost from the day I started playing Biddy Basketball, he was always telling me to shoot more, dribble less, box out and, of course, take no shit from anyone.

Once, when my high school team played Emerson, I was running down court on a fast break when I received a pass and went skyward to the rim. An Emerson player undercut me. I went flying over his shoulder. Thankfully, I didn't land on my head.

I quickly scrambled to my feet and went nose-to-nose with the perpetrator. There was pushing and shoving, insults and F-bombs. A referee separated us. I went to the free throw line and buried two shots.

After the game, my grandfather was waiting for me outside the gym, looking snazzy in his flannel blazer, white turtleneck and grey wool homburg, dashingly angled to cover his left eye.

He stared at me for a long moment, then withdrew a thick Dutch Masters cigar from inside his breast pocket. He bit off the end, spit it out and warmed the tip with a butane lighter. Holding the cigar with two fingers above and a thumb below, he took a puff.

"Why didn't you sock that kid in the snoot," he said.

"I woulda been thrown outta the game."

He gave me a resounding smack on the back of the head.

"Fuck that."

He then gripped my bicep. "Next time somebody cheap shots you, you hit 'em back. You hear me?"

"I hear ya."

He released his grip. "One more thing," he said. "You may not always do the right thing, but the question is: Can you live with the consequences?"

A few games later in an opponent's gym, a player going for a steal fouled me hard. I fell to the floor, jumped to my feet and decked him. A brawl ensued. The ref tossed me. Fans booed me. A cheerleader spit in my face. I accepted the consequences.

"I'm glad you knocked him on his keester," my grandfather said when I emerged from the locker room. He then reached into his pocket, pulled out a twenty-dollar bill and handed it to me.

"You showed fucking moxie," he said.

"Jesus, Grandpa. You sound like a gangster."

He palmed his heart. "Me? A gangster?" A snicker. "No way. I'm a pussycat."

Sitting now in McSorley's, my grandfather put his hand on my shoulder and said, "Well, guess your basketball career is over."

"I would say so."

But the next day, to my total surprise, I learned I had been selected in the eighth round of the NBA draft by the Kansas City Kings and in the fourth round of the ABA draft by the San Diego Conquistadors.

I later learned I got drafted by the Conquistadors, despite my poor play at Fairfield, because the Q's assistant coach Stan Albeck had scouted me at Duke and felt I "might be able to resurrect my game."

Bill Madden thought the same thing. A successful Manhattan sports agent, Bill had played college basketball at Yale. He phoned me and said he represented a number of NBA players, including Bob McAdoo. He offered to represent me.

I met Bill in his midtown office. Tall, blonde and hyper energetic, he sat behind his desk and said, "The Kings probably wouldn't offer you anything," he said. "But I think I can get you some bonus money and a free ticket to San Diego. Whaddya think?"

"It's more than I expected," I said, thinking how great it would be to visit California, a place I had never been and always wanted to see.

He extended his hand. I shook it. "Good," he said. "We got a deal."

We met again a few weeks later.

"You're all set," Bill said. He then made a scrunchy face. "I could only get you a thousand dollar signing bonus. I know it's not much, but the Q's aren't flush with money."

I nodded.

He smiled and raised an index finger. "Look at the positive side."

"What's that?"

"You'll be coached by Wilt."

"Wilt" was Wilt Chamberlain, an NBA legend. At seven-foot-two, his basketball claim to fame, among many things, was that he once scored 100 points in one game.

"You're kidding?! Wilt?" I said. "Holy shit!" I threw my hands up in the air and sang, "California, here I come."

The day I arrived in San Diego, I was met by a team representative who took me to my hotel. I expected to be ensconced in someplace grand like the Hotel del Coronado, a palace with ocean views, room service and gaggles of girls in skimpy bikinis laying around an Olympic-sized pool.

Wrong.

I was put in the Ulysses S. Grant hotel, an old and smelly property located downtown in a funky area—populated with druggies and drunks, hookers and homeless.

Skinny old ladies and palsied old men huddled in the lobby on frayed couches and chairs, adjusting their hearing aids as they talked of attending grammar school with George Washington.

My room afforded a view of a brick building. It smelled of mildew and Lysol. Through the thin bathroom wall I could hear coughing and farting, the gurgling and groaning of relic plumbing.

If that wasn't bad enough, I learned that Wilt had quit. He said he'd become disenchanted with coaching. His preference, he said, was to spend time playing volleyball with the girls—Wilt's Wonder Women—on the beach.

He may have had another reason: he was too busy scoring points in the bedroom since he claimed to have slept with over 20,000 women.

I did, however, meet Wilt. He was strolling one afternoon along Mission Beach, surrounded by a bevy of young, sumptuous blondes.

Wearing a pair of tight, bright red gym shorts and a white tank top, he displayed biceps bigger than loaves of bread.

I approached him and introduced myself.

"I'm trying out for the Q's," I said.

He stopped, stroked his goatee and stared down at me as if I was a Lilliputian. Then in a voice that sounded like an army regiment marching through a gravel pit, he said, "My condolences, my man."

Before I could say another word, he strolled off like someone who had the world by the balls.

Wilt was replaced by Alex Groza, a former player at CCNY who had been banned from the NBA in 1951 for point-shaving.

Six-seven and overweight, Alex had a long face and large ears. In all the time I spent in San Diego, he never seemed enthusiastic about coaching. He went through the motions and talked the talk, but he was the furthest thing from, say, Hubie Brown.

His practices were boring. He allowed players to smoke in the locker room and be late for practice. To my knowledge, few, if any, were ever fined.

We were a talented group that included Caldwell Jones, Bo Lamar, Stew Johnson, Travis Grant and Jimmy O'Brien. Groza cut a player or two every three or four days until there were thirteen players remaining on the roster, including me.

One more player needed to get axed to meet the mandatory twelve-man roster. My main competition to make the team was Billy Harris, a six-three shooting guard from Northern Illinois, nicknamed "Shotgun " because of his long-range proficiency.

Legend had it that the better a player played against him the better he became. Scoop Jackson of SLAM magazine dubbed Billy the best Chicago playground basketball player ever. "No one," he wrote, "every claimed to have seen, heard about or witnessed Billy having a bad game. Not one story, not one game."

Billy and I went at it pretty good in practice—him because he wanted to make the team badly, and me because I still had some pride.

One time I guarded Billy as he brought the ball up court, his body flowing with it, nursing it—a loose engine of muscle guided by wide eyes and instant recognition of potential paths of attack. He quickly performed a cross-over dribble, blew by me and went in for a dunk. A minute later, he caught a pass coming off a screen and buried a twenty-five footer. Thirty seconds after that, he drove the lane and scored on a reverse lay-up.

Backpedaling on defense, he shouted, "The doctor is operating."

He spent the rest of the scrimmage dribbling defenders into dizzied dilemmas, hitting pull-up jumpers, mid-range jumpers, layups, floaters. He wasn't just playing. He was performing as if on a magic carpet ride.

After practice, Billy and I sat together on a bus headed back to the hotel.

"Hey, man, was I dropping the fuckin' pill today or what?" he said.

"Yes, you were."

"I gotta make this fuckin' team, man. I know it's between me and you but no offense, cause I like you, but I gotta kick your muthafucker ass."

"Thank you for sharing that."

"Hey, man, I ain't goin' back to Chicago with my dick hanging between my legs. I ain't got no degree in brain surgery so this is my ticket out."

He shut his eyes tightly and pursed his lips, as if in recollection of his past. "You're different, man," he said. "I always see you readin' a book. You must be some kind of smarty pants. Probably gonna be some kind of muthafuckin' lawyer huh?"

"Not a chance. I'd rather clean toilets."

"Whatever, bro. Let's just agree to let the best man win, you dig." A mischievous smile. An extended hand. I grabbed it. His grip was strong. "Though you do know that that muthafucker will be me!" He laughed heartily. Strangely, despite his enormous talent, Billy only played one year with the Q's, averaging a little over eight points a game. Why he didn't have a great pro career was a mystery to anyone who'd seen him play. After the Q's, he left the U.S. and went to play in the Philippines. When he returned to Chicago, he coached kids in his old neighborhood. He died of a stroke in 2010.

I played so poorly I assumed Groza would cut me, but he didn't. In fact, he put me on the traveling squad and I traveled with the team to our first preseason game in Salt Lake City against the Utah Stars in the Cow Palace. The Stars were led by Ron Boone and Moses Malone.

I expected the same intensity in the Q's locker room that I experienced at Duke, where before a game the players were always revved up and bursting at the seams.

Not so in the Q's locker room. Guys were sitting in chairs looking bored, as if we were all waiting to board a plane.

Groza designed a quick game plan on a blackboard and told us to play good D, rebound hard and run the break whenever we could.

Then he said: "Okay, let's go play some basketball." There was no clapping, no stomping of the feet, no rebel yells. Boy! Was I disappointed.

I don't remember much about that game (I played very little), but one incident stands out.

I was sitting on the bench when a player next to me said, "I'm gonna drop a bomb."

I assumed he was going to fart and I slid away from him.

He signaled for the ball boy and asked for a piece of paper.

He wrote something on it and handed it back.

I watched the ball boy race across the back of the court and then up into the stands. He handed the piece of paper to a gorgeous girl who looked at it and gave a thumbs up.

My teammate turned to me and said, "Is being a pro athlete great or what?"

"Sure seems it," I said.

The day after we got back from Utah, Groza called me into his office, a small cubicle with a desk, some chairs and two large blackboards.

"I have to cut you," he said. Wearing a white polo shirt and baggy sweatpants, he grabbed a golf club and lined up a make-believe putt, wiggling his hips. "You do pass well, but your shooting is erratic." He took a deep breath and put down the golf club. "I hope you understand." A pause. "But, hey, you never know; a guy gets hurt I may wanna call you back." Groza never called. He was fired mid-season and replaced by Beryl Shipley. The team finished the year 31-54.

I left Groza's office and went back to the locker room and cleaned out my stuff.

I figured it was all over but the shouting.

On the way out of the gym, I ran into Jimmy O'Brien, the Q's starting point guard who would later become the head basketball coach at Boston College and Ohio State.

I told Jimmy what happened.

"Whaddya gonna do now?" he asked.

"Not sure."

"You going to try and make it with another team?"

"No."

"Why not?"

"I think my basketball playing days are over."

"You never know," Jimmy said. "Some coach might call you."

"He'd have to be fucking drunk," I said.

Chapter Sixteen

A coach did call and he wasn't drunk. His name was Del Harris, who I never heard of but who I subsequently learned was the coach at Earlham College in Richmond, Indiana.

Del introduced himself to me as the coach of the Iberia Superstars, a team that was part of a new league in Europe, owned and operated by American investors and featuring only American players.

"You'd be living in Castelldefels, Spain and playing against teams in Germany, Belgium, Switzerland and Israel," he said. "You get a free apartment and about ten thousand dollars. You interested?"

I was, but not because I still wanted to play basketball; I was more interested in seeing Europe on someone else's dime.

"I'm interested," I said.

"Great," Del said, in a deep voice that in later years would torment refs when he was coaching the Los Angeles Lakers.

I flew to Castelldefels, a pretty seaside town located just twenty kilometers outside Barcelona. I was given a one-bedroom apartment with a great view of the beach. In the morning, the sky was bright blue, the sun perfectly orange and the air cool and salty. At night, bells often tolled from a nearby church.

It was a peaceful place to live, and I treasured the privacy of it, the recognition that no one, except my teammates and my family, knew where I was or what I was doing.

The beauty of that freedom was that it provided me time to understand what it meant to be the real me—instead of the guy who for so many years had hid behind the cloak of being a basketball player.

In Spain I could be a person and not a personality. No one knew me. No one expected anything from me. I didn't have to act a certain way or put up any pretense. All I had to do was find myself and follow a plan. The problem was, I didn't have a plan.

The Superstars were co-owned by Houston businessman Allen Becker and Spanish journalist Carlos Pardo. We played our home games in the Palau Blaugrana arena and wore green and blue uniforms.

My teammates were all great players. Our roster included Pete Cross from the University of San Francisco who had played three seasons in the NBA with the Seattle SuperSonics and Kansas City Kings. Jeff Halliburton of Drake University who played with the Atlanta Hawks and Philadelphia 76ers. And Roy Ebron from Southwestern Louisiana who had a short stay with the Utah Stars of the ABA. All longed to get back to the "Show.' But none did. At least, not on my team.

One player who did make it to the NBA was M. L. Carr. Carr played for the Israeli Sabras and was the league superstar. The following year he signed with the Boston Celtics, where in six years he averaged 9.7 points and 4.3 rebounds.

The league format was for each team to play the others ten times, five at home and five away, for a total of forty games. The games were competitive, high scoring affairs with not much defense but lots of fast breaks and dazzling dunks.

While the games were exciting, the atmosphere in the arenas was dull. Some smelled like fried fish. Others like hard boiled eggs. The gyms were small and attendance was generally slight, at best a few hundred spectators. People clapped enthusiastically at slam dunks and blind passes, but they got more excited seeing a player slip on the court or a coach berating a referee. Once, in Switzerland, an irate fan threw a chunk of cheese. Thankfully, it wasn't aimed at me.

I sensed Del—tall, thin and white-haired—knew I didn't give a hoot about getting playing time. Once, he told me that sitting on the bench I looked like a bored lifeguard.

This didn't piss him off because I was, according to some teammates, the "coach's pet."

One time, walking through the streets of Barcelona, he said, "I get the impression you don't really seem to care much about playing."

"I don't."

"What 'do' you care about?"

"A lot of things."

"Like?"

"I don't know. I'm just curious."

"About?"

"Everything."

I was, in a way, a tourist disguised as a basketball player. Nobody knew me or my background. Nobody had preconceived ideas about me. I came and went as I pleased. Dressed anyway I wanted. Ate anything I craved. Thick sandwiches, milk shakes, banana splits. I sat on the beach and got tan. It was glorious.

We only played two, three games a week so I had a lot of free time. When I wasn't at practice or playing a game, I walked aimlessly around whatever city we were playing in. My only guide was my enthusiasm. I talked to people from different countries with different ideas, attitudes and accents. I listened to their dreams of transformation much like my own. I stopped in bookstores and bought a lot of books. I read the plays of Shakespeare, the essays of Thoreau, the poetry of Wordsworth. I was stupefied by their talents, became enraptured and involved in their lives.

In Germany, I went to a Munich Beer Festival and hopped around with men in their lederhosen suspenders and feathered hats, women wearing dirndl skirts and tight bodices. In Barcelona I hung out on Las Ramblas, drank sangria and danced the rumba. In Geneva, I decided to try fondue, which I had heard about but never tasted.

I went to a small and intimate restaurant. It had stucco walls, sawdust floors and framed pictures of snow-capped mountains. On a windowsill sat a tiny plastic statue of a little girl in pigtails, wearing a black vest, green skirt and white knee socks: Heidi.

The patrons were mostly men with big moustaches and big bellies. One was lifting his pinky as he raised his coffee cup. Another cleaned his teeth with a toothpick. From an overhead speaker flowed the celestial, celebratory strains of Siegfried Wagner.

I sat at a table by the window and perused the handwritten menu. It had the names of cheeses I never heard of: Emmental,

Gruyere, Appenzeller. I scratched my head.

The chef, no doubt noticing my perplexity, came out from the kitchen and introduced himself. His name was Christoph. In his late forties with dark eyes and a pronounced paunch, he wore a white chef's hat and a white double-breasted cotton jacket. The jacket was splattered with food particles.

"May I be of assistance, monsieur?" he asked, bowing slightly and smiling. His teeth were tobacco-colored.

"I'd like to try fondue."

"You mean you never taste fondue?"

"No, never."

He placed his hands on his head as if he had a migraine. I half expected him to shout "Sacrebleu."

"Then I make you fabulous one," he said.

He returned to the kitchen. Less than a half hour later, he brought out a bubbling pot of cheese. Joining me at the table, he tucked a napkin under his chin, ripped off a piece of fresh baguette and, using a long fork, dipped it into the pot. He tasted the mixture, kissed his bunched fingers noisily and exclaimed "Bon."

He then uncorked a bottle of white wine and poured himself a glass.

"It's Châteauneuf-du-Pape," he said, swirling the wine, smelling it and finally swallowing it. He then poured some wine into my glass, raised his and said "Salut!"

I sipped the wine. It was a helluva lot better than the crappy Lancers and Mateus I drank in college.

Throughout the meal, which was sumptuous, Christoph talked about his profession. About different foods and different wines. He rhapsodized about how much he loved cooking, saying how he came to it from "his babyhood in the South of France." He called himself an "athletic gourmet," because he said he had fast footwork and quick hands. He sounded as obsessive about food as I once did basketball.

When the fondue pot was empty, I was stuffed. Couldn't eat another thing. But Christoph said there was always room for dessert. He brought out bowls of fruits—pears, apples and melons, followed by a truffled chocolate cake covered with fresh cream. He nibbled at it and said "Ooh la la." We finished the meal with a wee glass of what he called a digestif. If memory serves, I think it was kirsch.

"That was the greatest meal I ever had," I said.

"Merci," Christoph said, grinning widely. "My goal is to win a Michelin."

I thought he was talking about tires.

One place I thoroughly enjoyed visiting was Israel. When we played the Israeli Sabras, my team stayed at the Tel Aviv Country Club, a gorgeous place with a nice golf course and tennis courts. Good food and friendly people.

When I had the time, I went sightseeing in Jerusalem. I walked through the Damascus Gate into the crowded Muslim Quarter where dozens of vendors sold fruits, vegetables, clothes, cameras, souvenirs and postcards while listening to some Koranic chanting from scratchy radios.

I went to the Garden of Gethsemane, the Western Wall, Mount Zion and the Church of the Holy Sepulchre, the place where many theologians believe Jesus was crucified and buried. The Sepulchre was always crowded with people praying, chanting and weeping.

One morning, I took a book and headed into Tel Aviv. The day was sunny and warm. I grabbed a seat at an outdoor café and ordered a cup of coffee and rugelach. The air smelled of toasted bread.

I sipped my coffee and was about to commence reading, when someone asked, "Is this seat taken?" referring to the empty chair across from me.

I looked up. Standing before me was a small, stoop-shouldered elderly man, possibly seventy. He had dark skin, a gray beard and wore his hair in long tendrils. His ill-fitting suit was black, his shirt was white and atop his head was black streamed.

"Mind if I sit?" he said. His voice was low and soft, almost musical.

I gestured at the chair. "Please do."

He sat and smiled. Deep furrows stretched down his cheeks, framing his mouth like parentheses.

We sat in silence for a while. Around us, military police dressed in swat gear patrolled. Young boys kicked a soccer ball. Teenage girls rode bicycles. From the window of an apartment building flew the Star of David.

I glanced at the man sitting across from me and grinned. He grinned back and extended his hand.

"Rabbi Asa Aaronson," he said.

I shook his hand, introduced myself and studied his face. He had deeply set dark eyes with tiny traces of gold.

"A pleasure to meet you," he said.

I sipped my coffee. The Rabbi blew on his.

"May I ask what you're reading?" he said.

"Tender is the Night by F. Scott Fitzgerald."

He nodded sagely. "A love story?"

"Kind of."

He drank his coffee. On the street cars buzzed by like hungry mosquitoes. Somewhere in the distance a police siren blared.

"You a student?" he asked.

"No," I said. "I'm a professional basketball player."

He folded his arms and leaned back in his chair. "Interesting."

"Not really."

He stared at me, as if waiting for a better, more elaborate answer. When I didn't give one, he said, "Why, if I may be so bold, is that so?"

"It's not what I want to be doing?"

He looked at me with the intensity of a hypnotist. "Then why do it?"

"It pays well."

He leaned forward, put his elbows on the table and clasped his hands.

"Are you happy?" he said.

"Relatively."

"Happiness only occurs when you find mental and spiritual contentment," he said.

I nodded.

"It is important," he said, "to know what you want and who you want to be." A beat. "What would you like to be?"

I thought a moment. "I'd love to be a painter, a poet, a singer, a writer, a musician—something that I can practice by myself, which is what I loved most about basketball, being alone and putting my entire heart and head into improving and succeeding."

"What's stopping you?" the rabbi said.

"From?"

"Doing what you desire."

"I don't have the talent."

"How do you know? Have you tried…a…another endeavor?"

"No."

"Why?"

I shrugged. A flock of pigeons flew beneath our feet and began nibbling crumbs.

"Can't really answer that," I said.

The Rabbi stirred a spoon round and round in his ceramic cup, making a clicking sound. "Always remember," he said, "You're only confined by the walls you build around yourself."

I nodded.

The Rabbi looked at me for at least a minute. I got the feeling, correctly or not, that he sensed something inside me that was not apparent on the surface. Perhaps, I'd like to believe in retrospect, he assessed potentiality in me that I myself did not.

"Trust me when I tell you," he said, lifting an index finger, "the fear of trying is what too often stands between a man and an extraordinary life. The best way to conquer fear is to look it square in the eye and make that stare a daily habit."

"You're a regular philosopher," I said.

He grinned. "No. Just a regular Rabbi."

I laughed. The pigeons rose up, their flapping wings sounding like applause.

"Where do you live when you're not here in Israel, playing basketball?" he asked.

"New York City."

His face brightened. "It is my wish someday to visit New York."

"Why New York?"

He chuckled. "From what I'm told people there love to talk."

"That's putting it mildly."

The Rabbi lifted his arms and spread them wide. "There is an old Jewish proverb that says no one is as deaf as the man who will not listen." A pause. A slight grin. "Keep listening, my friend. You learn more from hearing than talking."

He then grabbed my right hand in both of his. His hands were soft, veiny. "I hope I didn't talk too much," he said, "I have a tendency to be rather long-winded."

"No, you've been very enlightening."

The Rabbi stood and despite his age, he practically levitated out of his seat, as if his body was filled with helium.

"Be well, my friend," he said. "Mazel tov."

He took a few steps from the table, turned and said, "Don't worry about the future. You'll never be as young as you are today. Enjoy life now. Tomorrow will take care of itself."

He then walked away. I thought of him warning me against "the fear of not trying." The words reverberated in my mind. I wondered if I had the gumption, the knowledge and the smarts to try some new endeavor. Question was: what?

At least I realized that even though I had not found what I was searching for, I had hope that one day I might.

The season ended a few days later. It saddened me, not because we finished in last place, but because I hated to leave Europe, especially because of my side trips to Paris.

Paris revved my internal engines, the buildings ablaze with lights, the sun filtered through stain-glass windows, the street stalls brimming with mountains of mushrooms, bins of fruits and vegetables. I got drunk just breathing the atmosphere.

I especially enjoyed strolling the Left Bank, visiting the city's eclectic bookstore, Shakespeare & Company. I spent hours there, talking with the shopkeeper, an older gent, Alain, who liked to curlicue the ends of his Salvador Dali-like mustache.

Slowly sweeping his arm in the air, he said, "Perhaps there's a book here or somewhere that will alter your existence." His words escaped me then. But soon after they would prove prophetic.

When the store wasn't busy, Alain gave me the history of Gertrude Stein and Alice B. Toklas. He rhapsodized about Hemingway, Sinclair Lewis and Sherwood Anderson. "The air of Paris," he said, "awakens the senses and makes one want to think and write."

I purchased a copy of A Moveable Feast by Ernest Hemingway. Devoured it. Damn near memorized it. I savored Hemingway's simple declaratives that stripped everything down to the bare bones that could lift or break your heart in a single sentence. I marveled at his way of writing dialogue and descriptions that sparkled with emotional accuracy. I was so inspired by him I went to the Champs-Elysees Garden and took out a tiny moleskine notebook and filled it with descriptive sentences of the Eiffel Tower, the Arc de Triomphe, the Cathedrale Notre-Dame, along with portraits of the women in their stylish clothes and men in their Porsche convertibles. I even spent twenty minutes one day just watching a shirtless painter sketch a flower. I jotted down notes about his clothes, his hat, the way he sat on his stool, the way his brush moved across the canvas.

Soon my compulsion to record observations was so powerful

that it became one of shocking self-awareness, the realization that I could recede from the clear vision of myself after seeing twenty years of being nothing more than a basketball player.

By the time I left Paris, I had an epiphany that would change the course of my life. I decided, quite simply, that once I got back to the States, I was going to try my hand at this game called writing. But why writing? Aside from being able to do it in solitude, as I once practiced basketball, it was the incredible joy of putting into words thoughts, perceptions and emotions, mouthing them and rolling them around my tongue. Goosebumps literally appeared on my arms when I put together a sentence that made music, one that created a symphony of images and details.

There was only one problem: I hadn't spent my spare time growing up in the library or reading, much less writing. Did I have the ability?

Chapter Seventeen

One of the first things I did after flying back to New Jersey was reconnect with Peg, who was working at New York Life and living in Stuyvesant Town on Manhattan's East Side. She was sharing an apartment with a roommate. I'd sometimes stay overnight rather than with my parents in Union City.

It felt great to be back in New York. I missed going to Broadway shows and Jazz Clubs, hailing cabs and riding subways, eating meatball heroes at Manganaro's and hot dogs at Gray's Papaya.

Peg and I started going to dinners and movies and concerts. Together, we enjoyed the feverish pulse of the city, walking through a crowded Central Park, a boisterous Greenwich Village or just trekking across the Brooklyn Bridge, the wooden planks hundreds of feet above the rippling water.

We went where the breezes took us, going to art galleries and antique shops, drinking at Guy Fawkes' cozy bar on First Avenue, seeing the high-kicking Rockettes at Radio City Music Hall and listening to trumpeter John Parker as he walked around Chelsea Place restaurant, blowing Coltrane.

One night Peg and I went to dinner at an elegant restaurant on the Upper East Side. It had soft lighting and candle-lit tables. The waiters wore tuxedos.

The maître d' sat us in a corner table, put menus in front of us and said, "someone will be with you shortly."

"Nice place," Peg said, looking around at the décor. She was wearing a light blue blazer over dark slacks.

"Yes, it is."

"You look lovely."

She smiled. "Thank you."

A waiter came and I ordered a bottle of champagne.

"Very fancy," Peg said.

"Indeed."

Sitting around us were people who my grandfather called "East Side swells"—meaning wealthy people who probably owned big brownstones and even bigger bank accounts.

"A dinner here must be expensive," Peg said, the candlelight falling on her face, setting her loveliness against the dark interior.

"Probably costs more than my father makes in a month."

The waiter returned and showed me the label on the bottle. I nodded. He poured the champagne into long-stemmed crystal glasses.

"A toast," I said, lifting my glass.

"To?"

"Us getting married."

Peg's smile was incandescent.

We clicked glasses, kissed and drank.

"Champagne's delicious."

The waiter returned and we ordered dinner.

"What's your plan?" Peg said.

"You mean for a job?"

"Yeah."

"I'm…I'm thinking about becoming a writer."

Peg grinned. "Really?"

I nodded.

"What inspired you to think about writing?" she asked.

"It's more like who inspired me."

"Who did?"

"Pat Jordan."

I had read Pat's book A False Spring, a captivating memoir about his days as a great high school pitcher who failed to realize his pro potential. He subsequently turned to writing. Reading his book, I discovered myself. I was him in his words. I felt like Pat had lived my life.

I also read a number of Pat's profiles in Sports Illustrated—on Tom Seaver, Bo Belinsky and Jim Bouton. I liked how his profiles probed the psyches of his subjects. He hung around with them and observed them in different situations. He wrote in clear, cinematic language. His articles, even though they were obviously about sports, read like fiction, having the economy of phrasing and the exactness of tone, the vivid, evocative images and telling details, the surprising revelations and unique insights. To me, he was the sportswriting version of Hemingway.

I knew Pat lived in Fairfield. I had seen him a number of times in a Fairfield bar called the Nautilus, but we had never spoken.

"I'm going to call Freddy Barakat," I said, referring to my former Fairfield coach. "He knows Jordan."

"Sounds like a plan," Peg said.

The next day I phoned Freddy.

"Why you wanna speak to Jordan?" he asked.

"I'm thinking about becoming a writer."

Freddy chuckled. "Let me see if I heard you correctly?" he said. "You, a writer? Hell, I didn't even think you could write a grocery list."

He thought he was being funny. Sad thing was, he wasn't far off base.

"Richie, Richie, Richie," he said, softly. "Seriously, do you know the odds of getting a story published? A million to one. Perhaps more."

"Gotta take a shot."

"Don't cry if you miss."

Freddy got me Pat's phone number. I called him and asked if he remembered me.

"Of course," he said, "I saw you play a number of times at the U," meaning Fairfield. I asked if I could visit him. He said sure, then gave me directions to his office on Boston Post Road.

The office was on the third floor of a Victorian house. It was small and consisted of some director's chairs and a desk on which sat a typewriter and a cup filled with sharpened pencils. Painted horizontally on one wall was a large yellow arrow pointing at a huge question mark.

On the corner of the desk was a framed black-and-white picture of him standing alongside Milwaukee Braves pitching coach Whitlow Wyatt and the great left-handed thrower Warren Spahn. The picture was taken at Milwaukee's County Stadium in 1959. Pat was 18 years old, a pitching phenom who, only weeks before the picture was taken, had signed a $45,000 contract (nearly half a million in today's currency) to join the Braves. The money at the time was one of the largest bonuses, if not 'the' largest bonus, any young player received from the Braves that year. Sadly, his career never flourished. As a pitcher, he was considered a failure. Then he turned to writing. He seemed like someone I could relate to.

"What can I do for you?" he said, after a few minutes of talking Fairfield basketball.

"How does one become a writer?"

A handsome man in his late thirties, with dark wavy hair and a quick smile, he said, "Why? You thinking of becoming one?"

"Possibly."

"It's hard work."

I nodded.

"Question is: Do you have the talent?"

"Don't know," I said. "I've never written anything."

He lit a cigar.

"How would I get started?" I said.

"You can begin by studying the best. Get books by Gay Talese and John McPhee," he said, referencing two of the best magazine writers ever. "Study how they write scenes and use an economy of words."

"Okay."

"Thing is," Pat added, "you gotta decide if you wanna write news copy, game stories or profiles."

"I wanna write profiles like you."

"Why profiles?"

"I'm interested in what motivates an athlete to perform, to achieve greatness. Or, on the other hand, what makes them fail." A beat. "Like you and I did."

He puffed on his cigar.

"You might want to start by getting a job with a newspaper," he said. "It's a good place to learn technique and brevity. To understand that less is more."

"I don't wanna write for newspapers."

He blew out some smoke. "Why not?"

"I don't wanna cover games. I wanna write about people. Any suggestions?"

"Well, if you wanna break into, say, *Sports Illustrated*, you need to come up with someone they haven't thought of writing about. I mean, so many young writers try selling articles about athletes that everybody knows about. Forget it. The SI staff has that covered. You wanna get published—find a superstar athlete long forgotten who destroyed his career and maybe found redemption. Editors love those kind of stories."

"You like being a free-lance writer?" I asked.

"I do. Gives me the freedom of not having to work in an office. But it's not for everyone. There's no regular income, no check in the mail every Friday, no insurance benefits."

I nodded.

"And, truth be told, most free-lancers don't make much money."

"Sounds like a challenging profession."

"It is." A puff of smoke. "Sure you wanna try it?"

"Worth taking a shot."

We talked a while longer. About my athletic career and his athletic career. About how both of us were destined for greatness and both of us failed.

I said, "You miss baseball?"

A wide smile. "Every day. In fact, I still think of myself not as a writer who once pitched but as a pitcher who happens to now be writing. How about you? You miss playing?"

"Not at all."

"Really?"

"Yeah, somewhere between leaving Duke and entering Fairfield I lost my desire."

"I could tell."

"How?"

"Nobody who played as badly as you did at Fairfield could possibly have had any desire."

I thanked Pat profusely for his time and then spent the next few months reading everything by Talese and McPhee, studying their techniques, their novelistic approach. I spent hours and hours in the library trying to find a great ex-athlete Sports Illustrated hadn't profiled, someone whose career had been sidetracked. There were days I did nothing more than read old sports magazines for 8 to 10 hours, learning from writers like New York Times columnist Red Smith and Sports Illustrated feature writer Frank Deford how to turn a phrase and crystalize a sentence.

Finally, after three months of searching, employing the same single-minded focus, determination and obsession I once did basketball, I found the athlete I was looking for: Joe Don Looney. The aptly named Looney may be very well the greatest college football running back to ever fuck up a career.

The fact that he was once a star who failed in his pursuit of greatness resonated with me. I could relate to him. Understand him. In some ways, he was me.

The problem was finding Looney. I went to the New York Public Library and looked at rolls and rolls of microfilm, reading every story I could find on Looney and learning everything I could about him…except where he was currently living.

I called the University of Oklahoma. Nothing. I then called people whose names appeared in different stories. One person thought he was dead. Another hoped he was dead—"for his own sake," he said.

Just when I was resigned to never finding him, I saw a small article in the New York Daily News about how Baba Muktananda, a guru and founder of Siddha yoga, was attracting thousands of people, including celebrities like James Taylor and Carly Simon, to an ashram at the old Deville Hotel in the Catskills. One of the other prominent devotees mentioned was Joe Don Looney.

In the early 1960s, Looney had been an All-American running back at the University of Oklahoma. At six-foot-one and 225 pounds—big for his era—he was timed at 9.5 in the hundred-yard dash. As a senior, he had been a favorite to win the Heisman Trophy, and then go on to the NFL Hall of Fame. But he was rebellious and belligerent. He started at the University of Texas, flunked out, transferred to TCU, got kicked out, then led Cameron Junior College to the national championship, before attending Oklahoma, where in his first season he led them to the conference championship.

One day at practice early in his second season at Oklahoma, a Sooner coach accused him of not hustling. He told the coach to "Eat shit" and with a short hard swing, knocked him to the ground. The coach scrambled up to defend himself. Looney flattened him with another punch. That evening Oklahoma coach Bud Wilkinson informed Looney he was off the squad—permanently. He also told Looney his teammates voted unanimously against him. Replied Looney: "Who cares?"

Despite his craziness, the New York Giants still made him their No. 1 draft choice in 1964, twelfth pick overall. When Looney heard of his selection, he immediately quit school, flew to New York, and signed a $40,000 contract.

On the first day of training camp, Coach Allie Sherman ordered all players in bed by ten p.m. Looney refused to comply. He was fined $50. He complained that the penalty was unfair. Twenty-eight days later, the Giants traded him to the Baltimore Colts.

In Baltimore, he continued to miss practices, get drunk and start fights. The Colts quickly traded him to the Detroit Lions who just as quickly traded him to the Washington Redskins. He was cut almost immediately and was out of football until he made an abortive comeback attempt in 1972 with the expansion New Orleans Saints.

Then he dropped out of sight. But now I knew where to find him.

The DeVille Hotel was located 100 miles north of New York City. Once a famous and glamorous resort popular with Jewish families from New York that helped give the Catskills its nickname, the Borscht Belt. But by 1976, the place was a mess. There were crumbling cottages, a potholed tennis court and a swimming pool filled with broken bicycles and mangled shopping carts. Now it was an ashram, a retreat for those who wanted to study under Baba Muktananda.

Before I could enter, I was asked by a disciple of Muktananda—an emaciated guy in a white caftan who resembled the old actor Don Knotts—if I was looking for "a mental and spiritual awakening."

Putting on a sad face, I lied and said, "Desperately so."

"Then you must give yourself to us totally."

"Okay."

"And discard any anxiety or self-doubt."

"Roger that."

He smiled and said, "We welcome you to enlightenment."

For days, I walked around the Ashram showing disciples Looney's picture and asking if anyone knew him. Nobody did. But late on the third evening I came across a thin guy who, at best, weighed 150 pounds. His hair had sprinkles of gray and his eyes were darkly circled and deeply embedded in their sockets, giving him the look of a man relieved of an addiction.

I approached him. He was wearing a dirty white caftan and broken brown sandals. He smelled of disinfectant.

"Excuse me," I said. "By any chance do you know a guy named Joe Don Looney?"

"Who?"

I showed him Looney's picture.

He studied it.

"Looks like a wrestler." His voice was soft, almost a murmur.

"He was a football player," I said.

"Any good?"

"Could have been great."

He gave me a quizzical look. "What happened?"

"He got derailed."

He stared again at the picture, as if there was something about it that intrigued him. He said, "Come to think of it, I have seen this guy."

"Great. Know where I can find him?"

He smiled. "You're lookin' at 'em."

I was shocked by his appearance. It seemed impossible that

this skinny guy standing in front of me once carried huge defensive linebackers on his shoulders while running toward the end zone.

"What can I do for you?" he said.

"I'd like to write a story about your life."

"I'll talk to you about my football career but I'm more interested in talking about the Baba. He's the Vince Lombardi of religion."

Looney took me to his cabin. It was a small, ramshackle structure with broken windows. It smelled of B.O. and dog shit. There were a few cots and some mattresses scattered around. Joe pointed to a spot covered by a ripped dirty sheet and a thin pillow. No mattress.

"That's where I sleep," he said. "On the floor."

"What do you do here?" I said.

Joe rubbed his hands together like a man who had just won the lottery.

"I clean toilets," he said, "When I'm not working I listen to tapes of Sanskrit, meditate and chant. Sometimes for hours."

"You ever get bored?"

"Never."

His face suddenly lit up, his voice a cheer. "You gotta meet the Baba," he said. "Just being around him changes people's lives." A beat. "Look how he turned me from a madman to a happy man."

We met the Baba outside Joe's cabin. A short, bald man, he wore sandals and a long caftan. Strings of beads hung from his neck.

Joe genuflected before him, bowing his head and pressing his hands together in prayer. The Baba touched his forehead. Joe looked up. The smile on his face was radiant.

The Baba said, "My good son."

Joe stood transfixed. The Baba left, walking away—actually waddling—like a penguin.

"Just his touch alone puts me in a state of bliss," Joe said.

We went back to Joe's cabin.

"As a kid," he said, sitting cross-legged on the floor. "I never knew how to distinguish between right and wrong. Thanks to my early success in sports, rules didn't apply to me. People let me get away with murder. No matter what I did, coaches would turn a blind eye." He paused. As he did, I couldn't help but think of myself back in high school when I could get away with any shenanigan, however dastardly. "As I got older," Joe added, "the crazier I became. By the time I got to college I was pretty much off my rocker."

"You mean getting into fights?"

"I mean like getting into anything that would piss coaches off."

Joe took a deep breath. "Tell me," he said, "What are your goals?"

"I'm trying to become a writer."

"And this is your first story?"

"Yes."

He waved a hand before my eyes. His fingernails were dirty and broken. "May I make a suggestion?"

"Please."

"If you're going to write about sports, write about the guys who either recognized the insanity of it or have been destroyed by it. Sports is a bad drug. It can give you hallucinations of greatness that enables you to get away with things most people can't. It's only when you stop playing—and never forget sports is a playground for adults acting as kids—that you find out who you really are and what you really want."

He stopped talking for a moment, choosing his words carefully, then went on:

"Life is a matter of defeat, recognition and redemption. Defeat I understood from sports, but the vacuity of sport denied me a chance for self-awareness and self-awakening. When you're a famous athlete, constantly praised and heralded, you think you can get away with anything. It was only after I met the Baba that I was able to truly see and forgive myself."

He bowed his head slightly, then:

"Trust me when I tell you even though much of your story has been written, a rewrite is always possible." A smile. An outstretch of arms. "Look at me. Anything's possible."

Joe then hugged me and whispered in my ear, "Don't lose a minute's sleep about the you that doesn't exist anymore. Accept who you are now and who you will be." He kissed my cheek. "There is no greater sin than not being true to your dreams."

We separated. Looney now had both his hands gripped to my shoulders. He gave me a long, penetrating look.

"Pursue love in all facets of your life," he said. "Love always wins. Hate always loses."

He then slapped my butt like a coach. "Now go out in the world and do good, okay?"

Chapter Eighteen

I had found my story. Now all I had to do was write it.

Never in my life had I ever been presented with a challenge for which I was so unprepared. I might as well been thinking about climbing Mt. Everest.

I had never written a story. I didn't even own a typewriter, nor did I know how to type. I had to borrow a friend's Olivetti typewriter.

I decided to start by writing long-hand. I got some white loose-leaf paper and sharpened some Dixon Ticonderoga pencils. I played no music and took no phone calls. I wanted complete silence.

The words piled up. So did the pages. After five hours of sitting and writing and mostly erasing, then standing and pacing, sitting again and standing and pacing, literally walking miles, my right leg cramping and my eyes watering, I took an aspirin to soothe my pounding headache.

Everything I wrote sounded like crap. After a while, it hit me: What the hell was I thinking—that I, with no journalistic background, could write a publishable article? Wasn't that the gift of wordsmiths and journalists, brainiacs who knew the difference between a pronoun and a pro player, poets of paragraphs, sorcerers of sentences, wizards of words so magical I assumed they possessed a God-given talent, an aura, something like the glamour that went with being a fighter pilot or a jousting knight? I spent most of the day nibbling on my pencil.

Finally, the next day, I managed fifty or sixty words designed to be the lead, a term I knew meant the beginning of a journalistic article. I read those words over and over. Reworked them. Changed a noun here and a verb there. Edited out sentences. Added sentences. Subtracted sentences.

I reread the lead. Concluded it sucked. Rewrote it again and again and again. I crumbled paper and tossed sheets and sheets of it into a wicker basket. The pages spilled out like an overflowing toilet.

Everyone in my family tried to offer support.

Peg came into the kitchen of our small apartment in North Bergen, New Jersey and looked at me with my hands on both sides of my head, staring vacantly at the typewriter.

"You okay?" she asked.

I shook my head, puffed my cheeks and expelled a long breath. "Not really."

"You look so pained…you sure you want to pursue this career?"

"I do."

"Might be easier to try something else."

"Like what?"

"I don't know. Teaching?"

"Nah. I got to take a shot at this."

"Okay. Is there anything I can do for you?"

I took another deep breath and said, "Pray."

My father called.

"How's the story coming?" he said.

"It's not."

"Keep plugging."

"Not sure I can do this."

"What happened to the old athletic confidence?"

"I misplaced it."

"You'll find it."

"Where?"

My grandfather had a different motivational technique.

"Your father tells me you're having trouble writing your story," he said when he dropped by my apartment one night.

"I am."

He took a puff of his stogie and gave me a long hard look.

"Stop the bellyaching," he said. "Start warming up and get back in the goddamn game."

"Great pep talk," I said, smirking.

"What?! You expect me to be Bishop fucking Fulton Sheen."

He spun on his heels and left, leaving behind the smoke from his stogie.

I wrote another five, six, seven leads, each one beginning with meeting Looney at the Ashram. But then it dawned on me: Looney was famous in the 60s. Readers might not remember who he was. I had to explain who he was. I finally put a clean sheet of paper into my Olivetti and began typing a new lead with two fingers. I read and reread it at least twenty times.

The article began: "On October 14, 1963, the Oklahoma football team, soundly defeated by Texas 28-7 just two days before, grimly gathered for Monday practice. The temperature was in the 80s, but the players pushed themselves through a long hard workout. All except one—All-American running back Joe Don Looney, who stubbornly refused to exert himself."

I stopped writing and thought of something Pat Jordan had told me: "Think more, write less. Make sure to take the time to properly structure the story."

I put together an outline, selecting the scenes I wanted to include and in what order. I noted the details I wanted to incorporate, and how much background I wanted to provide. I kept questioning myself. Was I using too much verbiage? Was my construction adequate? Were the sentences stripped of clutter? I was driving myself crazy.

I wrote and rewrote and wrote and re-worked for almost a month. I finally finished. I then blindly mailed it to Dick Schaap, who was then the highly regarded editor of Sport magazine and a correspondent on NBC Nightly News and The Today Show. He didn't know me from Adam.

Weeks passed. I heard nothing. Then a month. Still not a word. But then, on Thanksgiving Day, the phone rang.

My father answered it. He looked at me and said, "It's for you."

I put down the turkey breast I was about to eat.

"Who is it?" I said.

"Some guy named Sharp."

I thought a moment. "I don't know anybody by the name of…. wait, wait, wait…you mean Schaap?"

My father shrugged. "Could be."

I leaped off my chair and grabbed the phone.

"Hello," I said.

"Hello," the voice said, "This is Dick Schaap."

Loudly, I said, "Yes, Mr. Schaap. Hi."

"I love your story," he said. "Who do you write for?"

Stunned by the call, I nervously mumbled "Ah…ah…myself."

"No," he said. "I mean what newspapers or magazines have you written for?"

"It's the first story I ever wrote," I said.

The line went quiet. For a moment, I thought maybe Schaap had hung up. Except I could hear him breathing.

"Is it really the first story you ever wrote?" Schaap said. I imagined him sitting in some magnificent Manhattan office, leaning back in a big chair, feet on the desk—maybe smoking a cigar and looking out a picture window at the East River.

"Yes…yes, it is," I said, walking in tight circles.

"Well, I very much enjoyed it and I'd like to publish it."

It took all my willpower not to scream 'Alright.'

"Does a thousand dollars sound reasonable?" Schaap said.

"For what?" I said, stupidly.

"For the story, of course."

I punched the air with my left fist. "Why yes…yes, it does."

"Good," he said. "I'll be in touch."

"Thank you, thank you, thank you."

I hung up the phone. My heart turned a cartwheel. The first story I ever wrote was going to be published! Hot damn!

A week later, I was invited to the Sport office located in the Citicorp Building in midtown Manhattan. I showered, sprayed, powdered and even combed my hair. It was the first time ever I would be visiting an editorial office. I didn't want to look like a schmo.

The office was a beehive of activity. Editors rushed from cubicle to cubicle, holding copy and shouting suggestions. Typewriters clanged and clattered. Almost everyone was smoking cigarettes.

Schaap's office was big and had large windows. Pictures of athletes festooned the walls.

Silver haired and raspy voiced, Dick's desk was cluttered with stacks of manuscripts. We talked briefly about my sports background, and then he suggested I meet with his former Cornell classmate, Ross Wetzsteon, the theatre editor of New York's Village Voice.

"Ross is a great friend and a great editor," Schapp said. "I often hire him to do some freelance editing. I'd like you to work with him." The story still needed work.

I hooked up with Ross at The Voice's Greenwich Village office. Bearded and grey-haired, Ross immediately went to work with me on my story. He stressed the need for details. "Be specific," he said. "Don't just write the pool is full of stuff. Be specific. Were there broken bicycles, mangled lawn mowers, etc…" "And don't just tell me, Looney is thin. Give me an example of how thin. His body, his facial features. Details. Details. Details."

I worked with Ross an entire morning. Using his advice, I reworked the story. Over and over. I probably did three rewrites. It appeared a few months later, in the March 1977 issue of Sport. The cover featured pictures of Joe Namath, O. J. Simpson and Bobby Orr. Funny thing was, I once dreamed of being on the cover myself, but now I was just as proud to see my byline the story.

The story got rave reviews. I received a call from Sport magazine's press agent, Sy Presten. Sounding like a bull frog with asthma, he said, "Your story is great, fabulous, and even good. I'm gonna have you on every radio and television show in the country."

Briefly put, none of that happened.

I met with Schaap again. He told me how Sport was a better, more influential magazine than Sports Illustrated because its stories had greater depth, were more artistic and better written. He said Sport had a history of hiring not only the best sportswriters, but the best writers—period. He mentioned Roger Kahn, Murray Kempton, Jimmy Breslin, Grantland Rice, John Lardner, Jeff Greenfield and David Wolff. The list went on and on. (Later talents like Larry L. King, Woody Allen and Pat Conroy would be added.)

"Wouldn't you like to be connected to that illustrious group?" he said.

"Sure would," I answered, smiling widely and feeling like a kid opening his wish gift on Christmas morning.

"Good," he said, shaking my hand. "Let's think of another story for you to write."

But Schaap retired shortly after that meeting and was replaced by Berry Stainback, a former Life magazine editor and the author of Joe, You Coulda Made Us Proud, a biography of New York Yankee first baseman Joe Pepitone.

Berry—curly blonde hair, intense eyes, spatula-like nose—was considered a brilliant editor, a talent only enhanced by his long liquid lunches at Jimmy Weston' restaurant, where he went to edit copy. His nickname was the "Duke of Lunch."

At our first meeting at Weston's I asked Berry if, being a novice writer, I should apply to the Columbia University School of Journalism.

"Fuck that," Berry said, sipping a scotch. "Writing can't be taught; it can only be practiced. You go to Columbia the only thing you'll learn how to write is a good suicide note."

He then handed me a small index card. On it was a quote from Ernest Hemingway. It read: "The good and the bad, the ecstasy, the remorse and the sorrow, the people and the places. If you can get so that you can give that to people, then you are a writer."

Instead of going to Columbia, I practiced writing every day, working with the same intensity I once did on the playground with a basketball. I wrote scenes of my neighborhood, portraits of people, and snatches of conversations. I found that dribbling words on paper and scoring literary points gave me the same eureka moments as hitting a game-winning jumper.

My passion to write became such that I couldn't wait to get to my typewriter in the morning and was reluctant to leave it when the sun set. I would get so engrossed in what I was doing I would forget to return calls, pay bills, even take a shower. I was, as athletes say, in the zone.

Berry urged me to seek out my own topics and pushed me to provide unique insights and perspectives since I was an ex-athlete. I first focused mostly on stories about unknowns, people who had never received much publicity, like Jim Valvano at the start of his coaching career at Iona College or Hubie Brown when he first began his pro coaching career with the Atlanta Hawks. Later I moved on to profile better known personalities like Larry Bird, Elvin Hayes, Julius Erving and NBA Commissioner Larry O'Brien. But those weren't as much fun. Almost everyone on the planet knew about them and their personalities. It was hard finding a new angle.

I owe Berry Stainback a lot. He along with associate editor Roger Director, who would later go on to be an Emmy-winning writer and producer for such shows as Moonlighting, Hill Street Blues and NCIS, taught me to care obsessively about language and about precision.

They had very high standards and they gave me a reading list: W. C. Heinz, A. J. Liebling, John Lardner, Jimmy Cannon, Roger Kahn: a veritable Murderer's Row of 20th century sports writing talent…Every time I worked on a story, I sweated like a coal stoker over words and syntax, hoping to achieve a measure of clarity and grace, to fuse sound with meaning, to be accurate and truthful. To give context.

Both Berry and Roger loved that, unlike many of the writers they worked with, it didn't bother me to have my copy heavily edited or criticized. My response was always, "After you get criticized by Hubie Brown you can handle any castigation."

Aside from Berry and Roger, I was lucky enough to befriend and get advice from Sports Illustrated editor Jeanette Bruce ("Make sure your story has a dramatic imperative"), and New York Times columnist Dave Anderson ("Make sure your story contains lots of details.") David Halberstam, the Pulitzer Prize-winning author of The Best and The Brightest stressed the need, when doing a profile, to do a lot of research.

"When you write an article," Halberstam said, "talk to as many people as possible. You never know who will give you the revealing anecdote."

I was able to reciprocate Halberstam's kindness by giving him basketball insights. He quoted me in his profile of Pete Maravich for Inside Sports magazine—"The End of Pete Maravich, A Prisoner Of His Own Skills."

"Fact is," Halberstam said to me at the time, "Maravich finds it easier to open up to you than me because you've played big-time basketball. That will help you as a basketball writer. You have credibility. When you write your stories, always give your fresh point of view. Always write with a larger message. A greater context. Arrange your sentences with the same precision as a photographer alters a person being photographed. You want to see all the sides, all the angles, all the gestures." I never forgot his words, and was greatly honored when he acknowledged me in his book, The Breaks of the Game.

Perhaps the best tidbit he gave me was this: "if your story is good, you'll learn something. If the story is great, you'll learn something about yourself."

In the summer of 1980—I was almost thirty—I received a call from Sports Illustrated to write a six thousand word "bonus" piece on former Los Angeles Laker coach Jack McKinney. Jack was making a comeback with the Indiana Pacers after an almost deadly bicycle accident that resulted in a serious head injury. He was reluctant to speak about it. But he made it known he would work with me because I was a former player.

My story on Jack appeared in the October 20th issue of Sports Illustrated. Seattle SuperSonic guard Paul Westphal graced the cover. In the same issue I also wrote the entire scouting report for the NBA's Midwest division.

SI's managing editor, Gil Rogin—thin, white-haired, distinguished looking—loved the McKinney story so much he suggested I think about becoming a full-time NBA reporter. I said that sounded interesting, except he should know that as an ex-player I would never go into a locker room with a pack of other writers and grovel around athletes who regurgitated some banal cliches. The way I saw it, if an athlete wouldn't deal with me on my terms, one on one, away from the locker room, then forget it.

Looking stunned, Rogin leaned forward in his high-backed chair and said, "Excuse me?"

Sitting across the desk from him, I said, "I don't go into locker rooms."

He rubbed manicured fingers across his chin. "You're kidding me, right?"

"No."

I don't think Rogin liked my answer. He looked at me the way King Arthur might have eyeballed a knight who turned down an opportunity to sit at the Round Table.

After turning down SI, I started getting assignments from other magazines, maybe fifty altogether, including GQ, Esquire, People, TV Guide and The New York Times.

Of all the stories I wrote, the one I enjoyed most was a profile for Philly Sport on Raymond Lewis—a basketball player whose name had been lost in the smithereens of time.

It began: "Wasted talent in sports—especially pro basketball— is an old and sad story. How good could Marvin Barnes have been had he not self-destructed? And Michael Ray Richardson could have rewritten the NBA record book—don't you think?—if it hadn't been for the nose candy.

Yet of all the National Basketball tragedies, the saddest and currently the strangest, is that of Raymond Lewis."

The article went on to describe how Lewis had been a cult figure at Verbum Dei High School in Los Angeles and a legend at California State-LA, where in his freshman season, 1972, he led the country in scoring with a 38.9 average. As a sophomore, he scored 73 points in one game. Said New York Knick scout, Dick

McGuire: "Raymond Lewis has more raw basketball talent than any college player in the country—and that includes Bill Walton."

At the end of his sophomore year, Lewis decided to leave college, declaring himself eligible for the 1973 NBA draft under the hardship rule, which at the time allowed college players to join the NBA early if they could prove "financial hardship." The Philadelphia 76ers, after naming Doug Collins as the team's (and league's) number-one pick, selected Lewis with the last pick of the first round. He was just 20 years old, making him, at the time, the youngest player ever to be drafted by the NBA. Most NBA coaches predicted that Lewis would become a legend.

But Lewis never became a legend. He didn't even take a shot or play a minute in the NBA. When he didn't get offered the contract he expected, he ultimately walked away from pro basketball, disappearing into the mist, never to return. Over the years, ugly rumors about him periodically surfaced—He was a junkie, a pusher, a pimp. There were even reports that he was dead.

He wasn't. I found him living in Watts in a small house where faded and torn yellow curtains covered the windows and doors. Inside, the rugs were frayed, the walls bare. The place smelled like cat urine.

The day I visited him, I knocked on the front door and he opened it, secured by a chain. He peered out with one eye, as if worried about a bogeyman. I introduced myself. He opened the door.

He was stocky, around 6'1", with a bloated face and drooping eyelids. I would have guessed him to be in his late 50s, but was still shy of 40.

He had been married to his wife, Sandra, for sixteen years. They had two children, Kamila and Rashad. Although Lewis seemed sad, he clearly loved his family. Laughter was a presence in the house. As was discipline. Twice, Lewis told his kids not to interrupt him when he was speaking. When I picked up his daughter's doll and handed it to her he reminded her to say "thank you."

Lewis told me he had worked a number of jobs. Clerk. Messenger. Handyman. But was "still taking it to the kids on the courts" where he was revered as a legend.

He said he wasn't a druggie or a boozer, but was unemployed at the moment. His goal, he said, was to get another chance at the NBA. Quite the delusion.

As crazy as it sounds, I admired Ray. He stuck to his guns. He was willing to face the consequences. His life, given the circumstances, turned out okay.

The article, which was included in the Sporting News Best Sports Stories 1990 anthology, was called "A Glimpse of the Phantom."

Sadly, Raymond Lewis later suffered a stroke and died of complications following the amputation of a leg before reaching his fiftieth birthday.

At that point in my career I was thinking about not writing about sports anymore—I was beginning to find it boring—but I kept getting unusual assignments.

David Hirshey, an editor at the New York Daily News, who would later become a highly respected editor at Esquire magazine and HarperCollins book publishers, called and said, "Got a great story for you, playing for the Washington Generals against the Harlem Globetrotters." The Generals served as the Globetrotters perennial opponent, scripted to lose.

I met with the Generals long-time owner, Louis "Red" Klotz, a small, energetic man with balding red hair who was also the team's point guard, best known for his ability to make long set shots.

"Here's the deal," he said. "All you gotta do is stand around and let the players do their thing while you act surprised. Dumbfounded."

"Dumbfounded, huh?" I said. "I can do dumbfounded."

"Good," he said. "Just don't do anything to embarrass the players."

Okay, I said. Deal.

Days later, I was in a locker room at the Westchester County Center in White Plains, New York.

I was so embarrassed by wearing the General's uniform that when I left the locker room and a kid asked me for an autograph as I headed into the arena, I signed it "Jim Nasium."

The teams took the court. The Trotters were led by Meadowlark Lemon, a clown prince who wowed the crowd with his silly antics, and Marques Haynes and Curly Neal who dazzled them with their ball handling wizardry.

Just before the opening tap, Lemon said to me: "Ain't gonna make you look too silly, son."

"Good to know," I said.

The thing is, he did make me look like a fool and I played along, letting him put the ball over my head with two hands, then allowing him to make me turn around just as he brought the ball back. Or he rolled the ball through my legs, spun around me and then dunked. With a wide smile and hopping around as if his feet were on fire, he gestured to the fans to give him some applause.

I had had enough. Next time, he went in for a layup, I

instinctively blocked his shot. The crowd went wild. Lemon's glared at me.

"What'd you doin', boy?" he said.

"Sorry," I said.

"Sorry, shit," he said. He looked over at Klotz, who immediately called a time-out.

"Are you crazy?" Klotz roared, as I approached the bench.

"It's been suggested."

"Didn't I tell you not to embarrass anyone? Didn't!? Didn't I?"

"You did," I said. "I have a bad memory."

"I can't let you back in the game."

I snapped my fingers. "Damnit," I said, feigning anger.

I took a seat on the bench and looked up into the crowd and saw my father. He was holding his nose with his thumb and index finger. I mimicked the gesture.

A few days later I wrote the story and decided that would be the last time I ever dressed in a basketball uniform.

But it wasn't the last time I played basketball. The last time came when Sport sent me to Boston to do a story on Martina Navratilova. At the time, she was playing for the Boston Lobsters in the World Team Tennis League.

Before I got to Boston's Walter Brown Tennis Arena, I checked in with a number of local reporters. They all told me Martina was a tough interview.

"She hates sports writers," one said. "Good luck."

He was right. For two days, she refused to speak to me. I said fuck it. If she doesn't want to cooperate, I'm going home.

But on my last day, I saw Martina doing a leg stretch. I walked over and said, "You're not doing it right."

She snorted. "How would you know?"

"I played sports."

She smirked.

"I played basketball at Duke."

Her eyebrows rose.

"I love basketball," she said. "I often shoot around on the court near my apartment."

I showed her how to do the exercise correctly, then said, "How about I challenge you to a game of one-on-one?"

She looked at me as if I suggested playing tennis with a snowshoe. Then: "Okay, big boy, you're on."

The basketball court was located behind her luxury high-rise in downtown Boston.

"Your ball," I said, taking the court.

Martina, wearing a satiny sweat suit, began dribbling the ball with her back to the basket. She maneuvered methodically and forcefully—left-right-left-right. I tried to impede her progress by putting a hand on her hip and pushing her back. But she was strong and kept advancing. I planted my feet and bumped her with my chest. No reaction. Then quickly she swung to her right, turned and tossed up a jumper. Her form was awkward; the shot was released from her hip. The ball hit the front of the rim and I was about to grab it when Martina charged in, pushed me out of bounds, retrieved the ball and scored an easy lay-up. An impish smile flickered briefly across her face. "I told you I was competitive."

My ball. Martina handed it to me and stepped inches away from my chest. She was, as basketball coaches would say, "bellying-up"—playing skin-tight D. I faked and dribbled to my right.

Martina crouched, bouncing on the balls of her feet, and made a swipe for a steal. I reverse dribbled, headed toward the basket, and went skyward. Martina recovered and, arms outstretched, leaped up to challenge my shot. Fortunately, thanks to my height advantage, I barely escaped having my shot rejected into nearby Framingham.

The lead fluctuated back and forth. Martina, who less than an hour earlier had undergone a grueling workout, was inexhaustible, hustling for every rebound and loose ball.

The game was to seven. With me in the lead at 6-5 I stopped and fired up a 20-footer. Swish. Game over.

"Damn," said Martina. "I wish I had time for a rematch, but I gotta go."

But before she left, we talked. She told me about growing up in Czechoslovakia. She said she wasn't a natural athlete and didn't possess the speed and quickness of her rival Chris Evert, who glided from baseline-to baseline.

So Martina adjusted her game and became a unique talent in women's tennis—a spectacular serve-and-volleyer who just didn't beat opponents. She laid waste to them.

"People often ask me how I developed my game," she said, wiping her face with a towel. "The answer's easy: hard work."

Aside from her determination, she had to overcome obstacles like leaving her country, abandoning her culture, adapting to a different society and learning a new language. And if that wasn't enough she had to deal with nasty press coverage about her weight and speculation over her sexuality.

"All things considered," she said, leaving the court, "I've done pretty well for myself."

"I'd say better than well."

She thought a moment. "You know," she said, smiling, "You're right."

I had my story.

Chapter Nineteen

In 1980, while writing the scouting report on the Midwest Division of the NBA for Sports Illustrated, I was at a Houston Rockets preseason exhibition game when I ran into the team's head coach, Del Harris, who had been my coach with the Iberia Superstars.

"Whaddya doing here?" Del said in a nasally voice similar to the old cartoon character Mr. Magoo.

"I'm writing for Sports Illustrated."

"Really?!"

"Yep. I'm doing the Midwest previews."

We stood behind the scorer's table, talking about the teams I had scouted. On the court some of the Rocket players—Moses Malone, Calvin Murphy, Rudy Tomjanovich, Tom Henderson— were warming up and leisurely shooting jumpers from around the perimeter.

"I always knew you'd wind up doing something outside of basketball," he said.

"Me too. Except I never thought I'd be writing about sports."

"You like writing?"

"Love it."

Just then a tall, thin balding guy approached us. He and Del exchanged pleasantries.

Pointing to me, Del said, "You know Rich O'Connor?"

The guy stared at me for a long moment. "I think we played against each other in the Greensboro Coliseum when I was at Northwestern. You played for Duke, right?"

"Right."

He extended his hand. "Rick Sund." A beat. "Think you beat us."

"We did."

"And you had a good game, if I recall."

I nodded. I had scored sixteen points.

"Rick's the general manager of the Dallas Mavericks," Del said. It was Mav's first season in the NBA.

I nodded.

"Have you seen the Spurs play?" Rick asked Del.

"No," Del said. "But Rich has."

Rick looked at me.

"Mind telling me about them?"

"No problem."

We went into the stands and talked while watching the game: Calvin Murphy hitting long jumpers, Moses Malone grabbing rebounds and Rudy Tomjanovich swatting shots.

I gave Rick a thorough analysis not only of various NBA teams but the strengths and weaknesses of individual players.

I told him I thought the Spurs looked strong. Forward George Gervin was almost unstoppable hitting mid-range jumpers, and guards James Silas and Mike Gale had an arsenal of offensive moves and no problem penetrating the lane. I told him I thought Kansas City Kings forward Reggie King had abundant skills but was often misplaced and their swingman Scott Wedman was a radar perimeter shooter. I noted that the Denver Nuggets center, Dan Issel, had lost a lot of weight in the off season and was more mobile, while his teammate, guard David Thompson, seemed fully recovered from the strained ligaments in his left foot and was skying above all defenders. Lastly, I said the Utah Jazz looked hapless, even though rookie Darrell Griffith from Louisville might make a good compliment to last season's leading scorer, small forward Adrian Dantley (28.0ppg).

Rick thanked me for the analysis and a few days later he called and we further discussed the teams in more detail. A week after that, he phoned again and offered me a job as the Maverick's East Coast college scout.

I was happy pursuing my writing career and I wasn't sure I wanted the job. But Rick convinced me it wouldn't be too time consuming, since most of the games I'd scout would be in the Big East Conference and the Atlantic Coast Conference so there wouldn't be much long distance traveling until the NCAA tournament. In the meantime, I could still write.

The thought of getting paid to watch college basketball games was, in the end, too good to pass up. I called Rick and accepted the position. I was paid fifty to a hundred dollars a game.

I scouted around fifty games a year, using a Maverick's scouting sheet, grading players in twenty categories, everything from their speed and quickness to rebounding, passing ability and shooting.

When I scouted St. John's, for example, I wrote how guard Mark Jackson was not a great shooter and a step slow, but he could still penetrate the lane and had excellent court vision. Guard Chris Mullin was also a step slow, weak on defense and couldn't really create his own shots, but he had good court sense; he knew how to use screens to get open and from three-point range his release was lightning fast. Center Bill Wennington, a seven-footer, wasn't that talented but he worked hard and would probably be a decent back-up.

What I enjoyed most, though, was creating a complete player profile. In a way, it was similar to the profiles I was writing for magazines, insofar as I had to observe a player's attitude on the court. Was he hustling? Was he selfish? Did he want the ball at crunch time? And just as I reported a story before writing, before creating a player profile I interviewed athletic directors, coaches, students, even fans about the player. I talked with anyone who I thought might be able to provide me with any insight.

I was interested in the player's background, his family. Did he have one or two parents? Was his home life stable? What were his friends like? Druggies? Preppies? What was his attitude? His goals? Did he get along with his coach? His teammates? Was being a pro his number one priority? Or was it about making money? I was, of course, not allowed to speak with the players themselves because of NBA rules.

Thanks to Sund, a totally dedicated and knowledgeable GM, I got to know Jerry West. He and Rick were best buddies, and the three of us often scouted games together.

I reminded Jerry how I'd once played one-on-one with him at the Duke basketball clinic and he had told me I might someday be "a helluva pro." He said he didn't remember the episode, but he was sure he had won the game—"Easily." And he was right.

Jerry, who played, coached and managed several NBA teams, most notably the Los Angeles Lakers was—and still is—as obsessed with basketball as Picasso was with painting or Mozart was with music. It's pretty much all he talked about.

In all my years working in the NBA—fifteen with the Mavericks, two with the Detroit Pistons—I never came across anyone in the NBA who worked harder or was more dedicated than Jerry.

Once, Rick, Jerry and I were scheduled to scout seven-foot center Rik Smits, who was then playing for Marist College in Poughkeepsie, New York. Along with a dozen other scouts, we were staying at the Grand Hyatt in New York City. The weather was bad—rainy and windy. Television reports indicated that roads were slippery. Virtually every other scout chose to stay at the hotel. But not Jerry. He was adamant about seeing Smits play.

So off we went, me driving.

By the time we got out of Manhattan and onto the narrow, winding Taconic State Parkway, visibility was so bad my chin was damn near resting on the top of the steering wheel.

Occasionally, we hit slick spots that made the car swerve to the left or right. Once, I thought we were going to slide into an embankment.

I was nervous. So was Rick. But Jerry just sat calmly, handed folded in his lap, as if enjoying a sunny, afternoon drive. No wonder they called him "Mr. Clutch." He was grace under pressure. The two-hour drive took nearly twice as long as usual.

As I looked over at Jerry I wondered what I would have become had I stayed with basketball. Would I have been as single-minded and as obsessed with it as him? Would I have made it to the NBA? Would I have been a star? Would I have become a coach and thus consumed with basketball at the expense of everything else?

The answer, I believe, is probably yes. But not once since quitting Duke did I regret the decision.

I'm glad I took the road not taken, glad I fell in love with the sound of words and the rapturous sensation I got when turning them into lucid form. I'm glad, too, that I took my grandfather's advice and embarked on a lifelong safari in search of purpose and fulfillment outside of basketball.

Not a day goes by that I don't thank my lucky stars for hanging up my sneakers and picking up knowledge and having experiences that I never would have had had I stayed focused on basketball, experiences that made me more aware not only of the world but also about life.

And yet, here I was working for the Mavericks. I was, in a sense, back in basketball, but now I was strictly on the outside looking in.

While working for the Mavericks I met Boston Celtics great Dave Cowens, an undersized center who played 11 seasons in the NBA, earning an MVP award and leading the Celtics to two NBA championships. Like West, he was a player I admired for his talent, hustle and tenaciousness. During his pro career he probably had more floor burns than any player in NBA history.

Beyond his athletic ability, I respected Cowen's lifestyle. He was his own man, a non-conformist. Instead of living in a big home in Boston, he lived over a toy store. Instead of buying expensive clothes, he wore plaid shirts and corduroy pants. Instead of purchasing a luxury car, he drove a small yellow Jeep. Instead of signing autographs, he offered fans a lecture on the stupidity of adoring athletes. After the Celtics won the Championship in 1974, Cowens celebrated that night by sleeping on a park bench in Boston Common. A few years later, he took a leave of absence in mid-season. Bob Ryan, the well-respected sportswriter for The Boston Globe, called Cowens "the most interesting character I ever met in sports."

I first met Cowens in Portsmouth, Virginia, at a post-season college workout for draftable NBA players. The games were attended by every NBA scout, general manager and many assistant coaches.

Cowens had retired and was newly elected as the Chairman of the Sports Museum of New England. Somebody told him I might be a good person to talk with. They probably thought Cowens and I, being non-conformists, had much in common. He called and we had lunch.

Cowens spoke about his goals for the museum and his years with the Celtics. I asked him why he quit the team just after the start of the 1976 season, a year after Boston had won the NBA championship and he had averaged 18 points and 15 rebounds a game.

"I just got burnt out," he said. "I didn't feel right about taking a paycheck when my heart wasn't into the game." He shook his head. "To this day, I still don't understand why people made such a big deal about it. I was just a guy who quit his job."

"But you were a superstar," I said, knowing he walked away from a $250,000 a year contract which back then was a big, big deal.

"That's the thing," he said. "I never saw myself as a superstar. I was just an everyday normal guy who happened to play basketball."

"What did your teammates think about you quitting?"

"Most were fine with it. A few thought I was crazy."

"Some thought you even crazier when you started driving a cab."

He smirked. "That was only for a few days," he said. "Some writers exaggerated it."

"What'd you do after quitting?"

"Whatever I wanted. I read. Traveled. Went back to Newport (Kentucky) and harvested Christmas trees. Fished and hunted and walked around the family farm."

"But you came back to basketball?"

"When I felt my heart was rejuvenated." He played a few more successful years with the Celtics and ended his career with the Milwaukee Bucks.

I told him how I quit Duke basketball. He said he understood completely. "You were your own man," he said. "I admire that." He ran his fingers through his red hair. "Don't ever regret what you did. Just because you've lost your motivation it doesn't mean you've lost your self-respect."

He then asked me what I was doing for a living. I said writing for a variety of magazines.

"A far cry from basketball," he said.

"Ain't that the truth?"

"And probably more rewarding."

I smiled. "Book it."

A few days after meeting with Cowens, I was at another pro tryout camp, I believe in Phoenix, Arizona. I saw Bucky Waters.

He was working then as an analyst for ESPN and Madison Square Garden Network and was preparing a segment on the upcoming NBA draft. We hadn't spoken since I had quit Duke.

I wasn't sure how I felt about seeing him. Should I ignore him? Would he ignore me? I knew it was inevitable we would bump into each other—and, soon enough—we did. I was waiting for the hotel elevator and when the door opened, Bucky was coming out just as I was about to step in.

We both stopped and grinned at each other.

Bucky still looked the same. Trim but with slightly longer hair.

"I hear you scout for the Mavericks?" he said, matter-of-factly.

"Yeah." I said, shifting my weight from one foot to another.

Bucky nodded.

"I watch you on television," I said. "You do a great job."

"Thanks."

We chatted for a while. And the more we talked the more I liked him. He wasn't bitter. He wasn't sarcastic. He was nice and easy-going, a good guy—very different than the coach I once knew. Then again, I was very different from the player he once knew.

We didn't talk about the Duke days. I guess we both figured the past was past.

"It was good seeing you," Bucky said. "Stay well."

I smiled. "You, too."

We shook hands and went our separate ways.

I left the hotel and went outside. It was warm and sunny, probably ninety degrees. I took a seat on a bench with a missing slat. I thought how I had been an immature fool to question some of Bucky's rules about going to class and studying. I felt even worse about quitting the team in mid-season. It had been a selfish, cowardly act, just as Bucky had said many years before.

I shake my head now at my younger self, as most of us do.

Not that I regretted my decision to leave Duke but, rather, my decision to do it the way I did.

Because of that immature decision, I've since learned to think things through more thoroughly before acting, to anticipate the consequences of those actions, and to battle against the corrosive sense of thinking I'm always right.

I think much of my learning and personal growth came through my experiences of becoming a writer and listening to other athletes who had to cope with success and failure. Through them, I discovered there's dignity and humanity in loss—courage in trying.

Trying—giving it all you've got—is what really matters. Winning is nice, but losing teaches you more. It teaches you about disappointment and disillusionment. It forces you to contemplate and reformulate your strategies and methodologies.

If I've learned anything from being an athlete and being around athletes it is that there is no teacher, no blueprint, no guideline and no general reference map that can put you on your path in life.

As I sat in the Arizona sun, I realized I my path in life occurred the minute I drove off the Duke campus and started spending time in New York City, where I had experienced complete freedom from basketball, a sabbatical, if you will, that made me aware that there was more to life than just running up and down a hardwood court.

Looking back, I'm convinced that my time in Manhattan was a defining period in my life. It was the first time I read, studied, observed and met different people living by different rules. Prior to that, I never imagined that such excitement, such variety could be mine.

Equally significant was the time I spent in Europe, discovering new cultures, new languages and new places, sidewalks burning with music and bookstores, restaurants and café, museums, parks, beaches, art galleries and historical buildings, all the experiences fused into one big, glorious joy ride, a ride that filled my mind with fresh expressions and my notebook with fresh sentences.

The irony is that when I came back from Europe I thought I was finished with sports. But now here I was, writing about athletes and scouting for the Mavericks.

Yet the work did not define me. I was no longer "the athlete." Basketball was still a part of my life, but it wasn't my entire life.

I'll acknowledge that the thought of basketball does, at times, still beat inside me like a second heart, but it's not what sustains me or gives me satisfaction, inspiration or motivation.

What motivates me now is the ability to confront and overcome new challenges. But what I didn't know then is that in the near future I would be ambushed by a challenge that would alter the entire direction of my life.

Chapter Twenty

In 1980, the same year I wrote the McKinney story for Sports Illustrated and started working for the Dallas Mavericks, a friend, Lenny Sherman of Royale Sporting Goods in Brooklyn, referred me to a woman named Helen Cohen who, he said, was starting a magazine.

I met Helen in a small Manhattan office across from the Chrysler Building between 42nd and 43rd Streets on Lexington Avenue. Short with dark hair, large glasses and abundant energy, Helen explained her idea: a magazine called SportsWise New York. It would focus solely on amateur sports. It would have profiles and humor stories and a calendar of events, along with service pieces such as the best local ski resorts, best tennis teachers, best sporting goods stores, best running tracks.

I asked Helen about her background. She was an honor student at NYU. After graduation, she sold advertising for a number of magazines, where she had been highly successful. And even though she wasn't a sports fan, she was using her own money to fund this venture. Why? Because she was convinced it had great potential.

After discussing our backgrounds, Helen said, "What I need is an editor."

"But I'm a writer."

"Doesn't matter. You know sports and you know writing."

I had totally lost interest in writing about professional athletes, who were now protected by agents and managers and team personnel, making it difficult to get a genuine interview. I detested the whole rigamarole. So the idea of editing a magazine totally dedicated to the so-called weekend athlete sounded intriguing.

"Do you have a staff?" I said.

"A few people."

"A few?"

"Three."

"How's your editorial budget?"

"Limited."

I scratched my chin. Then asked about overall funding and the salary. It was less than fifteen thousand.

"Let me think about it," I said.

I left the office and discussed the offer with Peg. I made it clear that, even with her working, the money from SportsWise would not provide for much caviar and champagne.

"Is it something you'd like to try?" she said.

"I think so. It would be different, editing a magazine."

"So? What's stopping you?"

I gave her a big hug. "I guess, with your support, nothing."

I called Helen and said, "I'm in."

My goal from the get-go was to publish a glossy magazine that came out six times a year. I was obsessed with recruiting top-notch editorial talent, just like Duke recruited top athletic talent. I hired a group of young, enthusiastic editors and art directors—kids right out of college—most of whom later went on to great careers: Maryjane Fahey designed award-winning covers for Cosmopolitan and Women's Health; Andrea Welch became an editor at The New Yorker; Michael Fleming, a Broadway theatre critic; and Bob Condor, a columnist for the Chicago Tribune and a senior producer for NHL Seattle.

We also hired a very savvy and supremely brilliant kid from Washington University in St. Louis, Brad Siegel. Brad headed our marketing department, and many years later became the president of TNT, TBS, TCM and Cartoon Network.

I guess I was as good scouting magazine talent as I was scouting players for the Mavericks.

We published the best freelance talents we could afford like Dave Anderson of The New York Times and Jackie MacMullan of The Boston Globe. We even published a story by Pulitzer Prize winning author James Michener. As illustrators, I hired Arnold Roth and LeRoy Neiman.

Neiman was a pisser. Famed for his brilliantly colorful, expressional paintings of athletes and musicians, models and movie stars, mostly for Playboy, he lived in a magnificent apartment with high ceilings and big windows over the Café des Artiste, right off Central Park at 1 W.67th Street.

One day I went to visit him with my art director, Mary Jane Fahey. We wanted to hire LeRoy to do a cover illustration.

LeRoy—thick black hair, curled-up black mustache—was smoking a long, thin cigar and standing before his easel wearing a smock dotted with red and yellow and blue splotches. The walls were covered with LeRoy's works. A half-naked woman sat provocatively on a three-legged stool.

"Hey," he said, waving cheerfully. "Where we going to lunch?"

"How's Giordano's?"

He threw up his hands.

"Perfect," he said. "Absolutely perfect. Love Italian food."

He looked at the model and said, "You may go, my pretty."

The girl hopped off the stool and gave LeRoy a big smooch.

LeRoy smiled at us and said, "How great is it to be me?"

He then excused himself and disappeared into another room. He returned minutes later wearing a pink shirt and white pants.

Twirling around, he said, "I'm ready."

We took a cab to Giordano's, a hidden gem on 39th Street off Ninth Avenue, at the entrance to the Lincoln Tunnel. It was the kind of place that if you didn't know it you probably couldn't find it.

Entering, LeRoy looked around and enthused, "Love it, love it, simply love it. So cozy. So Italy."

We took a corner table and ordered lunch. Mary Jane and I talked to LeRoy about doing a cover illustration of a skier.

He said he wanted five grand. Almost our entire art budget for the year.

I glanced at Mary Jane. She raised her eyebrows and pursued her lips.

"We don't have that kind of money," I said.

"What kind of money do you have?" LeRoy said, lighting a cigar.

"A thousand or so."

He twisted the ends of his mustache.

"Hmmm," he intoned.

He puffed on his cigar, and then tapped some ash into an

ashtray.

"Hmmm," he repeated.

Mary Jane and I looked at each other and grinned.

"Okay," he finally said, "I like you guys. You pick good restaurants." A gigantic smile. "I accept."

We ordered lunch. Between courses LeRoy took out his sketch pad and drew the waiter, an Italian kid who looked like a young Al Pacino.

At the end of lunch when the waiter started clearing the dishes he stopped when he saw Neiman's sketch.

"Wow!" he shrieked. "Wow! That's me?!"

"Yes, it is," LeRoy said.

"Can I have it?."

"Of course you can," LeRoy said, smiling. "For a few thousand dollars."

The waiter did a double take. Neiman kept the sketch.

Neiman did the illustration of the skier and after the issue was published we threw a party in his honor. It was held in a large penthouse on Sutton Place. Arthur Ashe attended. He was elegantly attired: blue blazer, crisp white shirt. We talked about his work in South Africa, where in 1973 he had become the first Black athlete to compete. But he refused to play before a segregated crowd, which forced the South African government to allow racially-mixed crowds at the South African Open, a significant act in a nation under the heel of apartheid. It was, he said, one of his proudest, if not the proudest moment, of his life.

"Just being on the court there made me feel…well, like a worthy human being," he said.

"You ever miss playing tennis?" I said.

"I still play."

"I mean professionally."

"Yes and no," he said. "But I'm busier than ever." At the time, he was writing for TIME and The Washington Post, while commentating for ABC Sports and captaining the U.S. Davis Cup team.

"Busier...and better?" I said.

He chuckled. "Much better. I have a great wife. I travel a lot. I've learned and experienced much. I hope to experience much more." He winked. "I'm sure you feel the same."

"I'm working on it."

"Don't stop. Don't ever stop experiencing people and places. It helps you grow as a person."

Not long after the Ashe party, I went to Lime Rock, Connecticut for SportsWise to interview actor Paul Newman. In between films, he drove racing cars and did very well, even finishing second in the prestigious 24-hour race in Le Mans.

Hesitantly, almost shyly, he talked about his Newman's Own food company which gave its profits to charity, and his Hole in the Wall Gang Camp which assisted children with serious illnesses.

Mostly, though, we spoke about how he lived his life.

"I'd be disappointed in myself," he said, dressed in a race car driver's outfit and holding a can of Budweiser, "if all I did was make movies. I think all of us should try different things. I mean, who wants to just walk a straight path? There's no challenge in that."

He grinned. His teeth shone. His baby blues blazed. "Thing is," he said, "the world is full of possibilities—things to learn, things to try, books to read, people to meet, people to help, skills to master, families to love."

"You seem to have accomplished it all."

He grinned. "I'm still working on it."

Taking a sip of beer he said, "You said you were an athlete. Ever think about racing cars?"

"Never," I said.

"Why not?"

I shrugged.

Paul gave me his best Butch Cassidy/Henry Gondorff/Eddie Felson laugh.

"You should try it sometime," he said. "It's liberating."

I thought of my grandfather who always pushed me to take risks.

"Maybe I will," I said.

"Good," Newman said. He then lifted his Budweiser and tossed it away. After a moment, he said: "Loved it."

"Thanks," I said.

"Oh, I'm sorry," he said, "You thought I meant the interview. No, no. I was talking about the beer."

He then laughed uproariously.

I drove that night through Connecticut and New York going sixty-five mph. When I got to the New Jersey Turnpike, I thought of Newman and I opened the window and put the pedal to the metal, the speedometer needle quivering between 100 and 105 mph. A cool breeze blew into my face. I felt loose, exhilarated.

I punched the air and yelled "Yes!"

I'll never, to be sure, become a race car driver, but that's not the point. The point is, thanks to Newman, I expanded my capacity for doing something previously unfathomable to me.

A few weeks after the Newman interview, Helen and I decided to create events to generate publicity for the magazine. In short order, we sponsored roller derbies, ski races, tennis tournaments and golf outings. But our biggest splash came in 1982 when we co-sponsored (along with Manufacturers Hanover Bank) the first Mighty Hamptons Triathlon at Long Beach in Sag Harbor on Long Island. It was a 1.5-mile swim, a 25-mile bike race and a 10-mile run. We were able to entice the most elite triathletes to participate— Dave Scott. Dave Horning. Stu Mittleman. And Allison Roe of New Zealand, who had previously won both the Boston and New York Marathons.

Helen thought I should participate and maybe even write about it. I wasn't too sure I wanted to put myself through such a vigorous training program. Sure, I was only in my thirties and still in decent shape, but participating in a triathlon seemed a bit crazy.

But Helen was adamant I should do it. (She could be quite convincing.) So I reluctantly agreed to complete—for the sole reason that it presented a challenge.

First thing I did was contact Jane Katz, a former Olympic long-distance swimmer. Jane was feisty and spirited, short in stature but tall with confidence, "The hardest thing about a triathlon is getting through the swim," she said. "Once you're out of the water all you need are your legs. The trick is not to use your legs while swimming."

She brought me to a public pool in the Bronx. I jumped in and did a few laps.

"How'd I do?" I said.

She raised her eyebrows. "You need help."

Jane demonstrated how to do the freestyle, butterfly, backstroke, breaststroke, sidestroke and the doggie paddle.

"Let's begin with the breaststroke," she said.

I started swimming, kicking off one end and returning to the other.

Jane grabbed me by the hair.

"Get out?" she ordered.

"I do something wrong?"

"Sure did."

She sat me on a chair and tied my feet together with rope.

I looked at her strangely. "What's this?"

"First, you were using your legs too much. Second, there's no ends to kick off of when you're swimming in the Sound. Now get back in there and don't let me see you kick off again."

Using every stroke she taught me I swam for hours. Afterwards, my arms were so sore I had to take Tylenol to relieve the pain.

After work, I went to Central Park and ran around the reservoir for an hour, then got on my bike and rode a few miles. I trained so hard I injured my right hip and developed knee tendinitis. Most nights I was in bed by nine o'clock.

There were times during training when, with my legs and lungs burning, I wondered if I was crazy putting myself through this exhausting ordeal.

I got to Long Island a few days before the event and stayed at the host hotel with the top triathletes.

One morning I ran into Dave Scott. Dave was the former swim coach at University of California, Davis and winner of the 1980 Iron Man triathlon in Hawaii and the United States Triathlon Championship earlier that year.

Twenty-eight years old and standing six-three and one hundred and sixty-three pounds, Dave asked me if I wanted to go for a quick run.

"Sure," I said. "How far?"

"Not far. Maybe fifteen miles."

"I think I'll pass."

Before running Dave made breakfast, putting fruits and vegetables and God only knows what other healthy stuff in a blender. I had three Entenmann's donuts and four cups of coffee.

Race day was sunny and hot. A small crowd, mostly family and friends, gathered at Noyack Bay where five hundred, mostly supremely fit athletes, both men and women, dressed in tight colorful bathing suits and white swim caps were stretching and hopping up and down while shaking their arms as if they had St. Vitus Dance.

I, on the other hand, wore a baggy pair of Tommy Bahama Hawaiian style trunks and no swim cap.

After some quick stretching exercises, I walked to the starting line. I stood next to a guy who was thinner than a swizzle stick. "I plan on winning this race," he said. "How about you?"

"I'm just hoping to survive it."

A gun sounded. Me and four hundred and ninety-nine other swimmers dove into the Long Island Sound. I immediately felt like I was swimming in a giant bowl of oatmeal. Moving slowly, I soon noticed a jellyfish the size of an apple, its tentacles splayed out around itself.

Jane Katz had warned me about jellyfish. She suggested I slather myself with Vaseline so they'd slide off me. It didn't work. The jellyfish stung me. It was like a bee sting.

Using every stroke Jane taught me, I gasped and gurgled. Swimmers sped past me with the smoothness and speed of Mark Spitz. At one point I looked up and saw so many swimmers ahead of me, I felt like a turtle amongst dolphins. But my competitive instincts kicked in and I increased my speed, using only overhead strokes.

When I got out of the water, I was huffing and puffing and covered with jellyfish bites. I got on my bike and started pedaling. Twelve miles into the ride, I experienced a cramp in my right calf so bad I had to dismount and stretch. The stretching provided little relief.

After finishing the bike portion of the race, I began running; well, I wouldn't actually call it running. It was more like ambling, the movement of a ninety-year old with acute arthritis. Once, I had to stop and take a deep breath. When I resumed running, I tripped over a small pothole, shredding my right knee. Blood leaked down my calf.

As I neared the finish line, my ability to pump oxygen was maxed out. I had to pep-talk myself: "You can do it, you can do it." I knew the decision to stop was less a bodily failure and more a conscious choice. My choice was to keep going.

I came into the back stretch, moving like a marionette whose strings had been broken. The route was lined with people cheering, both for the whippets and plodders. A few spectators offered slices of oranges. Others held out cups of water. I was too tired to reach for one.

Somehow I caught a second wind and despite my ragged breath, my throbbing head and my achy muscles, I crumbled to the finish line, falling to the ground.

I never found out in what place I finished. I was told it was somewhere in the middle. Dave Scott, as expected, won the event, finishing in two hours, twenty-six minutes and nine seconds.

Helen gave me bottles of Gatorade. "You need to hydrate," she said. I gulped down three bottles within thirty seconds.

Shortly thereafter, I drove back to Manhattan, feeling dead tired, but satisfied that I pushed my boundaries and finished the event. In one piece.

A few years after the triathlon, we decided to expand SportsWise into Boston and Philadelphia. It was a costly proposition. We needed an investor. Fast.

Through a number of contacts, we met with Andy McKelvey at his New York office on 1633 Broadway between 50th and 51st Streets. An entrepreneur who founded Telephone Marketing Programs, the world's largest seller of Yellow Pages advertising, Andy years later would create Monster.com and become a gazillionaire.

Andy was in his forties. He had a thin, narrow face and short gray hair. Leaning back in his high-back leather chair, he listened to our pitch about expanding SportsWise.

He thought the magazine had great potential and he agreed to invest. (He wasn't one to do much market analysis; he made decisions quickly. I don't think it took him more than a few hours to give us the go ahead.)

Andy was a very serious dude. He probably had only laughed a few times in his life. The only hobbies he had, other than creating businesses and making money, was collecting planes, yachts and women. He married six times.

Yet for all his energy and aggressiveness in business, he was reserved and somewhat shy. Once he started a series of meet-and-greet parties for wealthy people. Like Gatsby, he didn't even show up.

One night he asked me if I could get him into Studio 54, the nightclub which at the time was the hottest spot in Manhattan. Thanks to a friend who was friends with a doorman, I got us in.

The place was huge. It had high ceilings and spinning overhead lights and disco music so loud it boomed, pounded and exploded. People were dancing, prancing, strutting and posturing. There were guys in leather vests and aviator shades. Construction boots and cowboy hats. Girls in tank tops and miniskirts. Spiked heels and push-up bras. Everyone cruised the place like battleships on patrol. The whole scene blew Andy away.

He was awed by the throng of gorgeous girls. I introduced him to a striking strawberry blonde editor I knew from working at Sport. She had the slim body and chiseled features of an Alvin Ailey dancer. She looked at Andy and said hello. He was so tongue-tied, he stuttered.

I couldn't understand it. Here was a multi-millionaire who had probably more money than possibly anyone in the room yet he cowered like a bashful child.

"Let's leave," he said, after an hour.

"Why?"

"This place is too much."

Just then, actress Brooke Shields floated by wearing a skin-tight outfit. I said hello, and even though she didn't know me, she stopped and said hello back. I asked her if she was having a good time.

"Great time," she said in a voice softer than a lullaby.

We then chatted for a few minutes about the club, the music and the outfits.

"It's like Halloween for adults," I said.

"More like Sodom and Gomorrah."

"Be careful," I said. "The dance floor looks dangerous."

"Not compared to modeling."

She then wiggled her fingers in goodbye, turned and floated back into the crowd.

I looked at Andy. He stared at me as if I just performed a miracle.

"I couldn't have done that in a million years," he said.

"Done what?"

"Talk to a glamorous movie star."

"Nothing ventured, nothing gained."

"I wish I had your confidence."

"I wish I had your money."

"You have an athlete's confidence."

"I guess."

"There's no guessing. I see the world as a serious business enterprise while you see it as some kind of game."

I shrugged. "Life is a game. Either you play or you don't."

"True. But having fun seems more important to you than making money."

"It is."

"What perplexes me," he said. "is that as fun-loving as you are, you keep people at arm's length."

"Self-preservation."

"Explain."

"It goes back to the days when I was a highly recruited high school basketball player. I had all these college coaches bullshit and deceive me…it's made me cautious."

"Still? After all these years?"

"Yeah."

We left the club. As I drove home that night, I thought of Andy's words: how I didn't let people get close. He was right. I only open up and express my true feelings to a handful of people. If I had to define myself, it would be as a loner. Yet at the same time I'm social, very social. But I much prefer staying home and watching movies and reading books than hanging out with big groups or going to large parties. My favorite book of fiction is The Great Gatsby and my favorite book of non-fiction is Walden—both stories about loners who live their lives on their own terms.

I'd like to think I've lived my life by my own rules, having the freedom and flexibility to do what matters most to me, taking chances, being creative, finding meaning and, above all, having a purpose.

Purpose, I've learned, is what defines you. Gives you pleasure. Satisfaction. Uncovers the secret of happiness in all its truth and beauty.

Chapter Twenty-One

In 1984, after almost four years of publishing SportsWise, McKelvey summoned Helen and me to his office.

Leaning forward in his leather chair, hands clasped on his desk, he said, "I still like the concept of SportsWise but it's become too costly. You guys have worked hard and I admire what you've accomplished, but it's time I put my resources behind more lucrative projects."

Helen and I looked at each other and said nothing. The magazine was hemorrhaging money, and we knew this was inevitable.

Andy, wearing a rumpled white shirt and a loosened black tie, swiveled in his chair and glanced out a window that overlooked the rooftops of a souvenir shop, a cosmetics store and a corner delicatessen. After a few seconds, he returned his attention to us.

"My suggestion," he said, "is for you guys to find either an investor or a buyer." He pinched his nose. "Maybe try meeting with venture capitalists or a Wall Street firm."

He grabbed a small bottle of water and took a sip.

"I'll give you guys a month or so. If nothing develops…" his voice trailed off.

Helen and I left. We went straight to Victor's Café on West 52nd Street, sat in bamboo chairs and ordered cocktails. News like that called for a drink. Quickly.

"Whaddya think?" I said, after taking a big gulp of my scotch and soda.

"I think we need to find a buyer."

After ordering a few more drinks, we decided our best bet was to try and get funding or sell the magazine outright to Sports Illustrated.

"It's ironic," I said, my forehead supported by a splay of fingers "me going back to the place that years ago I turned down a chance to work as a reporter."

Helen finger walked a napkin. "Let's give it a try."

The next day we called Time-Warner—owner of SI, along with TIME, Life, People, Fortune, Money and just about every other magazine worth reading—and asked to speak with their merger and acquisitions director. We were given the name of Steve Blacker. The operator transferred our call to his office. He answered after a few rings. Helen told him of our situation. He said he was familiar with SportsWise and agreed to meet with us.

We met him at the Time-Life Building on 1271 Ave of the Americas.

A stocky, bald guy, Blacker took us into a large conference room surrounded by large windows. We sat in comfortable cushioned chairs.

For two hours, Helen and I pitched the features and benefits of SportsWise. Blacker listened carefully and asked the expected questions about costs and revenues, our plans for expansion.

He stroked his chin. "It's an interesting concept," he said, "but as you may and may not know, Time-Life just invested in regional TV Guide-like magazines. It was a failure. So as much as I enjoyed and admired your magazine we're going to have to pass."

Of course, Helen and I tried to change his mind. To no avail.

We then contacted some venture capital firms. We got praise but no money. Without a buyer or an investor, we decided, sadly, to fold the magazine.

This was, for me, a devastating loss. But like all my defeats in sports I didn't dwell on it. I accepted it. I questioned, as I did after every game in which I had lost or played badly, where were the mistakes. What could I have done better? Differently? I took consolation in Samuel Beckett's maxim "Ever tried. Ever failed. No matter. Try again. Fail again. Fail better."

When word of SportsWise's closing got out, I received a call from Dan Doyle. Dan was, among other things, a boxing promoter, mostly of Sugar Ray Leonard fights. I'd known him since we'd met during summer basketball camps at Worcester Academy in Massachusetts. Dan said he was starting something called the Shamrock Games, an Irish version of the Jewish Maccabiah Games, an Olympic-style sporting event for Jewish teens, except the Irish Games would include teens and adults.

Dan said he was aware of my background as an editor and a writer, my scouting for the Dallas Mavericks.

"You know a lot of people in sports and have a lot of contacts," he said. "You've been highly recommended." He then asked if I wanted to serve as chairman of the games.

"What do I have to do?"

"Organize fundraisers, generate publicity and write stories."

"Sounds easy enough," I said. "But what exactly is the purpose of the games?"

"To increase Irish tourism and raise sports awareness to generate money to build and improve athletic facilities in Ireland. Twenty-five percent of the Irish population is under twenty-five years old and they desperately need places to play sports."

"Do you have a corporate sponsor?"

"Budweiser. They're using the games as a vehicle to introduce Bud into Ireland."

"Good luck competing against Guinness."

"Don't doubt Budweiser," Dan said. "They have limitless money."

I asked Peg what she thought.

"Go for it," she said.

I then spoke with my father.

"Will you be spending much time in Ireland?" he asked.

"A lot."

"Will you be getting paid?"

"Just enough to keep me in Jameson's."

My father cheered. "Sounds good to me."

I met with Doyle—bald and pudgy, a feisty little leprechaun—at Ryan and McFadden's restaurant on the corner of 42nd and 2nd Avenue in Manhattan.

"I'll do it," I said.

Dan raised his hand and signaled the waitress. He ordered two glasses of Guinness.

When the beers arrived, Dan lifted his glass and I lifted mine.

"To Ireland," he said.

"To Ireland," I repeated.

We clicked glasses and drank.

Dan then told me that the chairwoman would be Sandra Worley Kelly, the sister-in-law of former actress and Princess of Monaco Grace Kelly.

Sandy was a banking specialist for Wilmington Savings Fund Society in Delaware. In addition to serving on the International Olympic Committee's advisory board, she worked at the Liberty Museum in Old City, Philadelphia.

The first time I met Sandy was at a fundraiser in New York City. Tall and slender, blond and blue-eyed, she not only resembled Grace Kelly but she also possessed Grace's style, sophistication and charm.

I approached her and introduced myself.

"Hi," I said, cheerfully. "I'm Rich."

She gave me a funny look. "Is that right?" Her voice reeked of debutante balls and trust funds.

Fumbling for words, I said, "I mean…I mean my name is Rich. I'm not wealthy."

Ever gracious and dignified, she smiled and said, "Glad you cleared that up."

I also met Eamonn Coghlan at the fundraiser. A native Irishman and a Villanova graduate, Eamonn was known as "The Chairman of the Boards" after he won the world-famous Wanamaker Mile at the Millrose Games in Madison Square Garden. In Ireland, he was more popular than Guinness. It was said—and still is said—that because of his victory he's the only man to ever unite all of Ireland—at least for one day.

A handsome bloke with green eyes and reddish hair, Eamonn was quite the charismatic character—a great speaker, fundraiser and publicity generator.

One night he and I went to Belfast to see Irish balladeer, Paddy Reilly, perform. The concert hall was packed. The audience was excited to hear Reilly sing his heart-wrenching song "The Town I Loved So Well." Whenever he sang it, people didn't just cry. They wailed.

As soon as Eamonn entered, he was swamped for autographs—men, women, teenagers, children.

He graciously signed as many autographs as he could.

When we finally got to our seats I said, "Must be nice to be a celebrity."

He grinned. "It is, most of the time. But it can be overwhelming."

His words immediately made me think back to my high school and college playing days when the admiration of fans was, to be sure, exhausting. I was happy I no longer had to deal with it.

To generate publicity for the games, we brought to Ireland a number of NBA head coaches, including Jack McKinney (Indiana Pacers), Billy Cunningham (Philadelphia 76ers) and Kevin Loughery (Chicago Bulls). Wherever they appeared, there were huge crowds.

The Games attracted thousands of participants, generating enough money to refurbish fields and improve athletic facilities. I'm proud of what we accomplished in Ireland.

When not traveling the country promoting the Games, I loved walking around Dublin—strolling Grafton Street, listening to the buskers or browsing in Greene's Bookshop, which was established in 1843, specializing in antiquarian books.

A friendly shopkeeper introduced me to Irish writers I wasn't familiar with—John Banville, William Trevor, Seamus Heaney. I wound up sending boxes of books back home.

Outside of Dublin, I enjoyed lounging in pubs in County Kerry before a fireplace burning peat. Or listening to a trio playing bodhrans, fiddles and tin whistles in County Kildare. I loved traveling to County Adare and seeing thatched cottages, visiting County Claire and standing atop the Cliffs of Moher and going to County Cork to kiss the Blarney Stone.

I especially liked hanging out in Killarney with the Lord Mayor, Paudie O'Connor, (no relation) who was and still is considered the greatest basketball player in Irish history. Paudie and I spent more than a few nights in Gaby's Seafood restaurant on High Street.

Gaby's had brown walls, rough planked floors, a small bar and stone fireplace. It served mouthwatering sauteed scallops and smoked salmon. But more enjoyable than the food was listening to "the lads" tell stories. They reminded me of the guys from The Spot.

Like The Spot guys, the lads had their own vocabulary. They never called a drink a drink. They called it "the cure," "the gargle," "the remedy," "the snort," "the tonic," "the refresher," "the cup of courage," "the breakfast of champions," "the hair of the dogma." One old timer called his Guinness "a pint of penicillin."

They also had their own aphorisms. "May you live as long as you want, and never want as long as you live." "May neighbors respect you, trouble neglect you, angels protect you, and Heaven accept you."

One night, Fergus, a gray-haired "former thespian" as he called himself, suddenly stood on a bar stool. He was wearing a Donegal tweed cap, a green waxed jacket and red silk scarf. He clapped loudly. Twenty-odd faces lifted in attention.

Holding his pint high in the air, he said in a dramatic voice reminiscent of actor Peter O'Toole, "Here's to Oscar Wilde. He showed us that good taste is a good reason to excuse a bad life."

All glasses were raised. Shouts of slainte. Fergus gulped his Guinness.

He then stepped down off the chair, put his arms around my shoulders and said, "Oscar may have been gayer than a dancing mouse, but the lad sure had wisdom."

After draining his pint, he added, "You know this quote: 'Live the wonderful life that is in you! Let nothing be lost upon you. Be always searching for new sensations. Be afraid of nothing.' "

"I like that."

"Know where it's from?"

"No."

"The Picture of Dorian Gray." A beat. "Have ye read it?"

"No."

"Jaysus, laddie, me tinks yer a bleeding eejit."

"You're not the first person to say that."

"Well let's hope I'm the last."

The next day, he literally dragged me to a bookstore and purchased me a copy.

The Shamrock Games ended a year or so before Peg got pregnant in 1986.

Peg and I looked forward to having a child. A few years before, she had suffered a miscarriage, which was devastating to both of us. It took months before we could get over the pain.

We were now both 35 years old, older than most of our friends who already had one, if not two or three, children.

When Peg announced she was pregnant, I had no preference

as to the child's sex, but Peg always wanted a boy because she LOVED the name Tim.

"Timmy has such a nice sound," she'd say. "It's endearing."

I still remember the first time I saw Tim's sonogram images; he looked so white and ghostly. The sight of him moved me to tears.

Driving home after seeing those images, I inserted a CD and we listened to Louis Armstrong sing "A Kiss to Build a Dream On."

Tim was now a life to build a dream on.

I remember calling my father and telling him we were having a boy. He listened, then said, "You're about to take on the toughest job you will ever love." A beat, then: "There is nothing on God's green earth greater than having a child. Especially a boy. Trust me, I know."

Unlike my father who, back in the day, was not allowed in the operating room during delivery, I was there when Peg was wheeled in on a hospital bed. The room was bright and cold. The doctors and nurses in scrubs moved in perfect synchronization.

Peg went into labor. She groaned. Her face inflated. Sweat soaked her forehead.

"Push…push," her doctor exhorted. "Keep pushing."

Peg pushed harder and harder.

Minutes later, there was the sound of a baby crying. Then a tiny body appeared—arms flung out, fingers and toes widespread.

I couldn't believe I was witnessing the actual birth of my son—Tim.

After Tim's arrival, things happened so fast all I remember is later looking behind a glass partition at Tim lying in a crib, sleeping.

Staring at him, I was determined that I would not, like so many friends, push Tim into sports. I would not deter him, but I wouldn't encourage him either.

My goal was to expose Tim, at an early age, to the things I learned about later in life: books, art, music, poetry, museums, plays. I secretly hoped he'd become more of a scholar than a basketballer.

I wanted to raise Tim as my father raised me. We'd be best friends, pals. Tim would always know that he could count on me, that I'd have his back. I looked forward to teaching him how to swim, ride a bike and drive a car. Help him with his homework. Go to movies, to concerts, to Broadway shows. We'd have long talks about school and girls. No holds barred.

Because I wanted to spend time with Tim I decided to take a shot at doing something where I wouldn't have to travel. But I wanted something different, something risky, something that would test my business acumen.

I went to see my old high school teammate Ray Vyzas, who was living nearby in Hasbrouck Heights, New Jersey.

When I got to his house, he was in his living room, standing on a ladder, fixing a ceiling fan.

"Do me a favor," he said. "Can you get me a screwdriver?"

"Sure."

I returned a few minutes later and handed him a glass filled with vodka and orange juice.

He twisted his face and said, "What the fuck is this?"

"You said you wanted a screwdriver."

He smirked. "Thing is, you probably don't even know what a real screwdriver is, seeing how inept you are with tools." He took a sip of the drink. "So? What'd you wanna see me about?"

"I'm thinking about getting into real estate."

"You mean becoming a broker."

"No. I mean buying, remodeling and selling business."

Ray almost spit out his drink.

"You?! Remodeling houses?! Are you fucking kidding me?! You don't know a fingernail from a roofing nail."

"I'm serious."

"So whaddya want from me?"

"I want you to be my partner."

Ray's eyebrows popped up so high they always touched his hairline. He got down from the ladder and gulped his screwdriver.

"This is one cockamamie idea," he said.

"Yeah, but think of how much fun we'd have." A beat. "Not to mention the money we could make."

Ray shut his eyes and kneaded the flesh at the bridge of his nose between a thumb and forefinger.

"I don't know," he said, softly.

"Whaddya got to lose?"

"My life savings."

I pushed my hand at him. "Aah, it's only money."

Ray scratched his chin, producing a sandpapery sound.

"Don't ask me why," he said, "but I'll do it."

We slapped high-fives.

The next day, I called Andy McKelvey and told him about my new venture.

"I love your entrepreneurial spirit," he said. "You always were a bit of an adventurous sort. But have you put together a business plan?"

"Yes," I said, knowing a business plan was as essential as a game plan.

"If you don't mind my asking, what's possessing you to do this?" McKelvey said.

"I want to test myself in a different business."

"You do know housing is risky, right?" McKelvey said.

"I do."

"And you do know that business success is predicated on initial capitalization and that most entrepreneurs fail because they're wildly undercapitalized."

"I've heard that."

"So?" A long pause. "Are you calling me for capital?"

"No. I have a million dollar credit line from Howard Bank."

He chuckled. "How'd you pull that off?"

"I went to see Don McCormick, the bank's president."

"Did you know him?"

"No. I just full-court pressed him." What I didn't tell McKelvey was that McCormick was a good friend of my friend, Dave Wohl, who was then coaching the New Jersey Nets. Don was a big basketball fan and Dave was investing with me.

"I assume this is like a game to you, right?" McKelvey said.

"Always looking to take a shot."

He snickered. "I guess you can take the boy out of the locker room, but you can't take the locker room out of the boy, huh?"

"I guess."

"So what can I do for you?"

"Gimme some tips."

"I'll give one big one."

"What's that?"

"Don't do it."

Ray and I started small. We bought an inexpensive single-family home in Cedar Grove, New Jersey, where Peg and I were living. We got to work most days around nine and put together a to-do list. Ray, whose father did all the maintenance on an eight-family building in Jersey City, had taught Ray about plumbing, carpentry and electricity. Ray would get right to work, tearing down walls and putting up sheetrock. I mostly fetched things, made coffee and stirred paint.

While working, we always played 60s Motown music, reminiscent of our high school days: The Supremes, Temptations and The Four Tops. For me, nothing was—and still isn't— better than the oldies but goodies.

Every once in a while Ray would catch me slapping paint on the walls while grooving to the music. He'd shake his head and mumble.

After we remodeled that first house, we put it on the market and made a profit of thirty grand.

We immediately purchased another home, went to work and made another thirty grand.

The business grew fast. The paperwork soon became overwhelming. Peg, a math whiz, became the chief financial officer. We also hired a receptionist/accountant. This allowed Peg time to get her real estate license so we could buy and sell properties at a bigger profit. Eventually, we started buying multi-family apartment buildings and soon purchased an office building in Glen Ridge, New Jersey. We named the company Tuxedo Realty.

Peg was given carte blanche to furnish the office, and she did so in style. She purchased expensive desks, leather chairs and plush carpeting. She put elegantly framed pictures on the walls.

The place reeked of success.

Soon we were buying properties at the Jersey shore, where there were even more lucrative opportunities.

Peg convinced a kitchen remodeler in Spring Lake, Matt Egan of Design Line Kitchens, to give us big discounts if we let him do all the work. It saved us a shitload of money.

But as lucrative as it was, I soon found it boring.

One afternoon, while sitting having lunch at the Grasshopper restaurant in Cedar Grove, I said to Ray, "You still enjoy this real estate racket?"

"It's hectic, but it makes good money," he said.

"I'm starting to get bored," I said. "There's too much red tape, too many building delays, too many permits needed for even the simplest repair. I wanna do something else."

Ray took a bit of his cheeseburger.

"Like what?" he said.

"Not sure."

"Well, that's specific enough."

We finished lunch and Ray went back to work. Soon after, I divested from the company. Ray continued buying and remodeling. He's done quite well.

While I was looking into new opportunities, I got a call from Rupert Murdoch's people. They asked me if I'd be interested in editing a new business-to-business magazine called SportsTravel. I said I'd listen.

I went to their offices in Secaucus, New Jersey, which was only a half hour from my home in Glen Ridge. The short commute made the job appealing, and truth be told, I missed the magazine world, the stories, the staffing and the camaraderie.

I met with Murdoch's group president, Sam Wolgemuth, a tall, handsome guy who wore custom-made suits and aviator glasses. His office was all polished mahogany and soft leather. He laid out his vision for the magazine.

"It's for people in sports who plan travel: high school and college coaches, athletic directors and travel coordinators. It will highlight hotels and destinations, give cost-saving tips."

I liked Sam. He was polite, had a nice manner.

After finishing his spiel, he said, "What do you think about becoming the editor?"

"If I take the job, I'll have some conditions."

"Like?"

"Like I'd want to hire the best editors and best art directors."

"Shouldn't be a problem." A beat. "Assuming their salaries would be within reason."

"That's the thing. They won't be."

Sam pursed his lips and nodded. "I'll get back to you."

I left.

Sam phoned a friend of his, Norm Sonju, then the president of the Dallas Mavericks. He questioned Norm about my qualifications, my character. Norm recommended me highly.

A few days later, Sam offered me the job and agreed to my conditions.

I quickly hired Andrea Welch, my former editor at SportsWise; Charlie Butler, a kid just out of Columbia University who would later write for Runner's World, Smart Money and the New York Times; Brian Silverman, a mystery writer, who eventually became editor of Frommer's Travel Guides; and award-winning designer

Amy Bothwell.

My goal was to create a well-written, high-gloss magazine and not some boring, snooze-worthy business-to-business publication. That meant spending big bucks for the best freelance writers, photographers and illustrators.

One of our first issues featured a cover shot of Magic Johnson sitting atop Jack Nicholson's shoulders, both wearing sunglasses and flashing big smiles. The issue contained stories written by heralded writers such as David Remnick (now the editor of The New Yorker), Josh Greenfeld (once nominated for an Academy Award for the screenplay for Harry and Tonto) Thomas Boswell (Pulitzer Prize winning columnist for The Washington Post), Bob Ryan (a columnist for The Boston Globe), Bud Greenspan (a documentary filmmaker) and Tim McCarver (the former St. Louis Cardinal catcher turned respected baseball analyst). The issue won a number of industry awards.

Other great issues followed, including stories by author and theater critic Ross Wetzsteon and my writing idol Pat Jordan. We were on our way to great things.

Then a problem arose.

After only publishing a couple of issues, Murdoch sold SportsTravel to Reed-Elsevier, a British publishing company. The Reed people didn't care much for sports. Even more, they thought SportsTravel was "too good and too glossy." They said it didn't have enough business-to-business angles. They thought I was trying to make it into a consumer magazine which is not what they wanted. They asked me to change the editorial format and focus more on straight business stories and less on humor and personality pieces.

I met with my team and told them the situation. We all agreed that we wouldn't change a thing, even if it meant losing our jobs.

After six issues, Reed killed SportsTravel. I, along with my entire staff, was fired.

Did getting fired bother me? Yes, because it put a lot of talented people out of work. But no because I took a shot at creating something different, something unique.

I was now without a weekly paycheck. But I was still making some money working for the Mavericks. Because of that, I was sometimes invited as a guest on New York radio shows, like the one called SportsTalk hosted by WABC's Art Rust Jr. who many consider the "godfather of sports talk radio."

Art's show was a new concept. Anybody who was anybody in sports appeared on his broadcast, including Joe DiMaggio and Muhammad Ali.

Art liked me because I was a big fan of Miles Davis, who was one of Art's closest friends. We often debated which was Davis' best album: Art preferred Birth of the Cool. I favored Sketches of Spain. We had some lively discussions.

He also liked that I gave silly answers to callers, saying things like "guy dribbles more than a two-year old" or "this player makes more passes than Warren Beatty" or "kid shoots better than Jesse James."

He suggested I consider doing sports radio.

"Not interested," I said.

"Why?" Art asked.

"I'd rather talk about books and movies."

After one show, I got a call from a headhunter who wanted me to interview for a basketball analyst's job at ESPN.

Once again, I said, "Not interested."

"It's a great opportunity," he said.

"Thanks. But no thanks."

It was a good thing I turned it down, because life for Peg and I with Tim was about to change. Dramatically.

Chapter Twenty-Two

We had prepared for Tim coming home by constructing a crib and painting Tim's room blue, purchasing a changing table, diapers, powders, hampers, monitors and a rocking chair for breast feeding.

Like most babies, Tim woke up a few times at night, but for the most part he slept well. He was never colicky.

When he was awake, he giggled and smiled a lot. Peg and I loved picking him up and carrying him around the living room, burping, hugging or singing to him.

Tim started walking after his first birthday. He toddled everywhere and we followed close behind, waiting for the moment when he might tip over and we'd have to swoop him up and kiss his chubby cheeks.

Looking back it's almost impossible to express the force of our happiness then—the sparkle that existed in Peg's eyes and the smile that illuminated my face. It was not just momentary pleasure. It was something we expected to last a lifetime.

When Tim was four, his red hair sprouting and his blue eyes twinkling, we noticed he wasn't responding to us.

He'd be sitting on the living room floor, playing with blocks and Peg or I would call him: "Tim."

No reaction.

We'd call louder. "Timmy. Timmy."

Again, nothing.

Then, suddenly, Tim would start shaking and throwing the blocks against the walls.

Peg would go over and hug and stroke his forehead until he calmed down.

One night after Tim was asleep Peg said, "Something's wrong. Very wrong."

I nodded. "I know."

We took him to his pediatrician. We sat for a while in a waiting room decorated with photos of smiling babies and smiling parents.

A few kids were there, some playing on the floor with toys and some sitting in chairs holding stuffed animals. One kid dismembered a G.I. Joe.

Tim sat quietly between Peg and me, holding our hands.

After a short wait, a nurse waved us into the doctor's office. The doctor, young and friendly, asked a few questions, made a few notes and occasionally ran his fingers through a forest of dark hair that fell onto his forehead.

He then took Tim's temperature and checked his heart, lungs and ears.

"Everything is good," he said, after the examination. "It's probably just delayed development."

On the drive home, I asked Peg, "What do you think?"

"I don't know what to think."

Tim's tantrums intensified. He would pick something up—a

glass, a chair, an ashtray—and throw it against the wall.

We took him to two more pediatricians. Both gave us the same diagnosis: Delayed development.

After leaving the second doctor's office, I said, "I'm not buying the diagnosis."

Peg, calm as always, said in a teary whisper, "Neither am I. Let me make some phone calls and find someone who can help us."

She made an appointment with a neurologist at St. Joseph's Children's Hospital in Paterson, New Jersey. The doctor was a trim and petite woman with a narrow, gentle face. She suggested Tim undergo a series of tests.

"The tests will take a while," she said. "Perhaps you guys should go to the cafeteria and have some coffee."

We did, although neither of us had the stomach for food or drink. I couldn't even sit down. I paced, slowly sinking into a blistering, wordless grief.

An hour passed. Then two, then three. I kept checking my watch. Jesus Christ! Where's the doctor?

I looked at Peg and she looked at me. We both had a hard time processing the situation, helpless to comprehend what was happening and too afraid to imagine what we might learn.

We waited and waited and waited. Hoped and hoped and hoped.

The cafeteria, with its grey tabletops and dim neon lights, was crowded with nurses and doctors. I sat down next to Peg.

"I'm worried," I said, "really worried."

Peg grabbed my hand and squeezed it. "I know, I know," she said, her voice a momentary comfort.

I stood again and walked out of the cafeteria and into a hallway where I heard monitors beeping and respirators wheezing. I passed an opened door and saw a hospital-gowned young boy curled up in a fetal position, moaning. Looking at him, I began to shake. I went back to the cafeteria.

Thirty minutes later, the doctor appeared. She walked us to her office.

Taking a seat behind her desk, she leaned forward and said in a soft and smoky voice, "Your son is…is…autistic."

I balled my fists into white knots, suddenly feeling as if my skeletal system was about to collapse. I could not believe what I was hearing. My son?! Autistic?! No fucking way!

I knew enough about autism to know that it was a malfunction of the brain that causes behavioral and emotional problems, manifested by everything from the inability to speak to the possibility of self-mutilation.

I glanced at Peg. She was doing everything in her power to keep from crying. But her eyes filmed over and she wiped her nose with a quick flash of her palm. I was so traumatized I could barely speak or breathe. All I could think about was that my son would live a tortured life.

"Understand," the doctor said, "the range of autism is wide. The symptoms and severity vary greatly. Some children are high functioning, others not so much."

"Can you tell us in which category Tim falls?" I said, my knees trembling like jackhammers.

"No," the doctor said. "It's much too early." She paused. "I'm sure at some point he'd need medication."

A long awkward silence followed. Then the doctor said, "Is there anything I can do for you?" She spoke these words so softly as if they were lines of an often-repeated prayer.

"Do for us?" I said.

"Recommend an autism specialist?"

Neither Peg nor I responded. We simply exchanged glances.

"Having an autistic child," she said, "can be very difficult, very demanding. Most likely, you will, at some point, need professional help."

Peg and I nodded. There were no more words needed because it no longer was about words.

We got Tim, who was wrapped in a blanket, sleeping soundly. I carried him outside to the car. Tears scorched my eyes and glazed my face. I wondered if I would ever stop crying.

Peg maintained her composure. But I knew her heart was rioting inside.

Driving home, I said to Peg, "What now?"

"We deal with it."

I wondered if I could.

I mean, I had lived, up to this point, an extremely fortunate life. I had excellent health, some prosperity, a good job, a beautiful wife and a childhood filled with love and attention.

Now I was confronted with the sobering realization that the things every parent desires for their child—normality, stability, opportunity, happiness, independence and good health—would be denied Tim.

I thought of my close friend, Peter Beckenbach, who had an autistic son, Errol. I'm Errol's godfather.

When Pete and his family had visited us, I had seen how difficult and exhausting it was dealing with Errol, his fixations and his tantrums. Often, I thought: How does Pete deal with this?

"It's tough," Pete told me. "As much as I love Errol he disrupts your life in ways you can't imagine. Most fathers bail on their autistic kids. They can't handle the problems and the pressures."

I understood pressure. I felt it many times standing on the free throw line in crucial moments of a game when 20,000 fans were waving towels and booing me. But I never felt intimidated nor did I ever lose my composure. I just stepped to the line, reached inside myself, and did what I was supposed to do: succeed.

But this diagnosis for Tim was something beyond anything I ever expected to confront.

I talked to my parents.

"Your full-time job now is to look after Tim," my father said. "Do everything you can to make his life enjoyable."

I nodded.

"Your needs now," he added, "are secondary."

My mother said, "Tim is your priority. Don't ever let anything else ever come before him."

Early on, Tim took lots of meds, powerful drugs to try to control his behavior. It was mostly trial and error. Some medications worked, while others caused him to have seizures and convulsions.

Dealing with his sudden outbursts and tantrums was not easy. Both Peg and I took turns being on high alert, watching for anything that might trigger his anger.

Funny thing is, in between his bouts of anger, Tim was usually quiet and content to play with his toys or stuffed animals, listen to music or watch videos.

From age four to age eleven, Tim was at home. Unlike many autistic kids, Tim was verbal, though he couldn't express his feelings or emotions—which is usually why he'd explode.

Around age twelve, Tim hit puberty. It was a tough time for

him. Some days he'd suddenly erupt into violence, biting and punching, throwing dishes and radios. He even threw a television through a picture window.

After he'd calm down, I'd hold him tight to my chest and repeat over and over: "It's okay, Tim. Daddy's here. Daddy's got you."

He'd fall asleep. I'd put him to bed, holding his hand and stroking his cheek. Often I'd wonder if he dreamt and if he did, what did he dream about. I'd never know.

Some nights when he couldn't sleep, I'd play music to help him relax, I'd play him Cleo Laine singing Stephen Sondheim's "Not While I'm Around." Quietly, I'd sing along: "Nothing gonna harm you/Not while I'm around."

One time he suddenly awoke and saw tears rolling down my cheeks. To my utter amazement, he sat up and hugged me.

Trust me, there is nothing more magical, more heart-inflating for the parent of an autistic child to have a moment like that.

Because of the need for constant vigilance, Peg was forced to quit her job. She did most of the heaving lifting, making sure Tim took his meds and kept his doctor appointments. She prepared his meals and washed his clothes. She took him on walks and to playgrounds. She got very little sleep. She was—and still is—Tim's Mother Teresa.

At the time, I was still scouting for the Mavericks but Tim's bills were mounting and I needed to find a full-time job.

I started calling friends about job opportunities, but as luck would have it, a job found me.

I got a call from Chuck Wrye, the publisher of Successful Meetings magazine. He said he very much admired SportsTravel and wanted to know if I'd be interested in becoming its editor.

"Of a dating magazine?!" I said.

He laughed. "No," he said. "It's a magazine for people who plan meetings."

I said I was flattered by his phone call but didn't know a damn thing about meetings, other than meeting friends for cocktails.

"Doesn't matter," Chuck said. "I saw what you did at SportsTravel. It was impressive, way beyond the pale of most boring business-to-business magazines. Bottom line: You know publishing."

I talked with Peg. I said the job might entail much travel, which could be an issue because of Tim's needs.

"You may not have a choice," Peg said.

"You're right. We need the money to take care of Tim."

I phoned Wrye and we agreed to meet in a Manhattan restaurant called Cowgirl, on Hudson Street in Greenwich Village.

Chuck was six foot tall with light brown hair. He wore a blue polo shirt, khaki pants and white tennis sneakers. He attended Yale, was smart, friendly and quick to laugh.

After describing the magazine, the market, the salary, the perks and benefits of the job, he said, "Does it appeal to you?"

"It might."

He raised an eyebrow. "Might?"

"I have one request."

"Name it."

"I want to hire the staff I had at SportsTravel."

Chuck took a minute to think. He stroked his chin and looked around the restaurant at the waiters and waitresses who were decked out in cowboy hats and boots. "All of them?"

"Yep,"

"Are their salaries reasonable?" he said, hunching his shoulders.

"Not by B-to-B standards."

"Meaning they're high.'

"Yes."

Chuck blew air out his cheeks. A middle-aged waiter passed by us looking like John Wayne after a long night in the saddle. From a jukebox Patsy Cline sang "Crazy."

"Is there room to negotiate?" Chuck said, now tilting forward.

"No."

He thought a moment. A vein pulsed in the hollow of a temple.

"Is this a deal breaker?" he said.

"Could be."

He scratched his nose.

I took a sip of my soda.

"Okay," he said, extending his hand. "We got a deal."

We shook.

"Please don't make me regret making this monetary commitment."

"I won't, but I may need more money for free-lance writers, photographers and illustrators."

Chuck tap-tapped his forehead.

"Aye yai yai yai," he said. "What have I gotten myself into?"

Chapter Twenty-Three

I could have asked myself the same question: What have I gotten myself into? Aside from taking a job about a subject I knew nothing about, Peg and I were still learning how to deal with an autistic child.

It wasn't easy. Tim had grown to over six feet tall. When he acted out it could be frightening.

One night, when I was scouting a game for the Mavericks, Tim got upset.

Standing in the living room he started hitting Peg, who is only five-foot-four. She put her hands up to defend herself, but his punches were hard and continuous. She pleaded with Tim to stop, but he wouldn't. Even worse, he couldn't. Like most autistic kids, he doesn't have the ability to verbalize his feelings when he becomes frustrated.

Peg finally untangled herself from Tim's assault, moved into the kitchen and phoned the police.

While she waited for them to arrive, Tim began throwing things—picture frames, crystal vases—around the room.

Peg tried talking to him, softly and comfortingly, but he was so angry he was beyond reasoning with.

The police knocked on the door. Peg answered it and quickly explained that Tim was autistic and not a drug addict or an alcoholic.

With Peg's help, the police calmed Tim down and then drove him and Peg to the Morristown Hospital Psychiatric Ward.

Peg phoned me at Madison Square Garden. I left immediately.

When I got to Morristown, Peg was sitting on a folding chair in a waiting area, her head lowered.

"How is he?" I asked, taking a seat. In the background I heard the moans and shrieks of patients.

"He's fine now," Peg said, lifting her head as slowly as if it was anchored by weights.

"You okay?"

"Yeah." Thankfully, she had no visible bruises. Just a bruised heart.

"I'm sorry I wasn't there," I said, feeling like a total loser.

Typical of Peg's niceness, she said, "You can't be there all the time."

"We gotta get him outta here," I said.

"Can't," Peg said, looking helpless and grief-stricken. "Doctors need to do an evaluation before he can be released."

We stayed at the hospital all night, saw patients walking around in white gowns, some in restraints.

A few days later, after Tim was given a thorough evaluation, a psychiatrist prescribed new meds. He was released.

The new medications helped. Tim seemed calm and relaxed. But for how long?

"What we need now," Peg said, "is someplace Tim can go and get help."

I nodded. Tim wasn't a kid anymore, he was a teenager and becoming a young man.

After doing some research, Peg found a private school in Nutley, New Jersey called the Phoenix Center that served the educational, behavioral and therapeutic needs of special students. They operated a day program, supervised by Dr. Doug Berrian.

A tall, thin man with wire-rim glasses and the personality of an energetic priest, Dr. Berrian fully understood Tim's situation and was convinced he could help.

"Our goal," he told Peg and me, "is to provide for these special needs kids the ability to have a good quality of life."

The Center was good for Tim. He got individual attention. He learned how to read and write and socialize with other kids.

But as much behavioral attention and direction as Tim received, there were still days when he'd fly off the handle and put his fist through a wall or attack a fellow student. That wasn't unusual for any of the kids at the Center, but at times Tim's antics were so bad that the principal, Jim Bagley, wanted Tim dismissed.

Peg and I pleaded with both Jim and Doug to give Tim a second chance—one of many second chances. Which they did. And little by little, Tim's behavior improved. But the staff at the Center, as well as Peg and I, knew Tim could explode at any moment when agitated.

When he'd come home from school in the afternoon, he'd usually be fine, his reddish hair mussed and his fingers blue from using crayons. Peg would give him yogurt and grapes, milk or cookies, then Tim would go into his room and contentedly listen to 60s music or watch videos like Pee-wee Herman or The Muppets.

Most days Peg got support and help from her mother, Josephine, and often from my mother and father who doted on Tim, as if he were royalty.

Tim, unlike many autistic kids, could still be very affectionate. He always greeted his grandparents with hugs, kisses and jokes. He'd ask my father, "Poppa, what do dogs put on their pizza?"

"No idea, Tim."

"Puppy-roni," Tim would answer in a high-pitched, excited voice.

Then: "Nanny, where do sheep get their haircut?"

Nanny, Peg's mother, would shrug.

"At the baa-baa shop," Tim cried, waving his arms like an orchestra leader.

He'd ask my mother, "Grandma, what time should you go to the dentist?"

"I don't know, Tim, what time?"

"Tooth thirty," he'd shout and do a little circular dance.

Even though he told the same jokes every day, his grandparents still got a kick out of them.

While Tim was adjusting to the Phoenix Center, I was editing Successful Meetings.

The magazine was owned by two entrepreneurs, the Bill Brothers, and the company was called, boringly enough, Bill Communications. Over the next sixteen years, Successful Meetings, along with a host of other Bill publications, including Billboard and The Hollywood Reporter, would be sold several times, first to Boston Ventures, then to VNU, the largest magazine publisher in the Netherlands, and, finally, to Nielsen, the global analytics company.

Thanks to the creative efforts of my former art and editorial staff from SportsWise and SportsTravel, Successful Meetings was transformed from a plain, boring magazine into one with a glossy cover, better paper stock and more in-depth and engaging articles. Their efforts, along with an experienced sales team, quickly turned the magazine from a marginally profitable publication into an enormously profitable one.

As a result, I was quickly promoted, within a year, from editor of Successful Meetings to the publisher of the magazine.

I got the promotion because I had a good reputation for managing people and the magazine was now highly profitable. But, even more, I got the job because…I asked for it.

It was a bold and brave thing to do. But I knew if I didn't ask I would someday suffer the pain of knowing I hadn't tried.

Over the next five years, I asked and was promoted to group publisher (7 magazines) to executive vice president (12 magazines) to division president (18 magazines, 12 trade shows and 300 staffers). My group generated $70 million in revenue and contributed 30% of the company's bottom line.

The presidency was a demanding and challenging job, insofar as I was now in charge of a variety of different magazines: Restaurant Business, Plastic Technology, Kitchen and Bath, Incentive, Training, Contract, Sales and Marketing Management and many others.

It paid enormously well, but it took time away from being with Tim, which I hated. Quite frankly, couldn't bear it.

Not being at home put a bigger burden on Peg and the grandparents. But I had to work. Tim's expenses were high and company insurance only covered a little.

As division president, I viewed the job the same way I viewed

Hubie Brown's challenge to me many years before when he questioned whether I wanted to test myself at Duke. Now instead of putting on a basketball uniform I was donning a three-piece suit.

One thing I had always promised myself was that under no circumstance would I become an ass-kissing corporate waterboy whose principal job was to polish his boss's ego.

From one day, I set my agenda to be a game-changer, a disruptor, an effective point guard who dished out assists.

As clichéd as the word teamwork is, I knew from my playing days that there is nothing better than many people working together as a cohesive unit. In sports, it's called creating "team chemistry." In business, it's referred to as developing a "corporate culture."

Tim's condition had taught me to be patient and understanding, and I showed interest in the needs of team members. I cared about their personal lives, their backgrounds and their goals. I wanted them to realize that there was more to life than just collecting a paycheck.

Once, I had a team member, an editor, whose father was sick in Florida. She came to see me about taking a leave of absence.

"I'm not sure how long I'll be gone," she said. "Will...will I have a...a job when I get back?"

"Let's do this," I said. "Take some time off to care for your father. With pay. After a few weeks, call me and we'll go from there. With the way stories are transmitted now via computer, maybe you could work from Florida."

Her eyes filmed over. "Are you serious?"

"I am."

She stood and gave me a big hug.

Some of my Nielsen superiors chastised me for being too

friendly, too understanding with my employees.

"You can't be friends with the people who work for you," one said to me. "You have to be detached. Never get close. They'll take advantage of you."

I blew off his advice and practiced what I preached. I continued to treat my team the way I thought best.

One day when I was in a division president's meeting in New York, Peg was in Cedar Grove with Tim, shopping at Foodtown.

The store was noisy and crowded, lots of people pushing carts and crowding the aisles. Tim was anxious to get home.

Peg rushed to the checkout counter. The people in front and behind her and Tim had carts loaded with groceries. They took their sweet old time putting them on the conveyor belt. The cashier was slow. Tim was impatient and like most autistic kids became agitated. He started moving his fingers as if frantically playing an invisible piano—never a good sign.

He kept saying, his voice rising with every word. "C'mon, mommy, c'mon mommy, let's go home!"

Peg tried to explain what was taking so long. Tim scrunched up his face and shook his head wildly.

Then, without a word, he darted away to the front of the store and put his fist through the store's big front window. Glass shattered. Shoppers shouted and screamed. Blood gushed from Tim's forearm.

Peg ran to his side and wrapped her sweater around Tim's arm. The sweater was quickly covered in blood.

Tim showed no reaction. No crying or yelling. He stood passively, simply staring at his mother.

An ambulance arrived. Tim was put on a stretcher and

placed inside. Peg held his hand. The ambulance raced to nearby Mountainside Hospital and into the Emergency Room. Doctors and nurses attended to him immediately.

Peg phoned me. I violated protocol at the president's meeting and I answered. I listened to Peg tell me what happened and then quickly stood and said I had to leave.

My boss glared at me and asked why I had to leave. I said nothing. I just left.

Only a handful of people at Nielsen knew about Tim's condition. My boss wasn't one. I wasn't ashamed of his condition, I just didn't want it known in business circles. When co-workers asked me if Tim was a basketball player, as if my athletic genes were automatically passed to him, I'd just say he moves to the beat of a different drummer. Many thought I meant he was a musician.

I ran to the parking lot, got in my car and drove across town in stop-and-go traffic, constantly beeping my horn while cursing and swerving in and around cars like a halfback going through the line. I finally entered the Lincoln Tunnel and came out on Route 3 in New Jersey, driving ninety, a hundred miles an hour.

As I neared Meadowlands Stadium, home of the New York Giants, I looked in my rearview mirror and saw the flashing lights of a police car.

For a moment, I thought about trying to outrace him, but decided against it. I pulled off to the side of the road.

I watched as the cop, a big, burly guy, walked over and tapped on my window. I rolled it down.

"License and registration," he said. His voice sounded like walnuts being cracked.

"Just gimme the ticket," I barked.

His face darkened. "What?"

"I said, 'Gimme me the goddamn ticket.'"

"Watch your mouth, buddy."

I rubbed my right eye with my right knuckle.

"You realize how fast you were going?" he said.

"Yeah, I do."

"What's the big hurry?"

"My son is autistic. He's in the hospital."

He regarded me with a skeptical eye. "What hospital?"

"Mountainside."

"What happened?"

"He cut himself…badly."

A patch of skin between his eyebrows tightened.

"This bullshit?"

"Call the hospital."

He stared at me for a good thirty seconds before responding.

"Okay," he said, "Get going. But watch your speed. Not going to help your son if you get into an accident." A pause. "You hear me?"

"Yes, sir."

He returned to his car and squeezed inside. Seconds later, he pulled back into traffic. I watched as he got off at the next exit.

I resumed driving just as fast as before, all the while trying to hold back tears.

I got to Mountainside and sprinted inside, gasping and sweating. I asked a doctor at the nurse's station about Tim.

The doctor—small and young, wearing a white smock, a stethoscope around his neck—said Tim had been released.

"How…how is he?"

"The cut required 40 stitches."

My knees buckled.

"Any tendons, ligaments severed?"

"No. He was lucky, very lucky."

I left the hospital and sped home. Tim was lying on the couch sleeping, his forearm heavily bandaged. I kissed his forehead, wiped tears from my eyes, then tiptoed away.

Days later, on a Monday, I was back at work. I called a team meeting. Still thinking about Tim, I reiterated to the "team" that my priority was for them to hit business goals, make money but, above all else, to enjoy their job and have fun. A lot of fun.

Unlike the other Nielsen presidents, none of whom had played big-time sports and who always read books on management and leadership, I managed by instinct. I never read a leadership book, but used the lessons I learned from being captain of every basketball team I ever played on.

I learned that a great leader sets an example, knows how to motivate people and gets them to work together to achieve group goals. At Nielsen I created a think tank where team members from different disciplines—sales, marketing, editorial, production—met once a month to create new and innovative strategies.

In the publishing world this was a big no-no. It was gospel to keep editorial and sales far apart. To me, this separation of "church and state" was bullshit, a liability.

To further generate camaraderie, I gathered the team together once a month in a conference room and ordered pizzas and subs and gave business updates—the good, the bad and the ugly. Team members could ask me any question, no matter how sensitive, and I gave honest answers, whether they liked it or not.

At the end of these get-togethers, I had my art director, Don Salkahn, present a video he created that showed team members dressed in costumes and performing funny skits—everything from parodying other staffers to impersonating movie stars. The videos were hilarious.

To establish this kind of fun environment, I was adamant—one could say obsessive— about finding potential staffers who would fit in with our group. They didn't have to be the smartest people. A resume was important, yes, but it was never the determining factor. I wanted people who understood the culture I was trying to create.

I disdained the in-office interview. People were stiff and uptight. They gave cliched answers. For the most part, it was a waste of time.

My strict rule was any potential mid-to-high level hire had to be taken out to lunch and/or dinner by different team members. And, ideally, given a cocktail or two—but never if someone objected.

I strongly believed in Hemingway's dictum that, "you never know someone till you drink with them."

I often hired people based solely on instinct.

Once while having lunch at the Abbey Tavern in New York with my H.R. Director, John Mulvey, I observed a waitress serving a table of five twenty-year-old guys, all of whom were loud, obnoxious and shouting obscenities. I noticed how this waitress never lost her cool, never showed displeasure. She just did her job, pleasantly and professionally.

I turned to John and said, "See that waitress?" He nodded. "Watch how she's dealing with those assholes. She's exhibiting perfect customer service."

John sipped his beer. "And?"

"Talk to her about a job."

He looked amused. "We don't have a cafeteria."

"See if she has any other skills than waitressing."

"Oooookay."

As it turned out the waitress, Lorna Manning, had some computer skills.

A few days later, I met with her in my office. She was a tall girl, with an open face and thick black hair. Attractive. Irish. From Limerick.

After complimenting her on his waitressing, I said, "I understand you have computer skills."

"I do," she said, in a lyrical Irish accent.

"Interested in doing some part-time clerical work?"

For a moment, she looked surprised. Then her face quickly brightened.

"Absolutely," she said enthusiastically.

"Okay, then," I said, extending my hand. "Let's give you a try."

We hired her as a part-time receptionist, working on some financial spreadsheets. She did well. Was very attentive to detail. Very upbeat, positive. The entire staff enjoyed working with her. Soon she was promoted to my assistant. Shortly thereafter, she moved into marketing and traveled the world representing our magazines. Clients loved working with her because she exhibited the same kind of professionalism in a corporate setting as she once did in the Abbey Tavern.

Another time, when I was at an industry cocktail party I saw an editor from another publication, Ron Donoho, standing on a stage telling jokes and singing songs. I knew right away he'd fit in with my team culture.

I elbowed my editor, Andrea Welch, and said, "Check that guy's writing clips. If they're any good, hire him."

We did. And like Lorna, Ron became an integral and popular part of our team.

I was proud that our office often seemed like an exuberant locker room, full of laughter and wisecracks—unlike so many offices where the pervasive tone was one of silent joylessness. I often said to the team: "Hey, guys, if we do this right, it'll be like high school with money."

A few times a year we played games in the hallways. Once, a Nielsen senior executive came up to our floor and saw team members playing bocce and miniature golf. Rock music blared in the background.

"What the heck is going on here?" he asked, his eyes wider than baseballs.

"Just a team timeout," I said.

He stared at my editorial director, Andrea Welch, who was bent over and getting ready to roll a bocce ball.

He pointed at her and said in a shrill voice, "What's she doing?"

"Looks like she's aiming at the pallino."

He gazed at me, totally baffled.

"What in God's name is a…a pallino?"

"The target ball."

"This is crazy," he said.

"No," I said. "This is fun."

Our shenanigans included holding monthly contests, like bringing in your senior class picture from high school. The team then voted on the prettiest face, the silliest smile, the worst haircut, the ugliest tie, etc. The winners got fifty dollars each.

We also, every few months, went bowling and played volleyball and softball; we threw Christmas, Halloween and Thanksgiving parties where everyone had to bring homemade food.

One time an editor brought an unrecognizable dish.

Rob Carey, an editor, tasted it and said, "What the hell is this? Fish or fowl?"

"Whatever it is," Andrea Welch said, wiping her mouth, "it's foul."

Sometimes we included clients in our events, which became a much sought-after invitation. I remember once we did a costume bowling party with a group from Dolce International, the world's leading conference center company. There was lots of beer, cheering and gutter balls. Afterward, the company's founder and chairman, Andy Dolce, said to me, "In all my years in business, I don't think I've ever seen a crazier and happier group of employees."

Yet for all our hijinks, we still managed to "bring in the numbers." And even though the performance of my division was important, what was more important to me was that I was back in competition, competing against other Nielsen presidents to see who had the most productive group.

That's not to say I didn't cooperate with the other presidents. I did. It's just that I saw them in the same way I saw players from North Carolina, Virginia or Maryland—as opponents I had to beat.

I enjoyed my job at Nielsen, enjoyed watching our team jell and succeed and produce quality magazines.

If nothing else, it gave me a distraction from Tim's problems.

Unfortunately, Peg had no such outlet. She, along with her mother Josephine, and my parents, dealt with Tim's tantrums and sometimes his punches every other day. It was tough duty.

But Peg always stayed calm. She was determined to give Tim the best life she could. She had a swimming pool installed for him, along with a large trampoline and a swing set.

Tim thoroughly enjoyed being pushed high on the swings, soaring into the air, holding tight to the chains and squealing with delight. Or bouncing up and down in the enclosed trampoline, falling and getting up, falling and getting up, all the while smiling and laughing.

I'd help as much as I could, but with long work hours and long business trips, I couldn't give Peg the breaks she deserved.

Looking back, I'm suffused with guilt and shamefully accepting that I didn't hold up my end of the bargain. Not with Tim, of course, but with Peg, who deserved more. Deserved better.

I wasn't always there when she needed my help, my support and my understanding, because I was in California or Europe on business, romping around with clients and sales reps. And there were plenty of times when I was at home that I'd forget to pick up laundry or food. Too many nights I came home late from work when I could have gotten home earlier. Bottom line? I made too many mistakes and was too inconsiderate. A true knucklehead.

When Peg and I got divorced on June 7th, 2006, after twenty-five years of marriage—Tim was 20—it was not, as many people thought, because of Tim and the stress of dealing with him. This couldn't be further from the truth. Peg and I never argued about Tim, never disagreed on how to raise him. We were always in sync. We divorced for no other reason than I failed at being an equal partner.

How do you forgive yourself for being such a selfish person? You don't.

I have asked myself, more than once, why I wasn't a better husband. The simple question doesn't provide a simple answer. I can only say this: I should have been a better man. But I wasn't. Shame on me.

To this day, I have the greatest respect and admiration for Peg. She is one of the finest people I've had the honor to know. I try to care for her in every way that an ex-husband can.

The only regret she and I have regarding Tim is that he'll never have a "normal life." He'll never be able to live alone or have an in-depth conversation. He'll never have a girlfriend or get married. He'll never have kids. I think of this almost every day. It breaks my heart.

But Peg and I have done our best to expose Tim to the world. He's visited zoos and museums, gone to movies and concerts, toured the Liberty Bell, Grant's Tomb, Wall Street, even Teddy Roosevelt's mansion.

We took him on trips to Florida, Rhode Island, New Hampshire, Pennsylvania, Connecticut, Massachusetts, Delaware, Washington, Baltimore, New Jersey and, of course, New York.

Tim loves New York. He's thrilled at riding the subways and taking cabs, walking through Central and Bryant Parks. He particularly enjoys Washington Square Park where he likes listening to the Maynard G. Krebs look-a-likes strumming guitars or blowing harmonicas.

Once a group of Rastafarians were playing steel drums. Grabbing my hand, Tim pulled me to them and started scuffling his feet like a square dancer. The Rastafarians smiled, increased their tempo. Tim increased his.

When the music stopped, one of the Rastas shook Tim's hand and said, "Ey, Mon, where you learn those moves?"

Tim, smiling, said, "Pee-wee Herman."

The Rasta, with matted dreadlocks down to his waist, replied: "I a Cowboy Curtis man myself."

The two then exchanged a high-five.

When Tim and I are home together, we play games every morning. Scrabble, Upwords, Trouble and Monopoly. We watch movies together. Raffi. The Muppets. Home Alone 2: Lost in New York. We listen, sing and dance along to The Beach Boys, Billy Joel, Jimmy Buffet and The Temptations. We look like the two Wild and Crazy guys from the old Saturday Night skit, featuring Dan Aykroyd and Steve Martin.

At lunchtime, we'll go to different restaurants. Tim loves eating out, loves trying to make conversation with the waiters and waitresses. He asks them the same questions over and over—about their favorite puddings, cakes and candies. He astounds them by always remembering their birthdays and their kids names and ages. His memory is amazing.

For some reason (nobody can figure out why) Tim has a thing about the number 49.

Once when we were sitting at Homer's restaurant in Sparta, New Jersey, Tim told the owner, Donna, who was older than 49, "You're 49."

Donna—blonde, beautiful, bubbly—immediately stood and shouted, "Excuse me, can I have everyone's attention." The place was crowded. Heads turned, eyes opened and people stopped eating. "Can you listen to what this intelligent man has to say?" She pointed to Tim. "Tell all these fine people what you just said."

Tim stood, his arms outstretched, yelled "Donna's 49."

Laughter and applause. Donna hugged Tim. He beamed.

What I admire most about Tim is that he never complains. Never, ever. Everything to him is Strawberry Fields.

He's always polite and affectionate. He never gets depressed or gets jealous or says anything malicious. He's quick to give gifts, as he puts it, "to the poor kids."

I always tell people Tim is a better man than I could ever be.

While I sometimes wish Tim could experience a little more of the world, I know that my world would be smaller and darker without him.

Chapter Twenty-Four

February 2005. I got a call from my former partner at SportsWise, Helen Cohen. She told me about a friend of hers who worked for the National Football League.

"Her name's Tracey Bleczinski," Helen said. "She's the Director of Consumer Products."

"And?"

"I'd like you to have dinner with us."

"Why? You want me to help you sell advertising?" Helen, at the time, owned a cheerleading magazine.

"I think you two would hit it off."

"What are you, Yente the Matchmaker?"

"Look," she said enthusiastically, "the lady is smart. She has a master's degree and took courses at the Cordon Bleu School in London."

"Wonderful," I said. "She can bake a souffle. Yippee."

"Don't be such a wiseass."

"All she'll want to do is talk about sports."

"Okay. It's settled. We'll see you tomorrow night at Beppe at six."

Before I could respond, Helen hung up.

The next day I canceled dinner. I canceled because I had no intention of ever remarrying. Why? Simply put, I thought it would be asking a lot of a woman to help me look after Tim, my number one priority.

Helen rescheduled.

I canceled again.

Helen threatened to castrate me if I canceled a third time. I replied I'd prefer to keep my shillelagh intact.

Helen and I got to Beppe's at six. The place was packed. People talking loudly, laughing hysterically. Tracey was late.

"Typical sports person," I said. "No consideration for time."

Helen stuck out her tongue.

Tracey soon appeared. She was wearing a black dress set off with white pearls. Stunningly beautiful and tall, maybe five-nine, she had shoulder-length blonde hair, large brown eyes and prominent cheekbones.

"You sure she works for the NFL," I said, "And not the Elite Modeling Agency?"

"Be quiet," Helen said.

Tracey joined us at the table and after an exchange of pleasantries, she said, "You follow the NFL?" Her voice was soft, with infections of the Midwest. She grew up in Kansas.

"No."

"Guess you're a basketball fan."

"No."

"How about baseball?"

"No."

She cocked her head sideways. "What games do you watch?"

"I don't watch games. I watch movies."

That led to a discussion about films, then music.

"You like country music?" Tracey said.

"Nope. I'm a rock and roll man, although I do love Gershwin." A beat. "Who do you like?"

"George Strait and Alan Jackson."

"Never heard of them."

"You're kidding?"

"Not in the least."

She smirked. "You need to be educated."

"Don't I ever."

The dinner was fun. Lots of chatter and laughter. Hardly a word about sports.

After Beppe, we went to the bar at Gramercy Tavern. Helen and I ordered B&B's, Benedictine and brandy. Tracey ordered Strega.

"What is that?" I asked.

Tracey smiled, her eyes shining like constellations. "It's the drink Tom Hagen sipped in the movie The Godfather when he had to tell the Don that Sonny was dead." She offered her glass. "Try it."

I took a sip of the 80-proof liqueur. Grimaced. "Jesus! This tastes worse than STP!"

"C'mon. It's not that strong."

"Not that strong?! It burnt my esophagus."

We had a few more rounds. Then Helen left to go home. Tracey and I took a cab back to my apartment.

"You like 60s music?" I said.

"Sure."

I slid a CD into my Bose player and out came the song "Stay" by Maurice Williams and The Zodiacs.

"When I was a kid," I said, "My father used to take me to a tavern in Union City called The Spot. Sometimes at the end of a drunken night, he and his cronies would lock arms, play this song and kick their legs up like the Rockettes."

"Your father sounds like a fun guy," Tracey said.

"He was."

I got quiet, thinking of Big Tom, my pal.

"Your father meant a lot to you, didn't he?" Tracey said.

"Meant the world."

"And your mother?"

"She's in her eighties and still as fun as ever."

Thinking of my parents, I got up from the couch and replaced the CD.

I played the song "I Only Have Eyes for You" by The Flamingos.

I extended my hand to Tracey like my father had extended his to my mother many years before at a high school dance.

"May I have the pleasure?" I said.

"Sure," Tracey said, standing and smiling and putting her hand into mine.

We danced the night away just as my parents had on the evening they first met.

A few days later, I called Tracey and invited her to dinner without Helen. She said she was hoping to watch Kansas (a number one seed) play Bucknell (a number fourteen seed) in the first round of the NCAA tournament.

We had dinner in my apartment. I ordered Thai food: Satay chicken, Pad Thai, chicken dumplings and spring rolls. I also got a bottle of Rombauer wine and, yes, Strega.

Tracey, who got her master's degree at Kansas, said, "KU has a great team. This should be an easy victory."

"Kansas is going down," I said, since I always rooted against Kansas for the simple reason I didn't think much of their head coach, Bill Self, despite his winning record.

Tracey smirked. "Not a chance."

"Wanna bet?"

"You're on?"

"I win, you pay for dinner. I lose, I drink Strega."

She extended her hand. "Deal."

We shook.

I said, "You should know better than to bet against an intelligent Duke guy."

Tracey grinned. "Not sure I've heard of that school."

"Well, unlike Kans-Ass it actually has academic entrance requirements, other than the ability to read a Denny's menu."

"Ha, ha."

As it turned out, Bucknell upset Kansas 64-63.

"What can I say," handing Tracey the dinner bill. "When ya got it, ya got it."

She snickered. "Got what?"

"Brains."

"As opposed to beauty?"

"Ouch." A smile. "Thanks for dinner."

"You're welcomed."

Despite my victory, I still drank some Strega. Yuck!

A year later, almost to the day, a long-time publishing veteran who I'll call Mr. Big was put in charge of Nielsen Business Media.

He demanded long-term, five-year business plans.

I, on the other hand, believed in having a strategic model, maybe two years out—no more. My reasoning was that, like a good coach, I knew situations could change quickly. If you've prepared your team well, as Hubie Brown had taught me, you can make the proper adjustments within a short time frame.

I mean, what coach talks about playing Maryland five years down the road? None. A great coach takes it one game at a time. I planned my business strategy one year at a time.

Mr. Big, of course, did not like my approach. Nor, as it turned out, did he like me. I was told he didn't care for my free-wheeling style—like letting my team play bocce or miniature golf in the hallways.

Unlike my past bosses who were reluctant to fire me due to my group's high profit margins and my team's fierce loyalty, Mr. Big didn't give a rat's ass.

I soon lost interest in the job. Indeed, I grew to hate it, the boring meetings and chicken-shit politics.

One night Mr. Big summoned me to a meeting at the Harvard Club, his alma mater.

The club, located in midtown Manhattan, was old and stuffy. It had huge chandeliers, oriental rugs, leather couches and high-backed chairs. Sitting in the chairs were old dudes in custom-made suits and silly bright bow ties. They looked like human fossils.

I was met in the lobby by one of Mr. Big's minions, a guy who genuflected every time before entering Mr. Big's office.

He took me upstairs to where Mr. Big—tall and overweight—was sitting like a pasha in an upholstered throne-like chair.

He pointed to a seat. I sat and crossed my legs. He stared at me for a long moment. I stared back. Nearby his minion stood poised like an attack dog awaiting his master's whistle.

Mr. Big made a steeple with his fingers, cleared his throat and said, "I'm letting you go."

I acted shocked, though I wasn't. I pretended to be upset, though I wasn't.

"That's unfair," I said. "I've exceeded my quota easily every year I've worked at Nielsen."

I pushed back not because I wanted to keep my job but because I wanted a good severance package.

He shifted in his chair and studied his fingernails.

"We'll be fair," he said.

I didn't respond. I didn't believe him.

He tugged on an earlobe. "You can leave now."

I stood, walked down a long stairway and exited through the front door. Outside, it was cool and windy. I took a deep breath, feeling like a prisoner who just got paroled.

I flagged a cab and just as I was about to get inside, another Nielsen president, John Kilcullen, appeared.

"What happened?" he said.

"I got fired."

"You're kidding me."

"Nope."

"Whaddya gonna do now?"

I smiled. "What I've always done. I'm gonna take a shot."

John squinted. "A shot at what?!"

"Who the fuck knows?"

I did get a generous severance package—after I threatened to sue, of course.

Within days of my firing, I received calls from a number of headhunters who suggested a host of job opportunities, all promising substantial salaries and bonuses.

I turned them all down.

"Why aren't you interested in a new job?" one headhunter asked.

"Because I have a job."

"Mind if I ask what it is?"

"Sure. It's taking care of my son."

At the time, Tim, now twenty, was living in a group home in Bear, Delaware called Advoserv, a nonprofit agency dedicated to providing housing, healthcare, meaningful employment and recreational opportunities for individuals with intellectual and developmental disabilities and special needs.

It was roughly a three-to-four hour's drive from my home on Lake Mohawk, New Jersey.

Now, without a full-time job, I was able to bring Tim home, pretty much anytime I wanted. Usually I got him every other Thursday and returned him to Advoserv on Mondays. Peg, still living in Cedar Grove, maintained the same schedule.

Thanks to my generous severance package, I was now free to do what I wanted for so many years—give all my time and energy to ensuring Tim had the best life he could.

At around the same time Tracey and I were still dating and beginning to discuss our future relationship.

We were at my house on Lake Mohawk, with a fire going, sitting on the couch with our feet on the coffee table, sipping wine. The room was fragrant with the scent of applewood.

Tracey had just come from work, so she was in a black dress and black heels. Her blonde hair was shiny and smelled like summer rain.

"Have you thought anymore about getting married?" Tracey said.

"I have."

"And?"

Some logs in the fireplace settled and crackled.

"I don't think it would be fair," I said.

"What wouldn't be fair?"

"You have to deal with Tim."

"I love Tim," she said. And Tim enjoyed and loved Tracey. Almost from the first time they met, the two of them talked about Pee-wee Herman and The Muppets and sang songs by Madonna and The Gap Band. It cracked me up to hear them sing The Gap Band's signature song "Burn Rubber On Me (Why You Wanna Hurt Me)."

Holding hands, they danced around the living room like the worst version of Astaire and Rogers. But seeing their smiling faces and hearing their laughter always warmed my heart.

"I know you love Tim," I said, "but he can be mentally and physically exhausting."

"I can handle it."

"It won't be easy. Even at this age he can pick up a chair and throw it against the wall." I paused. Took a breath. "Or you."

"I can handle it."

I sipped some wine and watched one log tumble and produce a burst of sparks. On the stereo, Dionne Warwick was singing "Here I Am."

"Ever think about having more children?" Tracey asked, staring into the fire.

"Don't think I'd want to."

"How come?"

"Wouldn't be able to concentrate on Tim. Why? You want children?"

"I've thought about it."

"And?"

"I'd be fine with whatever decision we make."

She then put her head on my shoulder. We were quiet for a moment, the fire hissing and a slow bubble of sap oozing from the end of one log.

"I'm okay with not having children," she said.

"I hope I'm not disappointing you."

"You're not."

"You sure?"

"I'm sure."

Tracey picked up her glass and drank some wine, then put the glass down slowly.

"Thanks," I said.

"For?"

"Accepting things as they are."

Tracey nodded.

I was quiet for a moment thinking about how much thought she must have put in on the subject. How much she was willing to sacrifice.

"So we're good?" I said.

"We're good."

"Okay, then. We'll be the three amigos."

"Works for me."

I lifted my glass. "Till death do us part."

"Or hell freezes over."

We clicked glasses and kissed.

Two years later we got married in Napa Valley. The year was 2008.

It's true what they say: time flies when you're having fun. For the next few years Tracey and I had a lot of fun. Tracey was happy working at the NFL. I was happy renovating the house. We both loved it when Tim would visit. We'd go to lunches and dinners, have barbecues, dance to music and swim in Lake Mohawk. I loved watching Tim run full speed from the house, his bathing trunks slipping down his backside, and jumping off the dock into the lake.

He'd rise from the water, shake his hands in the air and shout, "That feels good, Daddy, real good."

When Tim wasn't with us, Tracey and I went to Broadway shows and jazz clubs and Super Bowls. We traveled to Europe and Hawaii. All told, it seemed like a trip to the moon on gossamer wings.

Often, friends would ask me if I was bored.

"Bored?!" I'd say. "Bored with what?"

"Not having a job. A structured life." A beat. "You were, after all, a workaholic."

They were referring to the fact that for most of my career I held four jobs: in real estate, journalism, scouting and publishing. Sometimes all at once.

What they didn't know was this: despite wanting to succeed handsomely at every job I ever held, work was never any more than a means to an end, a chance to leave corporate America and live full time as Tim's father.

Some friends could never really gasp that I retired at age 55. Not because I was wealthy. I wasn't. Rather, it was because I wanted to live life on my own terms—to come and go as I wished and do as I wanted, when I wanted, which, to my knowledge, is what most people aspire to.

The thing is, I'm not totally retired.

I work, but only on projects I wished to take on and only with people with whom I chose to work.

I continue to write magazine articles, play the stock market, invest in real estate, consult to businesses. I was even asked by Brand New World Studios to be a consulting producer on a documentary called THE MENTAL GAME—ATHLETES IN CRISIS.

My real job, though, is just being Tim's father and Tracey's husband.

I couldn't ask for anything more; don't want anything more. Like my father, I strive to live a simple life.

This is not to suggest my life since "retiring" has been without heartache and heartbreak.

In 2013, when Tim was Tim 27, he woke up one morning at Peg's house with a bad cough. He was gagging and sweating. Peg took his temperature. It was over 100.

She immediately brought him to a doctor who said it was

probably a bad cold, maybe even the flu. He prescribed an antibiotic.

Peg called me and suggested I take Tim to my house because he had a bigger bed there and most of his games and CD's.

At the house, Tim went right to bed. I monitored his breathing. It was labored. Raspy. His forehead was hot and he was sweating profusely. I watched as he squirmed wildly and frantically, not comprehending why he was so sick. I thought he might be having a seizure.

When he woke, I cupped his head in my hand and tried to pour some water into his mouth sideways. It ran down his cheek and pooled on his pillow.

I took him to another doctor who checked his pulse, his blood pressure and his lungs. He removed the stethoscope out of his ears and said, "We gotta get this kid to the hospital—right now!"

Why? I asked

"His lungs are badly congested."

We rushed to the Emergency Room at Mountainside Hospital. Tim's vitals were checked. A doctor said, "Get him to Intensive Care."

"What's wrong?" I said, frantic.

"Don't know yet. We have to do some blood work, take an X-ray and get a nasal culture."

Tim was lifted onto a gurney and taken upstairs.

"The tests will take a while," the doctor said.

"Can I go with him?"

"Not right now."

I looked at Tim. I could tell from his eyes he was scared. I kissed his forehead. "You'll be okay," I said. "You'll be okay."

I slowly walked down a corridor, trying to fathom what was

happening. The medicinal odors that infiltrated my nostrils made me want to vomit.

I went downstairs to the hospital cafeteria. Doctors and nurses sat at a table, sipping coffee and chatting quietly. Across from them was an elderly man wearing a thick patch over his right eye. Nearby a young girl had her left leg in a cast.

After a few hours, my cell phone buzzed. It was a nurse saying Tim's tests had been completed. I raced out of the cafeteria.

Upstairs, I was met by the doctor. Looking resolute, he said, "Tim may have pneumonia or possibly pertussis."

"What's pertussis?"

"Whooping cough. But just to be sure we're sending a culture to the CDC."

"You mean it's that bad?"

A grave look. "Could be."

I shook my head. Couldn't fucking believe it. I wanted to scream so loud it would make the building shake.

Tim appeared, sitting in a wheelchair, barely able to breath. The normal flush in his cheeks had gone white and his lips had a tint of blue. "Daddy, let's go home," he rasped, "Daddy, let's go home."

"Soon, Tim, soon," I said, holding his hand.

Tim was wheeled into a private room. I followed. A nurse stopped me.

"You need to wear a mask," she said. "Pertussis is a highly-contagious respiratory ailment. Droplets are easily sprayed in the air and can get into your lungs." She handed me a mask.

"No way," I said. "Tim is traumatized enough. The last thing I'm going to do is scare him more by wearing a mask."

I looked at Tim.

His face didn't show emotion, but I could tell from the manic movement of his fingers—it was as if he were frantically playing an invisible clarinet—that he was scared.

"Okay," she said. "But I strongly advise against it."

Tim was put to bed and given IV antibiotics. The nurses put a cannula breathing tube in his nose and an oxygen mask over his face. He was connected to lots of electrodes attached to beeping monitors, measuring every internal event.

Tim could barely keep his eyes open. He said, "Daddy, I'm sick."

Choking back tears, I said, "I know…I know but you'll get better quick."

Around ten o'clock, a nurse, wearing a mask, entered the room and told me it was time to leave. Hospital rules.

"Not a chance," I said. "I'm sleeping here."

Her eyes widened. "You can't."

"Oh, yes, I can."

A hospital administrator was called. I pressed my case. I said Tim was trying to pull the tubes out of his nose and aside from making sure that didn't happen, Tim needed me and his mother to be with him 24/7. The administrator agreed.

The hospital had no extra beds. So on alternating nights Peg and I slept in a chair or on the floor or even squeezed in the single bed beside Tim. Twice I rolled off it and banged my head.

Tim had a tough time understanding what was happening. A big kid—now six-five, two-fifty—he looked brittle some days, as if he were about to dissolve. He kept saying, "Daddy, Daddy, why can't I go home? Daddy, Daddy, why can't I go home? I wanna go home. Please, Daddy, please. Take me home."

Stroking his sweaty forehead, I sang to him, reassured him that he'd be fine—even though I wasn't sure. Often I'd just stare at his sleeping face and wish the weeks would peel itself backwards until he regained the brightness that was there before the pertussis.

It was a tough few weeks. Tim kept pulling the tubes from his nose. He was given an additional antibiotic and it caused a bad rash. He couldn't stop scratching and sweating. His face was chalk white. He couldn't sleep at night. He ate very little. It was awful.

He was finally given different antibiotics. They worked and little by little Tim got better. He didn't need the breathing tubes or the oxygen mask. He ate better, slept better. Was even smiling.

To this day, I refer to that time as "my month of misery."

Not long after Tim was released from the hospital, Fast Company magazine did a cover story on the 100 Most Creative People in Business Worldwide. Tracey was ranked number nine. She earned that ranking because under her direction she had raised sales of NFL women's apparel by 76%. She did it by creating pop-up style lounges in ten NFL stadiums and designing a glamorous television ad campaign with brands ranging from Marchesa to Walmart. In short, she made NFL clothing for women chic.

After the story appeared, she was offered numerous other jobs.

"You sure you want to leave the NFL?" I said. We were sitting at the bar at the Gramercy Tavern, nibbling on cheese and drinking wine.

"I've been there 14 years," she said.

"And?"

"Maybe it's time for something new. A new challenge."

I grinned. "You mean take a shot?"

She winked and walked her fingertips up my backbone, one vertebra at a time. "If anybody understands taking a shot…it's you."

The opportunity that appealed to her most was becoming Senior Vice President of Consumer Products for the Ultimate Fighting Championships (UFC).

"Means I'd have to move to Las Vegas," she said.

I ate some cheese. "You know I can't move there. At least not full-time"

"I know."

The reason I couldn't move to Vegas was Tim. He was still living at Advoserv with the same three autistic residents who he called "the guys."

Why he didn't and doesn't live with me or Peg is because he has no siblings, and we knew that somewhere in the future he'd have to learn to live without us. It's a crushing thought. But living with others is the best thing for him.

And he enjoys where he lives and the same three guys he's lived with, now going on ten years.

"You could commute," Tracey said, pouring some wine into my empty glass.

"I could."

"Vegas has some great restaurants."

"It does."

"And there's great entertainment."

"There is."

Tracey took a sip of wine.

"So?" she said. "What do you think?"

I sang: "Viva Las Vegas."

We got an apartment in Vegas—Turnberry Tower, near the Strip. (We've since moved to Summerlin.) When we're not there, we live at the Jersey shore—in Sea Girt. Tracey travels a lot—to Russia, Brazil, London, China, you name it.

When she's back in town and Tim's visiting, we stay at home, playing games and ordering take-out food from Tim's favorite places—Five Guys, Andy's Pizza and Joe Leone's Gastronomia. Tim loves their chicken parmigiana and meatballs.

Talk about making a good life's decision. I often think that if I had stayed in sports I'd still be addicted to the game—probably be coaching somewhere—and not likely to have the time needed for Tim. Quitting Duke basketball was the best choice I ever made. It allowed me to experience New York, travel the world, try different occupations and, well…come to realize that the art of living begins with a total appreciation for life itself and the glorious things it has to offer…if you're willing to take a shot.

I recently told a friend that despite all of my life's adventures even the most mundane, most ordinary days now seem remarkable.

My favorite days are when we're at the beach, usually early morning. The sky is a blaze of pink and red. I watch Tim and Tracey standing at the shoreline. Sunlight brightens their faces. Ocean water laps their feet. Seagulls soar high above their heads.

I see Tim walk into the water, Tracey a few steps behind. A big wave rises. Tim dives beneath it. Tracey floats above it. When the wave passes, the two leap up like dolphins, look at each other and smile.

Tim, his eyes wider than saucers, says "Wow! That was a big

one."

Tracey, laughing, shouts, "A real big one!"

At noon, we walk to lunch at the boardwalk concession. The sand is hot. On the way there, Tim sings "Hey, good lookin', whatcha got cookin'?"

We grab a table overlooking the ocean, and order burgers and fries. The air is warm and salty. Sitting around us are tanned surfers and sunburned bathers wearing flip-flops and smelling of coconut oil.

In the distance a radio is playing and Jimmy Buffett is singing "Volcano."

Tim's face illuminates. "Daddy! Daddy!" he says, excitedly. "It's Jimmy Buffet!"

"Sure is."

Tim starts swaying his shoulders and singing, "I don't know where I will go when the volcano blows."

"You're rockin', Tim," I say. "Rockin.'"

"And rollin', Daddy, and rollin'."

Tracey and I start singing with Tim. Our voices rise. People around us smile.

When the song ends, I say, "Whaddya think, Tim?"

He lifts an index finger. "I think I'm gonna have ice cream for dessert."

Later, when we get home, Tim showers and has dinner. Usually pizza.

From a Bose wave radio/cd player there is always music—just as there was always music in my family's apartment when I grew up.

We listen a lot to Springsteen who, like me, is a Jersey street kid.

His lyrics move me. They're powerful, emotionally charged. I'm especially touched by the song "Glory Days" where he sings of a friend who sits back trying to recapture past athletic success. But time has slipped away and he's left longing for days gone by.

Thankfully, I've never experienced that. I never look in my rearview mirror to see myself as I once was: a great basketball player. The only time I look back now is to see how far I've come. How long it's taken me to find my purpose—which is making Tim's life comfortable and meaningful.

Not long ago, as I was sitting at my desk and writing this story, Tim stopped by my office and said, "Daddy, what are you doing?"

"I'm writing a book."

Tim, now thirty-seven years old and standing six-five, two hundred and fifty pounds, was wearing a hunter green T-shirt and bright red shorts. He scratched the back of his head. "Why you writing a book?"

"I wanna take a shot."

His eyes widened. "A shot at what, Daddy?"

"Finding my voice."

Tim made a sad face. He then walked over and gave me the same kind of bear hug I used to give my father—Big Tom.

"I'm sorry, Daddy," he said, his grip tightening.

"Sorry about what?"

"Losing your voice."

I smiled.

"No, Tim," I said. "Thanks to you I've found it."

Put on a Happy Face: My son Tim smiles as if he's swallowed the sun.

The Waterboys: Rafting with Tim on Lake Mohawk, New Jersey.

Nice Work if You Can Get it: Being paid to scout basketball games.

No Contest: After getting played and slayed by superstar Jerry West.

The Fun Couple: My parents Big Tom and Geri after their nuptials.

Lunacy: The aptly named Joe Don Looney at the Deauville Hotel.

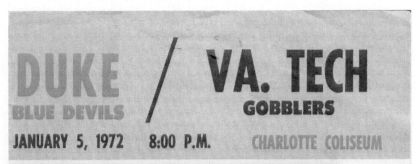

Taking a Shot: Displaying textbook form on my jump shot.

Goodfellas: My gangster grandfather (L) with his wife and cronies.

T&T: Tim and Tracey at the Breakers Hotel in West Palm Beach.

Penetrating the Lane: Driving past UNC star guard George Karl.
(photo by Jim Thornton, Herald-Sun Papers, Durham, N.C.)

The Irishmen: In Killarney with NBA coaches (L to R) Kevin Loughery,
Billy Cunningham and Brendan Suhr.

Fast Break: Dribbling toward stardom before abruptly leaving Duke.

The Cover Boy: (L to R) Gary Melchionni, Coach Bucky Waters and me. (media guide photos by Jim Laughead, Jim Bradley, Thad Sparks, Jim Wallace and Danny Farrell)

True Love: Tim with his dedicated and adoring mother, Peg.

Acknowledgements

I owe a great deal to a great many people.

I have to start with Pat Jordan. It was Pat's books and magazine articles that first inspired me to write. After I met him, he was very generous with his time and advice. Without his help, I probably would never have gotten a story published. His memoir "A False Spring" was named by Sports Illustrated as "one of the top 100 Sports Books of All Time." And in an article that appeared in the Wall Street Journal, writer Allen Barra wrote, "Who is the best sportswriter? The names that are mentioned most often are W. C. Heinz and Pat Jordan. I concur, but I'll take Jordan in a split-decision." For my money, Pat is sports writing's version of Hemingway.

I should also give a shout out to Pulitzer Prize winning author David Halberstam, who I first met in 1980 when he was doing a profile on Pete Maravich for Inside Sports. David spent a fair amount of time with me, talking basketball and writing. He suggested that someday I might want to write a book about my crazy experiences. Well, David, thanks to you...here it is.

I'm also grateful to brilliant and supremely talented authors/ professors, Charles Butler and John Capouya, for reading the book and giving me valuable suggestions and support. They both were always there when I needed a quick read and a quick edit. They never failed to greatly improve my prose.

A big, big gratitude goes to Glenn Stout. Glenn, who for over twenty-five years edited The Best American Sports Writing series and whose book, Young Woman and the Sea, about swimmer Gertrude Ederle is soon to hit movie theatres, is not only the best editor I've ever worked with (and I worked with some great ones) but also one of the nicest, caring and patient people on earth. Glenn never stopped pushing me to make this the best book it could be. His passion for language and craft is unsurpassed. If I had any pull with the Pope I'd have him canonized.

Bouquets also go out to the talented researchers/editors whose generous spirit and goodwill contributed much to the book: Andrea Witzig, Pat Murphy, Carmine Curcio, Steve Romano, Barbara Culvert, Ben Guest, Gail Bleczinski and my longtime buddy, Bradley Siegel, who is a major player in the entertainment business.

I'm indebted to Hubie Brown, a Hall of Fame coach and brilliant NBA broadcaster. Hubie is to the game of basketball what Einstein was to mathematics. I admire him enormously. Not only did he teach me how to enhance my basketball skills but he also taught me never to be afraid to face a challenge. His words became the gospel by which I have lived my life.

I must throw some hosannahs at the immensely talented artist, Gaston Mendieta, whose artwork graces the cover of this book. Gaston is what we call in athletic terms "a go-to guy who delivers in crunch time." What I wouldn't give to have his ability. His eye for color and design. He scores with every illustration he does. Gracias!

I'm deeply grateful to the dedicated team of Enhanced Communications, LLC. The company's namesake—veteran journalist, book author and publishing consultant John Hanc was the driving force in getting this book published. With his energizing enthusiasm, wise counsel and honest feedback, he helped me rethink and revise my strategies. He kept production moving smoothly and intelligently. He and his team were obsessive in their attention to detail and commitment to excellence. They were always available to answer questions and react quickly. Every staff member was a true professional, in particular Kevin Horton, whose creative production and layout skills resulted in this highly readable and inviting book you're holding in your hands now. I also pay tribute to Brandon Mariana and Tracy Stopler for their roles in helping me to…well, take this shot.

Bottom line: I simply can't imagine working with a better, more competent publishing organization. Thanks guys and gals for making this endeavor so enjoyable.

Above all, I want to genuflect before my wife, Tracey. She has done more for me than I can begin to articulate. She was my biggest cheerleader, my strongest advocate, always offering encouragement and calm, especially when I'd scream at the computer, which I did at least every other day. Tracey was not only my personal IT person, but my guide through months of whine and poses. I couldn't have done this book without her.

Last, I wish to thank my son Tim. So many days when I'd be pissed off about writing a bad paragraph and ready to throw the computer against the wall, Tim would come into my office and, apropos of nothing, say, "Daddy, what do dogs put on their pizza?" A big smile, then: "Puppy-Roni."

I'd crack up laughing and, after he'd give me a hug, I'd go right back to writing, thinking as my Irish grandfather would say, "What the fook is there to get excited about."

All the above enriched my life in different ways and at different times. The best way I can thank them is by saying, "Drinks on me."

Cheers!

About The Author

Richard O'Connor was a unanimous high school basketball All-American at St. Michael's High School in Union City, New Jersey where he scored over 2,000 points. He was recruited by over fifty colleges. He chose Duke and starred on the only undefeated freshmen team in Atlantic Coast Conference history. As a junior, he led the varsity in scoring. After quitting Duke, he played professional basketball in Spain under future Los Angeles Laker coach, Del Harris. Upon his return to the states, he became a writer and his stories appeared in over 50 magazines, including *Sport*, *Sports Illustrated*, *People*, *GQ* and *The New York Times*. His article on basketball player, Raymond Lewis was included in The Sporting News Best Sports Stories anthology. He is also the author of two mystery novels, Gaelic Force and Foul Shot. In addition to writing, O'Connor worked for the Dallas Mavericks and the Detroit Pistons, was a division president at Nielsen Business Media, chairman of The Shamrock Games and Founder of Tuxedo Realty. He lives in Sea Girt, New Jersey with his wife, Tracey and has one son, Tim, who gives his life meaning and purpose.

Also by Richard O'Connor...

FOUL SHOT

BY RICHARD O'CONNOR

Silk Swell is the best college basketball player in the country. By all accounts, he will be the number one pick in the upcoming NBA draft. His coach, Bobby Price, who is heralded as the best in the business, thinks Silk might be shaving points. But why would he? He's expected to make millions once he signs an NBA contract. Price hires private investigator, Jake Ryan, to look into things. Ryan delves into Sewell's murky past. The further he digs, the deeper he descends into a dark world populated by scoundrels and gangsters. Ultimately, what he discovers shocks him--and will shock readers.

Praise for Foul Shot

"His tale of corruption and foul play in the college ranks is a fast-paced read that rings all too true in today's world of bottom-line sports programs."
San Diego Magazine

"Jake Ryan is a hard-boiled private eye for the millennium. One of the most promising detective fiction debuts in recent years."
Success Magazine

"A great book. The dialogue is like Robert Parker's, the characters are like Elmore Leonard's, but the ending is entirely Rich O'Connor's: very surprising."
Mystery Journal

"If you like college basketball you will love reading Foul Shot. It's a great novel with lots of mystery, intrigue and excitement."
Rick Sund
VP Basketball Operations, Detroit Pistons

"Absolutely great reading. Extremely difficult to put down once you start. A great book for the pure basketball junkie"
Keith Grant
Director of Player Personnel, Dallas Mavericks

"O'Connor's characters come to life in a fast, exciting social commentary – on both sports and society. A wonderful book"
Lifestyle Publications

Made in United States
North Haven, CT
10 August 2023

40174827R00217